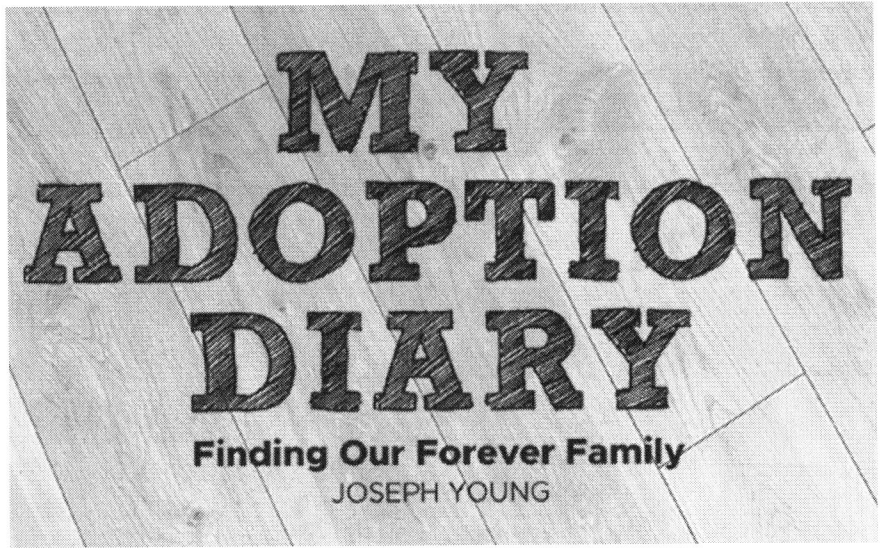

A superb diary describing all emotions, across the adoption journey of his family from the beginning until the end. It's a superb insight into the personal side as well as the process.

JOSEPH YOUNG

First published by Joseph Young by Amazon

Editing Support - My mother, Chrissy P, Danny J and Dr Taylor.

All rights reserved. No part of this publication may be reproduced, stored in a retrieval system, or transmitted in any form or by any means, electronically, mechanically, photocopying, recording or otherwise without prior permission in writing from the author.

This book is factual and based upon the recollections of the author. Names and locations have been amended to protect the identities of the family.

Contact to the author can be made via Instagram on *@joeyoung_adoptiondiaries* or via Facebook on the authors direct page *Joseph Young - Author & Blogger*

Copyright © 2021 Joseph Young

TABLE OF CONTENTS

ABOUT THE AUTHOR	7
ACKNOWLEDGEMENTS	8
THE PROCESS	10
AGENCY SEARCH	13
THE APPLICATION	23
STAGE 1 - TRAINING	30
STAGE 2	43
STAGE 2 - TRAINING	45
HOME VISITS	59
APPROVAL PANEL	82
STAGE 3 - FAMILY FINDING	87
FAMILY FINDING - JACOB	108
LINKING - JACOB	112
LIFE APPRECIATION	115
MATCHING	123
INTRODUCTIONS &	126
MATCHING PANEL	126
PHYSICAL INTRODUCTIONS	149
FOREVER HOME	174
ADOPTION APPLICATION	215
THERAPY SESSIONS	225
LEGAL PROCESS	244
FOREVER FAMILY	272

*'I would lay down my life for any of my children.
When you are a father, I know you will understand what I mean.'*

This is a quote from my mother and now that I am a father, I can fully understand and resonate with the true meaning of this.

Firstly, thank you very much for purchasing my book. I did not go into this process with any intention to write and publish a book, yet decided mid-way through our process to do so, with the intention of helping others that are already in the process or anyone thinking about it.

I must also confirm that I do not have a masters in English literature, nor am I a Best-Selling Author with a huge resource, so please be kind when reading my (northern) English.

This is the story/diary of myself, my amazing partner (turned husband midway through the adoption journey) and now our beautiful little boy, whom we completely adore and love unconditionally. We can now certainly resonate with the fatigue-based memes on the parents' pages on Facebook that we once mocked.

I really wanted to share my diary of events, the emotions that we went through and finally the roller coaster of a ride that we had. When we started the journey, we couldn't find much literature out there that helped us outside of the process only. There seems to be little out there that describes the emotional journey and I wanted to share that in the belief that it is important to know that you are not the only people out there feeling confused, overwhelmed and quite often fraudulent.

It was also apparent from our own experience that there are some misconceptions about the adoption process and adventure. I am hoping this will dispel some of those and answer fundamental questions that you may have. More importantly however, if this can help anyone thinking of going through this adoption journey or wanting to go through it, then I have done what I set out to.

This book is fundamentally based on my experience and through my lens.

I have also changed names, places and other details that can identify others. Of course, it is imperative that confidentiality is held in the highest regard to safeguard our family and other people that have supported us through this journey.

It is also really important that I stress that our experience **will** be different to yours, however I am sure the fundamental processes will be similar. This may differ depending on your agency or local authority, so please clarify with them directly.

I really hope you enjoy this book and could I ask that if it helps you, could you please share it with others who may benefit.

ABOUT THE AUTHOR

I am Joseph, or Joe to those who know me and live up t'north of England. I am originally from Clitheroe which is a nice market town in Lancashire and moved to join the Royal Navy at the youthful age of 16 years old. This was to the delight of my mother who had already shipped (no pun intended) 2 others off to the Armed Forces. I am the youngest of 5 boys so I bet it was pretty tough to see her favourite - of which I joke that I am - the last to leave home.

I completed 8 years mainly as a Physical Training Instructor and loved every minute of it. Those 8 years really shaped my adulthood and helped me become a strong and confident man. I now work in commercial property which is a world away from the fun role I previously held in the Navy. I often wonder why I left.

My childhood was great; it had some high and low points that were mainly due to my 'father' but on the whole it was very good – some I will go through further on in the book as they have a significant relevance to our story. I have the most amazing and loving mother who I idolise and love so much.

I am now married to Alex, whom I completely adore and love for his patience - amongst a whole host of other things - with me. I can be a tough person to live with, although I still maintain I have some desirable qualities, but quite how many, I am unsure.

Before I get into the diary element, let's set this out from the start, this journey has been tough. It's taken under 3 years of laughter, tears, arguments, tantrums, some good events and a tragic life event too; all of which have modelled and shaped this time of our lives. Overall, the outcome has been magical and one that has fulfilled our lives and showed me that there is a form of love that is way beyond any I could imagine

ACKNOWLEDGEMENTS

What I would also say is that this process has been amazing and a huge self-exploration for me, and I know for Alex too. Thank you to all the people in my life who have been part of it and thank you especially to those who have been part of our journey.

Alex, of course, has been the rock. Until death do us part, or until you bin me.

Mother, you are the most amazing person and role model. If I can be half the parent you have been to my brothers and I, then I will be super proud and know I have succeeded. Your advice, love and guidance is invaluable. I genuinely don't know what I would do without you.

To Alex's family who have been superb. You have been a HUGE support and we love you so much. I'm certainly not looking forward to the reciprocation of you winding up our child and then you leaving; just like I do with yours. I guess I have to accept my fate on that one.

Our friends and wider family; thank you for taking an interest in our journey, for being a shoulder to cry on and a friendly face to share a few drinks with when we have needed it. We have made a group of 'adoption friends' along the way who we really do call friends. You have been invaluable to us as a supporting arm and really hope we have been the same back. A special mention to K and N (you know who you are). You have been the most amazing friends to us, we love you lots.

Also, our neighbours and their little boy too. Without you, I think we would have struggled so much more than we have already. You have been amazing friends when we have needed reassurance, guidance and emotional support. You have done more than you may believe for us, so a huge thank you.

I would also like to thank the professionals who have helped us along the journey. Most of all, our social worker who has been the guiding force in our journey to being approved. Jacobs' social worker, who accepted us as a *'perfect match'* for him and helped, ultimately, to become a family. Lastly to some of the most amazing foster carers you can wish for. I couldn't do your job and I believe you are superheroes. Thank you, thank you, thank you!

Lastly, I am super proud of our little boy, Jacob. This story is about how we have found you, and most importantly how you have enhanced our lives, completely for the better. We will support you and most importantly, LOVE you forever. Our forever family!

THE PROCESS

The process that we followed…

This whole process is something that took us by surprise regarding the amount of 'things' that we needed to complete. However, in hindsight it's all worth it when you get that bundle of joy who completes your family.

It is worth stressing that your adoption agency may differ in process, so please ensure that you confirm with them their processes once you have selected the correct one for you.

Here is how it has gone for us…

1. **Honesty**
Be honest with each other and ensure it is something you both want to pursue. It is number 1 in my list because this will get you through your journey as a team (you, your partner and social worker) and family.

2. **Research**
Research agencies that would best suit your needs. They need you as much as you need them. Some specialise in different things. (older children, children with additional needs etc)

3. **Agencies**
Meet as many agencies as you feel comfortable with. Ask all the questions you have, however 'silly' you feel they may be. Trust me, they are not silly.

4. **Application**
Once you have chosen the right agency for you, get your application in. They will then confirm if you are suitable. This may be called an 'expression of interest'

5. **1st Meeting**
Once you have completed your application, you will be invited to meet some social workers for what seemed a little like an interview and confirmation that you are both on the same pathway with regard to adoption.

6. **Stage 1 – Social Worker interviews**
This will be meeting another social worker to discuss your application further in depth. This stage focused on the more material side of your life. For example, house set up, money & debt, DBS checks etc.

7. **Stage 1 Training Sessions**
If you are found suitable, you will then attend a training session.

8. **Stage 2 Training Sessions**
2 days training with other adopters. You will also be given the access to start looking for a child or children. I believe some agencies do 3 days.

9. **Stage 2 – Social Worker Interviews**
At this point you will have a number of sessions – usually 8 – with your social worker to access, well, **everything.** Be prepared to answer some uncomfortable questions that you may feel are close to conducting a therapeutic session. Also refer to point 1.

10. **Adoption Panel**
This is a panel that assesses whether you are approved to adopt a child or children.

11. **The Search**
The hard part… searching for a child that you feel that suits your needs and a child you feel you can meet the needs of. This is very emotional, so prepare yourself.

12. **Matching and meeting**
Once matched with a child, you meet them to confirm all parties (you, agency and child) suitability. You will also have a 'life appreciation day' with all significant people in the child's life (doctors, social workers, foster carers, nursery etc)

13. **Matching Panel**
Formal confirmation of the matching panel.

14. **Introductions**
Starting the process of introductions and moving to your forever family.

15. **Placement Day**
The first day your child(ren) moves in with you, officially.

16. **Ongoing support meetings**
As suggested, this will be ongoing support from significant people, but mainly with the social workers.

17. **The legal stuff & court**
As it suggests, really. This will be the formal and legal application (and hopefully the acceptance) of the adoption order which then completes your forever family.

18. **The rest of your life**
Well, I don't know what that looks like yet, but can't wait to enjoy it.

I hope that gives you a very swift and at least basic overview of the process. The whole thing will test you, it will make you cry, it will make you laugh, it will be an emotional and learning process… but it is well worth it.

Be prepared to experience so many emotions.

AGENCY SEARCH

This is our journey. I sincerely hope you enjoy reading it, but mostly, I hope it helps you understand the process and encourages you to do the most amazing thing….

Once upon time…. (I've always wanted to start a book that way)

18th December - The Start

Alex and I have been speaking about adoption for about 4 months now, properly. We have been together for 9 years even though we debated the official date. We were on and off for a while due to us both exploring who we were. However, that aside, I have always wanted a child. Since being young I've dreamt about playing football with a little one, going swimming, teasing him about his first girlfriend (or boyfriend); something I never got to do with my father. I don't swear very often, but 'Don' (my so-called father) is a complete d**khead and a person that has really inspired me in the art of 'how not to be a parent'. On the other hand, if I can parent anywhere close to how my mother has, I will know I have done well. My mother has been the most amazing person throughout my life and I would do anything for her. I can't describe the love I have for my mother. It's impossible.

Prior to us really starting the discussion about children, Alex had never really expressed a huge desire for us to have children or to get married. We always have conversations at parties and gatherings with friends as to when we are going to get married. Alex jokes that I don't earn enough or that he doesn't believe in it. To that end, we have never needed to get married. It is just a name change really!

We have decided that in January we will really ramp up the adoption process to look at some agencies. It's about time we did, or I will end up too old and even fatter!

25th December - Christmas Day

We had a really good day today at Alex's sisters. Adoption was a big topic around the dinner table as you can imagine. Jenny (Alex's sister) has two children with her other half (Jock) whom she has been together with for many years; we have just found out that he was adopted at a young age too. He's not spoken about how he feels properly to me, but I am told by Alex (via his sister) that Jock is a little frustrated that he never knew until later in his life.

Today too, as the adoption has been on my mind, my emotions have been a little funky; my brain has been going into scenario-overdrive. An example is that I've been thinking this could be our last Christmas without a child. The process can take as little as 6 months but of course can take much longer too. I can't wait for the journey to begin. We must get started.

The Journey Begins

4th January - The Journey Begins

We have been searching for some agencies today. I have been doing some sneaky searching without Alex, but we did it together for the first time this evening. We have looked at some LGBTQ+ friendly groups, local authority groups and have even explored some private charity organisations.

We have booked an LGBTQ+ event with a private agency called After Adoption (which is private) and also Adoption Counts, which is a local authority one. The Adoption Counts agency is the first event on the 24th January of which I am actually very excited to attend but also pretty apprehensive too because I don't want our dream to end before it starts. There isn't much more to do now until the 24th, so it's the simple matter of waiting. I will try not to bite my nails or talk myself out if it.

23rd January - Feeling Nervous

I am quite nervous regarding tomorrows information evening. We have continued to research the process and try and understand what we may come up against on our journey, however we are struggling to find much more than process driven information. We are very naive and our minds have been riddled with stories of what people 'think' the process is going to look like, however we are trying to erase those thoughts and preconceptions and enter tomorrow with a very open mind.

Speaking of tomorrow, I want this to be everything I have dreamt of and some. I am sure tomorrow we will find out if the expectation levels are to be met.

24th January - Adoption Agency Selection Evening

The nerves are still very high regarding this evening. I am going to work today, however sure my mind will be preoccupied playing over what tonight may bring.

Later today….

I was correct about thinking about the event all day! In fact I have struggled to concentrate at work today so it hasn't been my most productive one. I've chatted to one of my colleagues about it too and she has been very supportive and reassuring. It has been a welcome release to have someone to chat to.

We have now been to the Adoption Counts (local authority) event tonight and it was, well, interesting!

> *'Welcome. Firstly, we are **not** your friends.'*

That was the opening line from the woman who led and facilitated the session. I couldn't believe that was how someone would start such an important topical meeting. She was dressed quite casually, had a sour face and looked as though we had stolen her evening from her. I'm still in a little bit of shock at the tone of it all. Maybe she was having a bad day!

With us in the hall were approximately 20 other couples. We thought when going in, that we were going to be the only same sex couple (not that it would bother us) but that wasn't the case. It was reassuring to see a real mix of people there, from single adopters, male and female couples, different age groups and same sex couples.

Personnel in attendance aside, the overall meeting was just COLD. Miss Sour-Face was very frosty and wasn't really selling the idea of adoption to us or the others in attendance. The atmosphere felt uncomfortable and tense and I am sure someone left mid way through. I could see some other people nudging their partners or giving them a bit of the side eye, likely feeling similar to us.

What we did learn from this evening's meeting was about worst case scenarios regarding why children may have gone into the care system. It was shocking! Neglect, sexual abuse, physical abuse, verbal abuse, children fed bleach and more. It was a pretty grim evening and I have walked away from this thinking about whether I want to get into this. Alex is feeling the same way too. It has been really off-putting and dampened our mood regarding adoption.

I am also questioning us too. Do we have what it takes to support a child that may have such complex needs? Do we have the mental strength to be able to go through the process? How do we choose the right child for us based on the needs and what we can offer? And so many more…

Jesus, we have a whole lot of thinking to do!

25th January - Frustration

I didn't sleep much at all last night. I am very frustrated with the meeting that we have just attended. I can't but feel put off by the whole event. However, we can't drop out at the first hurdle, so have booked into see After Adoption and the LGBTQ+ event. We want to know if this attitude and frostiness is across all agencies or whether it is just this one. I can't help thinking that Miss Sour-Face wouldn't make a good salesperson, but I can understand her wanting to whittle out the tentative prospective adopters.

13th February - After Adoption - Agency Evening

We are going to see After Adoption tonight which is a private agency. My understanding was that with private agencies we would have to pay for the service, however it turns out that we don't. I am really hoping the experience tonight goes much better than the previous one. I'm going to try and be positive.

We arrived at After Adoption and as we entered we were greeted by this absolutely lovely lady with a very welcoming demeanour. She offered us a drink and directed us to the conference room where prospective adopters were gathering in readiness for the start of the event. Immediately it felt different and the atmosphere was much better. When the room seemed to settle and no further people were coming in, we had a small presentation welcoming us and offering some information about the agency. The team who presented were 'soft' in manner and it made us feel very much at ease. I think one of the opening lines was *'there are over 84,000 children in the care system, so thank you for being here today'*. To be thanked for being there made us feel we were doing the right thing. Similarly it made us confirm we were exploring the correct route for us and not others like surrogacy, for example. We have maintained that adoption is our preferred route for the reason of giving a child a loving home that needs it.

Further into the session they described most of the scenarios as to why a child may be placed in the adoption system and become a 'looked after child'. It was an eye opener for us because we had always thought of worst-case scenario of them being removed; which had incidentally been backed up by the previous meeting. For example, we assumed the birth parent was a drug addict or was an abuser of sorts and although that clearly happens and is highly prevalent in the adoption world, there were similarly a number of examples and videos shown of birth parents who had been on the receiving end of domestic abuse or had learning difficulties. These were scenarios that I would say were no fault of their own. It really changed my view on why a child may be in care and I am really glad it did too!

Additionally, we received a twenty minute 'talk' from a really nice couple that have already adopted. This was a superb insight into their process of their experience of their adoption journey to have a child. What was fantastic and candid was that they shared their positive experiences and the not-so-positive experiences too. The couple was a male and female married couple who biologically couldn't have children, so they wanted to adopt as opposed to surrogacy or IVF. They adopted a little boy of 4 years old. They told us a little bit about the backstory of the little boy, yet they did caveat that telling the child's back story is your (our) choice.

The couple also explained some of the emotions that they had experienced along the way. I think they touched on every emotion and feeling; some happy, some sad, some exciting and some frustrating too. That was a very important part and intriguing piece of their talk. Processes are processes, but feelings are something you can only gain from experiences.

Once they had finished, the session ended with a Q&A and with some 121 time with any of the social workers should we have any questions. Alex and I went into this meeting with the intention – should we get a better experience from the first one – of asking lots of questions. When we got our opportunity and in the heat of the moment we forgot what we wanted to ask. It was probably due to the adrenaline and high we were on from the meeting.

Top tip for next time – we must write down any questions we need answering.

14th February - Valentines Day

It's certainly not like me to be romantic, but Alex and I went out for dinner tonight and predictably the main topic of conversation was centred around last night and the next event we are going to attend. This is the LGBTQ+ one and the last event we have set up.

We tentatively had a discussion about what kind of child (although it's a rubbish way to put it) that we would like and be able to offer a home and life to. It was a severely premature conversation, but one that we just got caught up in. The topic was actually a very tough one as morally there is a lot of conflict with what you feel is 'right'. We settled on being open to a boy or girl but would like them to be under 2 years old. We are not even sure we get to choose yet, or even how you would choose if that is the case; it's one more to add to the question list for next time.

We also discussed whether we feel we have the right credentials the agency would want for adoptive parents and personally we are questioning ourselves too. Do we feel we can do it? I am sure that it's normal to have doubts, but it does dent the confidence a little.

We are looking forward to the next event. We have lots of questions still; probably more than we have ever had. Here are some to remind me.

- What makes a good agency to go with?
- Do we need to have a certain income or level of savings?
- How do we find the right child that will suit us and vice versa?
- How does it work with the child's family – how do we safeguard all of us?
- What training is given?
- Is there any support after the child comes here?
- What if the child gets here and hates it?
- Do adoptions break down?
- What happens if you see the birth parents in the local community post the adoption?
- Do we find out the back story of the child?

I hope they aren't silly questions. I feel like we need to be on top form each time we meet someone.

22nd February - LGBTQ Night

This is the LGBTQ night. Alex and I have spoken non-stop about adoption. We have also spoken to some of our friends who have already adopted and have found out quite a number of snippets that we didn't already know. I bet these friends and their experience are going to be invaluable to us in the future with the support and guidance they can give. Similarly, I hope we can make friends with some other people who are adopting too. I've just joined some Facebook groups to see if we can get some insights and friends online.

We are setting off in ten minutes and I hope this event and experience will reaffirm the positive experience we had with After Adoption. I will ask those questions I wrote down too.

Brilliant news! The event went fantastically well and it all but confirmed – judging from conversation on the way home – that we will be going ahead and applying to be considered to adopt. This could be a life changing decision and I am feeling all the emotions scaling from scared to delighted, and everything in between.

As we arrived at the venue we headed upstairs and the room had 7 different stalls each with a different organisation there. It was a mix of adoption and fostering organisations which after speaking to many of them throughout the evening, helped us cement our view to adopt rather than foster first. This is commonly known as 'foster to adopt'. There is a risk of not fully being able to legally adopt the child in both scenarios, however it is less likely to have to relinquish the child back to the birth parents or family with adoption. A key learning was that you don't adopt the child from day one either. You can apply for an adoption order after 10 weeks post placement with you (when they come to live with you).

After Adoption were there and it was a pleasant surprise to meet them again. Representing them was the same women as the previous meeting; she also recognised us which was lovely. Adoption Counts were there too and they confirmed our thoughts and solidified our decision regarding not choosing them. This time Miss Grumpy was on the stand. Some of the other agencies were lovely and engaging but we just felt like the support, aftercare and connection was there with After Adoption. I think we should go with these and I think Alex agrees. Once we have had time to digest the evening we will talk about the evening in detail.

23rd February - After Adoption Email

We've now spoken a lot about the evening, and it is a resounding 'yes' as to whether we want to continue the process to adopt a child. We are going to send After Adoption an email and to confirm what the application process is but before we do, we have also decided to let our emotions from last night settle down to make sure we are not jumping the gun. I am quite an impulsive character, so we need to just be sure and fully committed. A decision like this is not one to be taken lightly.

We also organically continued the 'type' of child discussion again. It sounds a little bit like shopping and making a bespoke build child, however last night they told us that you have to be honest regarding the child's needs and what you feel capable of living with for the rest of your lives. They told us that you have quite a lot of say in the child themselves; you aren't just allocated one and that's your new family, you have to be 'matched' with a child based on their needs and what you can support.

19th March - *'When you know, you know.'*

We have been having a little bit of email tennis with After Adoption over the last few days. Alex has now sent over the email that formally advises them that we would like to proceed and work with them to help us become adoptive parents. We just feel that they are the right agency for us. Alex's mother said, '*you will know, when you know*' and she is correct. We get the feeling they care about the children *and* the adoptive parents, where others have not. Additionally, After Adoption have been quite forthcoming expressing the level of aftercare that we would receive and as people who have never been parents - especially of a child that is likely to have a challenging background - we feel we may need this.

Overall, they just feel like the right fit for us. We certainly haven't done this all on emotion and have considered other factors. We have looked at the reviews of others, the aftercare package and I even had a friend who worked there previously in the fundraising department who has said they are a very good organisation to work with.

We are very excited. It is starting to feel real and exciting.

3rd April - Expression of Interest

We received an email back today from After Adoption this morning. Post our discussions with a social worker which discussed our application and our current position in life (finance, house, relationship etc), we have been invited to register an *'Expression of Interest'*. We have also been given some direct feedback on the strengths of our application, and of course some things that we should look to work on to strengthen it further down the line. This included positives like the strength of relationship, the home set up we have prepared and also some negatives like our debt and lack of childcare experience.

Overall, it is fantastic to know that we are considered as potential adopters and the professionals have some form of confidence in us to potentially be parents.

The email detailed what the next phase is and when it would be due to start. There will be some formal training that needs to be completed within a 2 month cut off from the date we formally express interest and sign the documentation required. 'Stage One' training is to be a group training session with other potential adopters and led by the social workers from the agency. This will be in July, so it's a fair way off at the moment. We will have to take the time to do some further research and postpone the application to match the 2 month cut off criteria.

The Royal Navy used to have a term and it feels quite apt here. *'Hurry up and wait.'* Frustratingly, I guess that is what we will have to do now.

THE APPLICATION

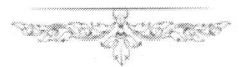

7th April - Application

We decided to just get the application forms completed and ready to send off when we are comfortable with the content. The recruitment person at After Adoption has advised it's okay to do that and that they will hold the application until we are within the two month time frame.

It is relatively straight-forward and has the subjects headings of:

- Applicant Details
- Residency Status
- Relationships
- Identity
- Employment
- Finances
- Health
- Legal
- General

The only difficult section here was based around previous relationships (I get jealous) however I guess this is what we will need to get used to. We have been told there will be lots of awkward and uncomfortable conversations and ones that will test us. I am sure for the greater good of what we are looking to achieve, we can suck it up and I can swallow my own insecurities.

I was chatting to my mother about the health section too and joking with her, but she said quite seriously that I need to lose weight. I am not fat; just not as lean any more. Granted I could do with losing a kilogram or two, but cheers Mum (I laughed about it). It's a bit of a running joke in the family as I once had abdominals, but that was a long time ago.

30th April - Perception and Patience

Even though we have had the forms for a while the recruitment team at After Adoption have been on leave and the detail required has forced us to take some time to reflect on the details and how we present ourselves. It is very important to us that we get the content and tone of our application right too. We are being very cautious regarding the perception we are giving off at each and every interaction we have had so far and we have continued that here in the application. Classically, we are overthinking everything. I think we just need to relax and be us. They will either accept us or not.

Anyway, the application has now been sent. So we can't change anything now.

3rd May - Application Received

We had confirmation this afternoon that the application had been received and it felt a large step forward had just been taken. This means we are formally in the process and it's official.

In the email that we did receive, one of the points refers to gaining references from work but Alex hasn't discussed it with them yet. Alex would rather tell his line manager and HR team rather than them getting a reference request out of the blue to find out. I have spoken to my employers HR team already and they are aware that they may receive a reference request. I haven't told my line manager yet, but I am pretty sure he will be very supportive. He has a few children himself.

All that aside, we are going on holiday tomorrow, so it's time to switch off. Maybe this will be our last full holiday without children. But in the meantime, we are going to take full advantage of the adults only, all inclusive resort.

21st May - Unexpected Proposal

The Mexican sun must have done something to Alex because he proposed to me whilst we were there. I had been sick for two days due to the Mexican food and a number of tequila's. Because of that I had been sitting on the toilet for most of that time feeling as though I was close to crossing the bar (dying). I was just washing my hands as we were about to leave for dinner and Alex stopped me, cuddled me and popped the question. I thought he was getting some Imodium out his pocket and certainly not a ring. He certainly hadn't planned to ask like that and I felt bad that he had to cancel the dinner table on the seafront which was where he had originally planned to ask. It was completely unexpected because he had always maintained that he didn't want to get married. It was a complete surprise and I am over the moon. With my pragmatic head on, I feel it's the right thing for us to have the same surname should we have a child. It will certainly help with their identity as part of our family.

It has been an amazing holiday and feels like this is another significant step to becoming a family.

15th June - Work

My line manager at work is now aware that we are working through the application for adoption. I am still apprehensive about speaking to him in depth about our application as I don't want his views to change regarding myself and my commitment to my career. He is a professional guy so I am sure it won't change his views, however there is still that fear it could via an unconscious bias. Unfortunately, I know from being in a leadership position in several roles that views can change based on many factors (even though they absolutely should not). Personally, I find it completely immoral for people to make decisions based on personal circumstance of this nature.

I spent some time on the phone with HR at work today too. I have politely asked them to ensure our conversation is confidential and asked them to send me across the adoption policy. It was very much an exploratory conversation to understand how the company will support and guide us through the adoption process, however it became clear that a policy is not fully in place and that the HR team are now exploring uncharted territory. Lucky for Alex the HR manager at his work is looking to adopt a child too, so he is in a strong position regarding the support he will receive.

I will pick up with them after we have read through the policies (probably after they have crested them). It is important that we understand the entitlements and support offered, plus we need to get to grips with what money we will have available so we can work out whether we can afford to have a child or not.

16th June - Adoption Leave Discussion

Yesterday's conversations with HR have also sparked the conversation between us regarding time off after we have a child join our family. I would love some time off with our child however both Alex and I know it's not practical for me to be off and for Alex to work due to money reasons. I have a worry that it will cause a missing connection with myself and the child but I'll just have to accept that could be the case. Frankly I am getting ahead of myself as we are just starting the process, so I will have plenty of time to find a way to deal with it.

17th June - Reference Requests

We have been asked to supply five personal references today. We knew this was coming so we had already identified and spoken to the people that we would like to supply a reference for us. Thinking about who we wanted was really important. We want the right people who can articulate about us in the best possible manner and people who know us very well, and in enough depth, to ensure we come across as great parents. It was also important to us to ask people who we value and respect a lot and people who would appreciate the journey we are embarking on.

There are restrictions on who you are allowed to use, and they also wanted a mixture of people from family and social circles. We have asked our parents, Alex's sister's partner (Jock), a Padre who is a good friend of mine, Alex's best friend, plus a couple of our very good mutual friends too. They are all superb people who we are confident will support us and that will say lovely candid things about us to endorse and enhance our application and suitability.

It was a great experience asking these people and one that we will cherish as a happy memory bringing them onboard our journey.

After Adoption has asked for an address so they can send out a reference questionnaire. We asked about the questionnaire and what out references are to expect. We are told it is pretty simple and basic and that it asks about our relationship, current situation and how they feel we would be as parents, ultimately endorsing (or not) our application.

A silly side note, but I worry (but laugh) about how much Jock would love to just write a full essay of jokes and silly banter back to the agency. I know he won't of course but it is still fun for him to tease me about it.

26th June - Admin & Training

There have been a few emails between us and After Adoption. They are of little substance as they have all been requesting factual details and past information. For example, past addresses, information about my time in the Navy etc. The level of information and detail required is staggering and it seems like there are always questions to be answered. I wished we could just do it all in one go and get it done with.

We also have the stage 1 group training coming up soon, which I am really looking forward to. Due to overthinking, I am a little apprehensive that we are going to be judged on everything we say and do. I bet the social workers are going to be watching everything we do and listen to all the comments we make and views we express. I am quite an emotionally driven person, so I may have to be careful how I answer questions. I must remember to engage the brain before blurting out my answers or comments.

27th June - Adoption Medical

Today we completed our medicals at the local GP surgery. Before going today I had some minor anxieties bubbling about my health and suitability, but there was absolutely no reason to. I don't have any health concerns other than a few extra pounds around my midsection, but you never know what they are going to assess you against. Overall, the medical was very basic physically (height, weight and blood pressure), however I am aware the doctor has other questions to complete and send back based on medical history. Again, there is nothing from my side that I believe is a concern, but you never know.

Alex has been worried as he has (and still does) suffer from anxiety. This tends to rear its head when there is some major change; house moves, job promotion offer, etc. Having a child will be a major change and we don't know how it may affect Alex, however after talking about it in some detail we will just have to deal with it should it arise. I worry about him and even if the adoption agency came back and said it was enough to stop the process, I wouldn't hold it against him. He has learned to manage it very well through the techniques he has read about (listing, breathing, reading etc) and I have also learned to spot the signs and what I can or should do. Mostly for Alex, I should do very little other than to just be there for him to unload his thoughts. I find being in the situation where he is anxious really tough for me personally, but it must be so much harder for him to not have someone to discuss it with. I've got it the easiest out of the two of us.

29th June - References and Homework

After Adoption messaged back today to advise that they had received some of our references back already. A couple of the references who we approached, called us to check what they have written with us and to make sure that we are happy with it. Jock was one and although he has been winding me up about what he will put in the letter, he has been very magnanimous with his words. He really does know how much we want to have a child but I also think he is excited at the prospect of having a niece or nephew.

We have also been given some 'homework'. It's a reading list of a few books. We have bought a couple straight away as any help and guidance we can get will be great. The list they have suggested for us to get through are:

- Attachment Handbook for Foster Care and Adoption by Gillian Schofield (*note from After Adoption -* I think section 2 is most relevant for parents as the rest is more for professionals)
- A Child's Journey Through Placement by Vera Fahlberg
- Why can't my child Behave?: Empathic Parenting Strategies that Work for Adoptive and Foster Families By Dr Amber Elliot
- Becoming Dads: A Gay Couple's Journey to Adoption by Pablo Fernandez
- The Simple Guide to Child Trauma (Simple Guides) by Betsy de Thierry

We have also searched for some other books or blogs that may talk us through the emotional side of the process, yet we can't find many. We can find lots that talk through the step by step part, however.

STAGE 1 - TRAINING

12th July - The Day Before Training

We are due on the training course tomorrow and Saturday. I have taken an annual leave day for tomorrow as I am still not sure of my entitlement and neither are my work place. I am very excited about the training course, and I am confident we will present ourselves very well. We have been overthinking the day and how much we will be assessed, so much so that we've discussed what we need to wear to make the right impression. Should I wear a shirt, or jeans and t-shirt (my staple). We eventually have come to the conclusion that we just need to be 'us' and not something or people that we are not. We have been told to be 'us' so many times by the agency so we must stick to that advice. They say it is very important as it helps them form our profiles which effectively support the search for a child to 'match' with.

We want to be accepted based on our merits and not a false perception either. Even if we did go into it and try to 'please' them, I don't think that would be sustainable for the whole process. It's definitely the right thing to just be ourselves. I am going to have an early night tonight and make sure I am fully rested for tomorrow. I am sure it is going to be mentally draining.

13th July - Stage 1 - Training Course Day 1

I unexpectedly slept like a log, although I wouldn't have thought that would have been the case. This whole process and outcome means so much to me (and Alex) that I have played over every scenario I can think of in my mind as to what and how the process may play out. Maybe for that reason it exhausted my brain and body enough to sleep so well. I am not sure Alex slept much though. He never does in situations like this.

We arrived in good time and signed in. The nerves left us when we had finally got there and got a nice welcome from the co-ordinator. After the welcome from the After Adoption team, we were seated in a training room with another 15 or so people. It was set out in 5 round tables and we sat across from some lovely people, who we got to know over the course of the next few hours. The room felt a little edgy and nervy at the start of the day but we all soon relaxed into it as the sessions started. It was also refreshing to see the type of other people there. There were single people, a couple of same sex couples (both male and female) and also a few heterosexual couples. There was also a gentleman who was deaf and a couple with very limited English understanding; they had an interpreter to support them. It was great to see that all people from different backgrounds are considered to adopt a child as I would assume that there are lots of different children from many different backgrounds requiring a forever home. Due to that they must need to be very open to who they consider.

The day started with an introduction to adoption. There were some facts and figures about adoption. Shockingly, there are approximately 74,000 children in the care system with about 4% 'making it out' (adopted or back to their birth family). How can there be so many children that have been put in that situation? The social worker presenting said that number has grown by about 2% in the past 12 months and is projected to continue to grow. It makes me very sad and frankly quite angry to hear that.

My initial thoughts were very negative towards the people and 'parents' that could put their children through this, however there was an exercise completed today that changed my opinion a little. The exercise consisted of us being asked to verbalise why children were in care and also to express our opinions regarding the parents. We did this in a small group of people and then presented them back to the whole group. Pretty much all the answers from across the board seemed to be negative; in fact I can't remember a positive one that was offered.

'Drug addict, physical abuser, sexual abuser, Jeremy Kyle watchers, violent people, prison goers, horrible people, sick minded' etc etc. We were also asked to verbalise how we felt about those people too. The tone went along the same route, being negative and 'deserving' of the birth parents. One man said, 'surely it's their own fault their child

would be removed if they have chosen to neglect them'. It was hard to reject that notion. What was refreshing from the Social Worker though, was that they did NOT judge anyone for their answers and their feelings; after all this was about helping educate us on the reason and process of adoption.

On the whole it was very negative when in reality, there were some very varied and often unavoidable reasons for a child to have to be removed or relinquished. We were shown some video footage of some of the birth parents effectively doing an interview. I am very sure everyone in their room changed their opinions at that point. It showed a woman who had been in an abusive relationship. She came across as a very respectable woman, she was well spoken and appeared to be in a lovely house and 'normal'. She had been abused by her boyfriend, physically, and felt so trapped that it was unsafe for her and her children. It got to the point where a social worker had been asked to intervene and the child had been placed in the care system. The sadness in the woman's voice was so upsetting and it really hit a chord on my heart strings. Another video showed a woman who struggled with severe mental health problems and she has been taken advantage of by men. Both stories were very tough to listen to and it was by no fault of their own this had happened to them and their children. The final story that was shared was about a child whose mother had died after a long battle with cancer. Hearing these unexpected narratives was heart wrenching and opinion changing.

We, of course, also learned about some of the horrible stories too and boy were some horrible! I found it very important and useful to learn about both groups. The common message from the social workers was that all of the children in the care system will most likely have some form of trauma they will have to contend with at some point in their lives. Often it manifests in different ways; behaviour, autism, learning difficulties, attachment struggles, foetal alcohol syndrome etc. We then spoke in quite some detail about the children and some of the different examples describing their adoption journeys.

When that session finished we had some lunch and at that point I was certainly ready for it. Not because I was hungry (well, I was too) but because my mind was frazzled. We got to speak to some of the other people attending and started to get to know them. We had learned that it was likely we would be on further training with them so we all wanted to connect properly because we thought it would be good to have a support group that we could all share ideas, experiences and also offer each other some moral support should it be needed. It was recommended by the social worker to make connections, so who better than people on the same journey as us. I am glad the other people there also had the same intentions too.

Over the lunch break, Alex and I connected with 3 couples. They were two guys, two ladies and one male/female couple. All of us were around the same ages, give or take a year or two, so it was quite natural to connect. We spent most of the break asking the basics about each other and learning a bit about each others back stories. We also spoke about the process to date and how they were finding the adoption journey. All of them seemed to have positive experiences which boded well regarding the decision to work with After Adoption. I felt very comfortable around these people and I instantly knew we would get along.

After lunch we went through the subject of Therapeutic Parenting and lots of ways to work on it. We learned about some models to support therapeutic parenting. A lot of it seems to be common sense to me, I think. We spoke in lots of detail around being patient, having lots of understanding, listening and also identifying challenging behaviours. We spoke about some physical and psychological ways to form connections with your child. It was the psychological piece that I found most interesting. Lots of 'cause and effect' stuff and how an action of the past can manifest in the coming few years or beyond. Many of the actions to be a therapeutic parent centred around *'being your inner child'* and actually having fun with your little one(s).

I don't need any encouragement bringing out my inner child and based upon the experiences we have had with children within our family, I can certainly conclude that I am a big kid. This should come naturally to me.
To show some examples of how to bring out the inner child, we played some games. I particularly enjoy watching Alex immerse himself fully into the part of pretending to be an animal. He actually surprised me because he is not an extroverted person in groups of unknowns, however he played the monkey and frog so well in front of lots of people; I secretly think he was having loads of fun with it.

After making a fool of ourselves (and having fun), we did some work using building blocks. This was a visual representation to show that if there are missing blocks when building a structure then it can lead to instability or in some cases collapse. It was a tool to help us understand that many children that come from the backgrounds we spoke about earlier will often have some form of 'block' or 'blocks' missing. The big message (I think) was to be conscious that our child may have some 'blocks' missing that may need some repairing through a variety of channels. Some of those may be through therapeutic parenting, professional therapy, school and even what I deemed to be the basics; love, attention and safety. The term *'meeting the needs of the child'* was used a lot of this section.

Towards the end of the day, I was flagging a little. There was a lot of information to take onboard. Many of the scenarios played out across the day got me thinking, over-thinking and running a hell of a lot of scenarios through my head. It was exhausting. The day certainly made me think about whether I thought I was ready, able and 100% committed. I had some doubts today if I am honest. I am worried that I may not have the skills to help a child that has come from such a traumatic life.

I have a feeling that I won't struggle to sleep again tonight.

14th July - Stage 1 - Training Course Day 2

Reflecting on yesterday gave me a hell of a lot of doubts about my ability. There is so much more to consider than I originally thought. What we also reflected upon when discussing the day was that we felt very guarded in how we presented ourselves; maybe we were conscious that we are being constantly assessed. We thought this would happen before all the training started.

It was nice that we arrived a little early today because it gave us a few minutes to grab a coffee and settle in. We got speaking to the group we did over lunch yesterday and it was suggested we have a beer and some food afterwards. We of course said yes. It would be nice to meet them in a more social setting and get to know them. It sounded as if the intention would be to create a small network group of similar minded people which we of course think is a great idea.

Once the sessions got started we had a recap of yesterday's topics and an open forum to discuss our feelings. What we learned from the conversation is that many of the other people were feeling the same as us regarding the difference in parenting a child that is adopted, over a child that hasn't been.

Next up was a discussion about honesty. I thought it was a bit of a bizarre session, but once it was over I understood why it was an essential topic to cover. The social worker explained why it was important to be honest throughout the process, the home interviews and - more importantly - why it is important to be honest with ourselves. They said that they have seen enough people come apart when not fully telling the truth from the start. It was also described that it is often a self-exploration process and it can feel close to your own therapy session when discussing your past. I am not looking forward to that bit as I don't want to speak about my 'Dad' at all. He is not part of my life and I don't want him to be at all. I will have to cross that bridge later I guess.

After the break we did a session that discussed different 'types' of children and how to choose the right one (or ones) for you. We explored the process of family finding and how to find and search for a child. We completed an exercise that had us go through a checklist that picked out what we believed we could take on in regard to a child. For example, the checklist would ask if we wanted a child with 'learning difficulties, physical impairments, HIV, sexual abuse victim' and so on. It was quite a shocking list and one I really wanted to compartmentalise and tuck away in my brain quickly. I didn't really want to think about the things some of the children could have gone through. The big takeaway for me here was based on a comment made by the social worker.

> *'Be honest, in fact be very honest. You will not be judged if you feel that a category or need is not for you and your future family. Being honest from now on is critical to be able to lessen the likelihood of a breakdown in a match in the future'*

I felt it was quite tough to rule out certain children based on them having a disability or situation beyond their control. When we had finished our checklist, I had very heightened emotions and I felt mentally drained and low due to the fact the profile we have created from the checklist was one of a child with close to zero additional needs; some would term it a 'normal child' (which we were told isn't the case for any adopted child). As tough as it was, we were very honest with ourselves just as the social worker had advised us to be. She was very reassuring explaining that there are children out there with all sorts of profiles and there will be one (or more) potential adopters that matches with them.

At lunch we then had some more time to speak with the social workers and other potential adopters. We were unsure whether it is taboo to ask why others are wanting to adopt, or to naturally gravitate towards the subject we had just covered. We discussed the profiles of children we had just drawn up and just as the social worker had reassured us, it was great to hear that other potential adopters wanted different needs. In the group we had people who were happy to disclose that they wanted to go down the route of having a child that had additional needs, some wanted older children, some wanted siblings and us, whilst we would like a little boy between 1 and 2 years old with very few additional needs.

After lunch we had a session on *'How do you find a child?'* and it was enlightening to say the least. Originally, I had thought that when you had been signed off as adopters, you were then matched with a child on the recommendation of the social worker. This is not the case at all (but can be too). There are quite a few ways to search for a child and be matched, however.

We were told about the following ways:

- **Social worker recommendation** - based only on our profile and a child profile, you will be offered some profiles that the social worker feels match yours and their criteria and needs.
- **Website** - There is a website that has profiles that you do a search on by filtering your criteria. She said it's like a dating website - taking away the obvious - but you add in all of your desired criteria and it will show you all the profiles that match that search. You then click the profile and 'express interest' should you want to know more. The profiles have some significant detail on them about the child. If your interest is reciprocated by the social worker of the child, then you can open a chat and take it from there.
- **Finder events** - This is where you go to an event where lots of the children requiring a forever home are there playing. When you go to this, you are invited to interact with the children whilst they are playing and if you form a connection, you are invited to express interest.
- **Profiling event** - This is where you go to an event where social workers present profiles of children and you present yours in return. The social worker described this as like an 'exhibition stand'.
- **Foster to Adopt** - This is where you foster a child first and then move to adopt them at the appropriate time. There is a risk to this however, as the child may move back to the birth family.

The one that jumped out to us was the website search. This is because we can check out the profiles yet still keep the emotional connection at arms length. Some of the other people with us preferred other routes, but it's each to their own, I guess.

The final session of the day was a session with two ladies who had adopted a couple of sisters. As soon as they entered the room it was clear and obvious to see how much of a happy family they were and how attached the children were to their mothers. It was so nice to hear about the journey of this family. They spoke about their journey from when they applied up until the present day explaining the good, bad and challenging experiences. They explained the process was tough, draining, rewarding and very much a self-exploration journey too (we have heard the self-exploration term a few times now). They told us about the search process and how emotionally demanding that could be due to the profiles pulling on heartstrings and some explaining a high level view of the harrowing circumstances described within them. A pull out point that they stressed was to stay as detached as much as possible and do not under any circumstance feel like you 'have' to adopt the child. I took quite a few points away from this session and really enjoyed knowing that the process does produce happy families.

Finally, we were told about some 'friends and family' days that are designed to help our friends and family understand the journey that we are going on. This is so they can understand a little bit more about the children, some possible needs of a child that we may have and also to help them understand how they can support us as adopters. The social workers have highly recommended that we have people attend and quite frankly I can see why if the last couple of days are anything to go by. I have been educated to see there will be many additional things to think about when adopting a child. They are different to other children due to potential and likely trauma of some form. I will certainly be asking my side of the family to go and take advantage of this opportunity to learn. It can only be positive learning.

Once we had finished the day, a few of us went for a drink and some food at the pub that was a couple of minutes walk away from the adoption training centre. It was nice to discuss the adoption journey outside of the training room, but most importantly for me, it was nice to start making a friends group. I feel like it could be invaluable having people that are going through the same process as us. I think it will be important for the children too, to have a network as they grow up. They are all absolutely lovely people too.

We have agreed to keep in touch via a WhatsApp group.

15th July - Sound Board

I called my mother today to chat through and help me process the last few days. I tend to call her when I need a fresh view or vent and she is always a really good soundboard when I am overthinking things. I have now had some time for the information to settle and I appreciate the 30 minutes on the phone as it was good to talk through it all with her. I have found it refreshing to have someone else other than Alex to discuss our journey with. Mum and I just spoke about what we did on the course and we both had opinions on certain topics that we had covered. She is always a good leveller of the mind and sound board.

Alex and I also received some WhatsApp messages through from our new friendship group. The conversation has been very intelligent, pleasant and an open forum for each of us to ask questions. I like that we have all respected boundaries too, so it has not been intrusive . It's interesting to assess the dynamics of the group. We have all naturally and politely been feeling out the amount of information we want to share and ask with one another. I certainly don't want to ask a direct question to one of the group about why they are adopting or something similar. I am sure when people are comfortable we may offer more information than we are at present.

18th July - Worksheets

We received an email today to remind us about the worksheets that we have to complete. I totally forgot about them (even though we are pretty much finished completing them). They are effectively a massive set of questions that walk the social worker through our life to-date and sundry.

They are due before the end of stage 1 which is creeping up on us quickly.

We are up to 36 pages of questions and answers at present and there is still some way to go. The main subjects that we have answered so far are:

- Family background and early experience.
- Adult life; work, health and other issues.

- Relationships and support networks.
- The home, financial circumstances and lifestyle.
- Motivation to adopt and expectations of placement.
- Understanding the needs of adopted children and adoptive parenting capacity.

These sections have really asked us to delve into our life and I found myself thinking about things that I hadn't for some time; especially family background. I have had a really hard time emotionally on that section. The bits where I've had to think about my 'father' have been especially hard for me. I really don't want to speak about him, yet this process means I have to address my underlying emotions regarding him and the past. An example of one of the questions and answers:

Q: Describe your father and the nature of your relationship with him. If you had to choose five words to illustrate this, which ones would you choose? Can you recall any examples to evidence the words you have chosen? Did the nature of your relationship with your father change at all during the course of your childhood?

A: I do not have a relationship with my father. I can only remember bad things about him from being violent, aggressive, a drunk and abusive. A manipulative person when we met him again in our teenage years.

There are of course many more questions and each one engages a different emotion. If you were to ask me the same question regarding my mother - which it does - then you get a completely different answer and one of pure joy and respect.

Overall, some of this was tough and it was a roller coaster that I don't think I was fully prepared for. It has brought up repressed and compartmentalised memories that I haven't even discussed with my mother. Ones that she may not even know that I am aware of.

I hope the social workers respect that fact that I don't want to talk about him and leave it at that, however I get the sneaky feeling that it won't be the last time I will have to think about him and address my own demons about the whole situation and relationship.

21st July - Friends and Family Training

Today we received information regarding the 'friends and family training' sessions. Both Alex and I have spoken to the people that we would like to attend. It's pretty much all of the people that we have asked to be our references as they are the people that are most likely to have high level contact with the child. All of them have been very receptive to wanting to attend and learn; which I am very pleased with. It shows how supportive they all are regarding our journey to having a family. We are very lucky to have such great friends and family.

23rd July - Taking a Break

Now that we have pretty much completed stage 1 training and all of the paperwork, Alex and I have been discussing stage 2 and the timing of our wedding which we have now set for December. After quite some deliberation, we have unanimously decided that we are going to take a break from the process and for no other main reason than timing of the wedding and that date of stage 2 training, which is in January. It makes sense to switch off and recharge . Frankly it hardly changes much of the forthcoming agenda anyway and only postpones the home visit meetings with our newly allocated social worker. It is a guy call Patrick.

In stage 2 we will have 8 sessions (9 if required) with Patrick. He facilitated parts of the training that we have already completed and he seems like a really nice guy. Hopefully we hit it off with him and the following process goes well. Also, with him being assigned to us, we are interpreting this as a very positive sign that things are going well.

Another reason for taking the break - bar the wedding - is that we really want to make sure we are financially and mentally ready, plus we really want to have the same surname for the child when they arrive home. We don't want to add another layer of complexion to their overall identity by having to explain that we have different names.

Between now and January we will still have interactions with After Adoption as there are still actions that need to be completed. The friends and family training, online training for us and formal checks, like DBS checks, for example; so it isn't a complete close down.

4th September - Stage 1 - Sign Off

The DBS checks have been returned and we can now officially be signed off for stage one. We have chased this up to check when sign off will be because we want to complete as much as we can, so we can switch off and concentrate on the wedding. Even though there is very little to do at this time, it always seems there is a hell of a lot on that ever-growing list of actions to complete. I guess having long lists of things to do will only increase with a child. My best mate constantly tells me enough how busy and tired he is and at the present time I can't resonate with him.

6th September - Adoption Friends

We had a lovely surprise today because we have heard from our adoption friends on our WhatsApp group. They are all progressing really well and doing a lot of their home visit meetings with their allocated social worker at present. We have been pumping them for information regarding the questions being asked and their experience; however it seems to differ for all of them based on the answers they have given and their circumstances. I guess that means we can't read into the information too much although I am still sure some of it will help us navigate our way through our home visits when they come around in the new year.

I am feeling a little bit jealous of the others though. They are so advanced and are looking at some profiles of children via the website that we have all got access too. Additionally, their social workers have presented some profiles which indicated how far into the process they are. It also offers an indication that they are likely to pass their assessment in stage 2.

It must feel awesome to be in their situation, however we must reflect and accept that it was our choice to slow down and take a break from the process.

21st September - Stage 1 Sign Off

Just as I was switching off from it all we got a call and the delivery of some great news. We have now had an official sign off for 'stage 1'. It is fantastic to know that we have been deemed suitable candidates to potentially adopt a child.

In the same breath, it is actually quite daunting that we are an official step closer to being parents. It certainly feels that little bit more real now.

The news itself was delivered via a voicemail and a follow up email to tell us. It wasn't all party hats and party poppers, but delivered quite transactionally and monotonically (as if they have done it a thousand times) with a 'congratulations'. Patrick then moved straight on to what the next steps will be when we return to the process next year. I think as it is such a big milestone we wanted it to be a bit more engaging, exciting and emotional from them, but even though it wasn't, it won't stop us from having a drink tonight to celebrate.

Stage 1 complete. Brilliant!

22nd September - Celebratory Hangover

We had drinks last night. My head hurts! We celebrated with our lovely neighbours and they were very excited for us. They are great neighbours and friends. I just know they are going to be very important to us in the future.

Anyway, I hope we can now switch off fully until January when we restart the process. It has been mentally draining enough so far so time to recharge.

STAGE 2

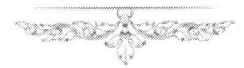

5th January - New Year & Re-Start

Alex messaged After Adoption this morning to check in and see if we need to do anything to re-start with the stage 2 process. They have advised that we now are again actively in the process on their system however it will not officially restart until the 18th January. This is due to the timings as we have 6 months to complete stage 2. The 18th January is the first day of stage 2 training and so maximises the window to complete it.

It will be great to see the other guys from our group and see how they are progressing with the home visits and the questions. They have shared some of it via WhatsApp on the group and it all seems pretty simple, but as previously mentioned, it's all different depending on their situation.

8th January - Panel Date Questions

We received an email from the agency today to confirm stage 2 training is on the 18th January. They have also asked us if we have a preferred date (April in Manchester or May in Birmingham) for our Panel which would confirm we are suitable to adopt a child. Of course this is very premature but they need to get it in the diary at the earliest opportunity. I think it also will help make sure all sections and assessments are done in good time too.

This has just got very real all of a sudden. I can certainly say I am a little apprehensive whilst simultaneously elated. This is going to completely change our lives from what we have now. Currently we have freedom of choice to do as we want when we want. I am pretty sure that will change quickly, however.

Overall I am pleased that we have some form of timeline for the next stage. Sign off at the panel is only one more step. There are quite a few stages post 'panel' that will take some time. For example, the phase of finding a child and matching with them too plus the introductions and things that go with that. I think it's fair to say we still have plenty of freedom for now and I am sure we will make the most of it. The process certainly has taken longer than I thought it would.

We have accepted the 23rd April in Manchester for the panel. We wanted the earliest date because after all, we want to complete our family so the sooner the better.

STAGE 2 - TRAINING

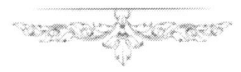

17th January - The Day Before Training

We both have some nerves regarding tomorrow, quite similar to the time we did stage 1 training. The good news is that we will know most people attending this time and we have confirmed with our adoption WhatsApp group that all will be there. I am happy that there won't be so much small talk and we can feel a little more comfortable from the start.

18th January - Stage 2 - Advanced Adoption Training - Day 1

In a slight change of emotion from last night, I was really excited about today before we set off. I was excited to see the others from our little 'support group' (as we have now called it) and to get an update regarding their progress. It also presented an opportunity to learn about the more challenging parts that they have come up against at the home visits. If we can gain an insight into the questions we will be asked we can prepare better.

When we arrived there were hugs all around. I am a hugger, so I am cool with that. We all seem to have that connection to each other and I am very appreciative that we have. I know how lucky we are to find good people to share our experience with. I bet having these friends will be invaluable when we all have children.

After a quick welcome and some housekeeping - training days wouldn't be the same without the fire alarm detail and other boring admin - we move into the first of four sessions before lunch. The sessions were...

- Attachment Theory
- Neurological Information and Brain Development
- Self-Awareness
- Introduction to Safebase parenting programme

In the attachment theory session, I was particularly drawn in to the content and I really enjoyed it. I quite enjoy trying to learn the 'why' about things I don't understand.

'Young people need to be attached to a primary caregiver or givers for normal and social development'

We had done a little on this in stage 1 training, but this went into a little more of the scientific detail and in hindsight, it linked well into the second session (neurological information and brain development). It was discussed that children become sensitive and responsive within social interactions, yet children that have come into the care system may not have ever had the opportunity to form them (not all, but likely most). The only time they may would be with the foster carers and then their new forever family (us, hopefully)

This was then flipped and linked into 'separation anxiety'. It was discussed the journey may include lots of separation anxiety at the start of a placement as the child may lack trust of their new base / family, until they understand it is secure and safe. This is due to a number of factors, but my take was that it was linked heavily to losing the secure base of their foster carers. The social worker facilitating the session said that it can manifest in many ways; anger, crying, quiet or loud behaviour, bad behaviour, and lots of talking about their foster carer if they are older. It is also common to see lots of regressions of age relative things. The wider group really engaged with this and asked a lot of questions, so it was clearly a hot topic. Who wouldn't want to know how to connect with their child?

The second session regarding neurological information and brain development was high level information and not massively in depth. I think the title exaggerated the content somewhat. This section touched on trauma and the effects it has on the brain development and neurological pathways that are created (or not) when the child has the interaction they have. Those interactions could be good (e.g playing with them) or bad (e.g watching and hearing people fight). The social worker then explained how this can affect various things such as learning, expressions of emotions, basic understanding, physical attributes and so on. This session was an awareness session and one that really emphasised that adopted children or children in care are NOT the same as other children and that we must be conscious of that. This was linked back to attachment and therapeutic parenting.

Session three's subject was based around self-awareness. Until this session I hadn't really thought about this in much detail. We discussed our current feelings as a group and then went on to speak about how we may feel in certain scenarios. I enjoyed discussing what the social workers have seen as trends in other adoption families, drawing from their experiences. Self-care and partner care was a big subject here too.

'You need to look after yourself and your partner too. If you are struggling to function, then it will be tough to parent a child who will require a lot of support and guidance. Ensure you are meeting your own needs too'.

I thought that was a powerful message. We also delved heavily into self-awareness with regard to parenting an adopted child. A few key messages here were around patience, understanding and not to be too self-critical.

Before the guest speaker was due, we had a session introducing us to the Safebase Parenting Programme. This programme is based around therapeutic parenting interventions for young children up to teenage years. It is based on Theraplay®; therapeutic playing and was offered to us should we want to pursue it. It seems a little far away yet to decide as to whether we will need it or not, but it's good to have the knowledge the support is there if we need it in future.

Finally, we had a guest speaker due but they couldn't make it at the last minute, so we went straight into lunch. Once we had all collected food, our little support group sat around one big table which gave us all time to chat through the morning and again generally have a chat about how the process was going. I really enjoyed this time because all the others - who were now ahead of us due to our break - had all received similar experiences but personalised to their circumstances. We also heard about one of the couples who had already discussed with their social worker a child that had been identified and one that matched one another's profiles. It was very exciting news!

After lunch the agenda was as follows:

- Theraplay®
- Attachment & Education
- When considering your child
- Guest Speak - PAS Speaker (Post Adoption Speaker)

I think it was one of the social workers that was presenting this section - I missed the introduction because I was writing some notes - but they introduced the session as *'a child and family therapy for building and enhancing attachment, trust and self-esteem. The sessions are designed to create active and emotional connections between parent and children'*

The session on Theraplay ® was again similar in content to the session we did in stage 1 training but had the connection to the training we received this morning. It was connecting some of the dots as to how therapeutic playing can help connect some neurological pathways and help with attachment.

When we had completed that we discussed 'Attachment and Education'. Attachment had been spoken about a lot already, so it was again linking it all together and also linking it to education. It was suggested that many children have anxiety or other mental health concerns regarding attachment and school as they are no longer with their new primary carer(s). There were some tools suggested to reduce and combat this, like talking about school and even pretending to be at school. It was effectively putting some school routines into the household routine that replicate the school one in an effort to maintain a structured schedule. For example, we could tell our child that he is going to school in a few weeks and that they do registers in the morning to check who is at school. Then we would replicate that by doing a register. 'Andrew, Teddy, Car, Bear, Pillow etc'. They also suggested having a band that they can wear on their bag or wrist and if they need to feel connected, then to use that to confirm the connection is still there. We would also have one too, so we can suggest that we would use it when we wanted to think about the child throughout the day, reciprocating the connection back to the child.

The education part of a subject that we all engaged to a high level due to the level of importance it has. As a parent (I would assume as I am not one, yet) I would want my child to have the best possible education and one specific to their needs. The social worker discussed the requirement that you should ensure the school was ready and geared up to best meet the needs of your child and for us as parents to be quite demanding of that point from the school. In addition, it was noted that the school receives a grant of £2000 per year as a 'pupil premium' to support your child (and others) with their additional needs, so again it is recommended that you are quite forthcoming of how this is spent; although the final choice is the schools. When your child is at school, they receive regular LAC (Looked After Child) reviews up until the adoption order is complete. This is an opportunity for the school to use the grant to best suit any recommended action points from this. Finally, as a LAC and adopted child, they will get priority on any school in your local area, but not a guaranteed place. I am really pleased that there is this advantage because we can place our child in the best school suited for them.

After a small break we moved on to the subject of 'when considering your child'. This session was just a repeat of the previous one, but in different terminology. It went into some further detail on the search process too. Yet this time we were given some profiles of children and were asked to read through them. This was a superb exercise for me personally as it really set the tone on the kind of things we were likely to see within them. I couldn't believe some of the information in there and it was hard to read them. Some of them discussed neglect, sexual abuse, physical deformities and others were very tame in comparison.

At the end of this part we were also advised that we could have access to the online database and would be invited to any of the activity days if we wanted to. We just needed to confirm with them that we wanted access and invites.

19th January - Stage 2 - Advanced Adoption Training - Day 2

I was quite tired mentally going into today as there was a lot of information to take in, but my thirst for more information was still there. I want to know as much as I can to make sure we are good parents. When we got home last night I bought a couple of books on child trauma and a book on therapeutic parenting. Conversing over coffee in the training room this morning before we started the sessions, it seemed like some of the others were feeling and doing the same too.

We had quite a few things on the agenda today, but they were only short sessions. Once we had finished the wash-up from yesterday and any questions, we moved onto the day's agenda. I've listed below.

- Where are we now?
- Identity & Embracing the Past
- Life Story Work
- Guest Speaker - Adoptive Family

Session 1 - Where are we now? This focused on the stage of the journey we are at and what the next steps are. It was a good session for me because with this whole process, there is so much going on that it is hard to keep up with the next steps. We are slightly behind a few of the people here - and all of our friend's group - and the next phase for us is the home visits and questions. Our social worker Patrick, will be doing these with us. These are the sessions that we have gained some insight into from our group. They have suggested that they are nothing overly exciting or worrying; just a hell of a lot of questions about our past, present, and other things like beliefs. After the home visits, you go to a panel to be signed off as suitable to adopt and then follow on or continue with your search for a child(ren). We have now got access to the search site too. I am reluctant to look at it right now, but I am inquisitive to have a look soon. Alex isn't keen at all to look at it just yet. He fears - and rightfully - he may find a child he really likes and wants to pursue but we are too early in the process; so his hesitation is justified in my view. I can resonate and respect that.

After the search is completed for a child and the social workers agree it could be a potential synergy of profiles, there is a 'matching panel' that confirms (or not) the match. Should it be agreed the process moved onto introductions to the child and then placement into your home. All of this seems some way off yet, but I am sure we will get there soon enough. To put into perspective, some of our group are currently exploring matches with children and we are only a few months behind.

Session 2 was about 'identity & embracing the past'. I found this a tough session personally. When we were prompted to discuss this section, I unexpectedly cried in front of everyone when trying to ask a basic question about the subject. I feel so embarrassed for doing that in front of a lot of people and a little worried that I have exposed a weakness to the social workers. The bit that got me was about identity, what makes you who you are and how it can affect you as a person; past, present and in the future. The social workers just were not getting into enough detail for me and I kept asking 'why?' to back up their claims. Ultimately, I think it was getting me worked up and I feel maybe my questions - in hindsight - were actually questions to find answers I wanted for myself. Ever since I left the Royal Navy I feel like I have lacked a direction and most importantly, a purpose. I have really struggled with that and emotionally compartmentalised it enough to get on with life. I also feel that not having a father to grow up with has subconsciously hurt me a little, even though I am very happy with the way I grew up with the guidance of the most amazing woman on earth; my mum.

Once I had composed myself the group discussed the reasons why it's important to acknowledge the identity of the birth family with the adopted child. The take-away for me was around transparency with the child but at an age-appropriate level. I would rather feed correct information over the long term and not give the child a massive shock. I mean, the child is going to be adopted by 2 guys and so clearly there will be questions asked from the child and his/her friends at some point in their lives. I am pretty sure that we will be very clear and transparent from the beginning with our child, unless the social workers suggest otherwise for what ever reason.

Session 3 was titled 'Life Story'. This session was a continuation and link with session 2, but explained that the local authority will produce a life story book to help the child with their identity as they grow up and begin to understand what adoption really means. A life story book is a chronology of the child's life that is to help with identity formation and can help with various other aspects of adoption. For example, separation anxiety, attachment, understanding their reality and to help identify and understand positives and even the negatives about their birth family.

I found it very interesting that the social worker and the manual suggested that you should not gloss over the reasons for a child going into care as this can cause longer term issues for the child. It is important to be honest, but also age appropriate when discussing the child's life story and identity. Personally, I would have thought to be careful about the information you share with them; that session changed my views on that. I wouldn't like information about my birth family withheld if I was in the same position.

'Life Story' was followed with a meet and presentation by a couple and their two adopted boys. The two dads held a very open conversation about their journey and were very candid about the positive, negative and other events that happened throughout. I was particularly interested when they discussed the 'introduction' and the 'coming home' elements. I have this huge fear that whichever child we eventually (and hopefully) bring home, that we/they will struggle with a connection, or they will resent us. I am sure that wouldn't be the case as the social workers will be very diligent in relation to matching a child to us and vice versa.

The two dads discussed everything from starting the search process to present. They said they had changed their minds on so many occasions regarding the 'type' child they wanted and then ended up with a child that was different from their first view. They originally said they wanted a baby boy or girl, but then ended up falling in love with two older sibling boys and that's what they had eventually been placed with. At the start of the placement they expressed that they saw the children presented a lot of typical pleasing behaviours which eventually turned into testing boundaries and some challenges. The social worker told us that this is quite common. The pleasing is often fear and attachment related but is usually an unconscious behaviour the child doesn't know they are doing. It was believed that it was the boys trying to form a secure bond and a place where they feel safe. It was all very interesting. They went on to discuss other things that I hadn't considered in much detail. Things like school, food, days out, money, clothing, meeting family, seeing friends and so on. They also spoke about a really interesting point regarding the boys mentioning their birth family, how they deal with that and also how it really affected them emotionally. They said it was a hard feeling and one that they had to accept quickly, regardless of how jealous it made them feel. The conversation was never shut off and was discussed should the boys want to discuss it. All at an age appropriate level.

The session ran over into lunch, so we could ask questions to the parents in a more informal and private manner should we want to. It was just amazing to watch the two boys interacting with their parents too. They just showed complete love towards each other and that was fantastic to witness. It has eased some of my worries about attachment in adoption.

After lunch we went through the agenda of:

- Contact & Maintaining Links
- The Abused Child & Safe Caring
- Health
- Mechanics of Placement
- Living with Adoption
- Support
- Wash Up

'Contact and maintaining links' was the first session after the break. We discussed the importance and rights that a child has in regard to maintaining some form of contact with their birth family. This doesn't mean meeting them necessarily (although the social worker said some do) but could be in other forms. The main 4 ways of 'contact' are:

- **No Contact** - This is extremely rare, but this means there is zero contact with the birth family. Often this is due to safeguarding and safety reasons.
- **Meetings** with birth family (adults only) - This is a one-off meeting with the birth family and this is strongly advised to do this meeting should you be offered the opportunity. It has many benefits, but mainly so you can reassure the child that you have met their birth parents and can positively speak about them where required. It is also good for the birth parents as it can reassure them about who their child will be placed with.
- **Indirect / Letterbox Contact** - This is the most common. A letter is sent once, or twice a year to share information (safely) about your child and how they are progressing. These can then be shared in later years, if appropriate.
- **Direct Contact** - As it sounds. This is direct contact with the birth parent or some of the birth family. This process is always in a support and supervised session.

Out of this session, the one I think I would prefer the most is the letterbox contact and if it was deemed necessary, I came around to the idea of the one-off meeting with the birth family. My instant reaction to the meeting was negative due to a worry about safety, however the more it was discussed I started to understand the benefits of the meeting for the child. I just think I will be running anti-surveillance drills going to the meeting! The Armed Forces mentality never leaves you!

The overall message that resonated was around building strong and honest relationships through open communication for the benefit of all parties.

Part of this session discussed the use of 'social media platform' and modern technology. We looked at this from all sides, birth parent, us and the child. A hot topic here was the safe use and sharing of information about your child on social media, especially pictures. You see so many people posting pictures of their children on Facebook or Instagram and our friends just think it's a nice way to document their lives and share with friends and family. As an adoptive family, it must be much harder if there are safeguard reasons.

There was a huge section regarding vulnerabilities and is advised that...

'we know children have emotional, social or behavioural difficulties because of their earlier experiences of trauma and/or separation of loss and this could mean that, for instance:

- *They may be suggestible and easily led. E.g. by a paedophile posing as a young person in an internet chat room or by a manipulative relative.*
- *While searching online for their birth relatives, they may make contact with strangers who could use these opportunities to exploit or dupe them*

Plus lots more examples...

These two examples alone were certainly enough to make me sit up and take notice. I know it's going to be important to monitor the social media use of the child, but also not be over restrictive to cause other behaviours like lying about the use. It was a very interesting section of the training.

'The Abused Child & Safe Caring' was the next session. The figures (that were way out of date when we went into the training, but had likely increased) absolutely hit me for six. They categorise them into 4 reasons, but with a 5th of 'multiple' as to why the children in England have been subject to a Child Protection Plan (CPP).

- 17,930 were subject to neglect
- 4,670 were subject to physical abuse
- 2,030 were subject to sexual abuse
- 13,640 were subject to emotional abuse
- 4,870 were subject to multiple of the above

This actually makes me feel dejected, upset and very sad. I am writing with tears of anger because I just don't understand how anyone can hurt a child or believe that what they are doing is acceptable. I heard about a case of someone in Cheshire (not at the training) who lived in an expensive new build property, who were classed as 'well to do' people on the outside, yet they had their toddler chained up under the stairs, only to be discovered by a builder doing some work on their house. How could they? B*stards! I am not sure I was mentally ready for that kind of detailed information and looking around the room, I am not sure many of the others were either.

Once they had let those numbers and statistics sink in (which took a few minutes from us all) we moved onto discussing the traits and signs that a child would tend to show when in one of those categories. It was one of the most gruelling conversations and training sessions I have ever been in. My personal belief system and emotions were really fighting hard for me to not express in a public forum what I really think of some of these people who can do that to another human, even more so to a child.

As we were wrapping up that session a comment stuck with me. *'Often your child can confuse you for someone in their past life especially if they are young. This may mean that they could accuse you of something that you had never done. Just be prepared for this and know they are confused'.* I couldn't imagine that happening and being OK with that. I bet that is one of the most hurtful things to be accused of from a child, even if it is borne out of confusion and not true.

We took a break after that session. We all needed it.

Once we got back from the break we discussed 'Safe Caring'. This topic was only short but was designed to ensure you thought about the child's past and how you can then support them through offering them a safe and caring environment. A couple of the tools were to have a support network, write a diary of any events and who was there (they could trigger an action), create boundaries and to make use of further training provided.

By this point in the day, about 2pm, I was starting to struggle with the amount of information and some of the difficult content that was being presented. I was feeling pretty overwhelmed, and it became hard to concentrate on the next stages.

We did however have to keep going as there was more training to complete. We moved onto the next subject surrounding difficult behaviours. It was another grim subject. *Masturbation, inappropriate sexual behaviour, self-harm, fighting, biting* were just some of the absolutely huge list that the manuals presented. I am still having some doubts that I can do this, and I bet that there are many others in the room thinking the same. This is not 'normal' parenting.

There just seems to be so many negative parts to adoption. I am sure they will tell us about the good stuff and the fun parts at some point; or at least I hope they do.

We were nearing the end and had some short sessions based on *Health, Mechanics of Placement, Living with Adoption and Support* all followed by a round up at the end. The health section seemed to be pretty self-explanatory and after the substantial sessions today, it was refreshing to switch to this section. This was not as emotionally draining and reiterated the rule that the Child Health Assessment must happen every 6 months until fully adopted.

We then moved to the mechanics of placement and through a large flow chart. It was quite self-explanatory again, however it would have been good to put some timelines to this for my own sake and setting of expectations. I guess that they can't put timescales to this due to all processes being different.

1. Family Finding - Identifying a potential child(ren) and expressing interest.
2. Matching Meeting - This is with the Local Authority (LA), child's social worker and our social worker
3. Life Appreciation Day - To gain further and more in-depth knowledge from people who are close to the child (doctors, school/nursery, foster carers etc)
4. Matching Panel - Adoption Placement Report submitted to the matching panel for approval (or not)
5. Match Approved (or not)
6. Introductions / Placement - A detailed plan to start introductions to the child as their forever family.
7. Placement - The child comes home, but the LA remains legal guardians. The adoptive family takes on shared parental responsibility.
8. Application to Adopt - post 10 weeks of placement you can apply for the Adoption Order to be granted.
9. Adoption Order - Full hearing at court to grant adoptive family legal rights as the child's parent.
10. Post adoption support offered.
11. Forever Family.

It seems simple to see it in this format, but I am sure there is a hell of a lot more complexity to come under each stage. From what we have been through so far, I am in no doubt that is going to be the case. It is never ending tick boxes and forms.

After this session we discussed *Living with Adoption*. This went through the stages most children go through as they pass through age groups. There was some detail on younger years where the child is often unconsciously unaware they are adopted causing confusion. The expressions of this confusion may present itself in a number of ways and behaviours. Moving to when they are teenagers and have a million questions internally and ones that they do express; plus many emotions that will likely follow too. All very interesting to see the stages of growth and the journey they often will go on.

Finally and thank God as my brain was mashed at this point, we discussed the after support that we would receive, post a placement being made. A lot seemed to be routine visits, health care meetings and more ad hoc support depending on the needs of the child. There seems to be a lot of support available, and after the level of detail we navigated today, I am thankful there is.

I've had enough for today!

20th January - Overwhelmed

My head is still pretty messed up from the last couple of days. I feel like there is so much to process and we are now aware of so many things that could go wrong or that could be really challenging it's making us think long and hard about the whole adoption process. As always when I feel overwhelmed, I called my mother. She is always good to help ground and reframe my thoughts by suggesting a different way of thinking. Just chatting through with her was enough help and because she has had 5 children and a wealth of experience, she is a great soundboard to ask questions or offer any reassurances. I felt much better when we finished the call. She's a good 'un (as they say).

HOME VISITS

23rd January - 1st Home Session

Today was a significant day in our journey as we had Patrick, our social worker, visit the house for the first time to start the sessions. I had to rush home from work which put me on edge fighting through traffic and to compound that with the nerves I was experiencing, it was pretty consuming. I am pretty sure Alex was nervous and anxious too because we were both pacing the kitchen waiting for him to arrive and doing nervous energy stuff. I eventually got a grip of myself and calmed down. Although we had met him on the training courses, we didn't get much of a sense of his personality and he presented himself as you would imagine, very professionally. We wanted to be able to feel comfortable enough to show our true personalities in our own home, so knowing a bit more about him would have been nice.

Patrick arrived a few minutes early and then sat in his car until dead on 5.30pm. We welcomed him in and offered him a drink, trying to create a good first impression. We finally sat down in the front room on the sofa and he got his note pad out and set the scene for the next few weeks and home visits.

The first visit was delving into our family, background and early experiences. Patrick described it as an easy way to get to know us and understand our past history, but by the end of it I felt as though he knew me better than Alex. I expected him to ask my inside leg at one point and if there was an ounce of something that needed to be explored in some further detail, then he dived straight in and into detail about the subject until he was happy with the outcome. At some points, I really wanted to question why he was asking questions that I felt had no relevance. Some of them made me feel really uncomfortable and were a shock to the system.

'Tell me about your father' Patrick asked.

'We [my family] don't talk about him, sorry' was my reply.

That was a red flag for him and immediately he was asking a number load of open questions which made me really want to shut down. He was there when I had my mini crying outburst at the training course, so I think he must have known there was a lot of history and emotion there. It was a really tough 30 minutes from there and I found myself answering questions and then taking a long drink or a bathroom stop just to compose myself. He must have thought I had diarrhoea. I also spoke about things that Alex and I haven't spoken about in the past. I am sure I saw some raised eyebrows from Alex at some points suggesting *'you've never told me that before'*. The topic of my 'father' was one I was happy to compartmentalise. I don't want to bring back bad memories as it was full of events and things that hurt my mother and family. She is my world and I can't stand the thought of her hurting, so balls to him.

He then went on to speak about my 'fathers' side of the family and any other children he had since my mother. It was another difficult subject to discuss and due to it being about people who I share a bloodline with but nothing else, I had little interest. I find it quite a bizarre dynamic and quite the dichotomy. To be candid, I may be quite unfair with them, however as I associate them with him, I find it very hard to create any form of an organic connection.

Eventually he gave up on asking questions because he knew everything about my mothers-mothers-aunties-dogs-first born child's best friend. When he shifted to Alex's family tree I was quite relieved my time was done. Alex got away with a million questions because his family is very small and he had a very stable upbringing. It was nice to hear him speak about his mother and father and the relationship they had when he was growing up. I found interesting to hear of the relationship he had with his sister too as it seems different now; they are now best friends and very close. I learned quite a bit about him in that session and I am sure he did with me too.

Overall, I am still trying to work out whether what I said was not too damning to our application. I want don't Patrick thinking that I am unstable or that I bury my emotions. I am exhausted and it's only 8.30pm. The nervous energy, rush to get home from work and then this barrage of unwanted questions has really taken it out of me. It seems to be a running theme when we have a session with a social worker or training. I bet the fatigue gets worse with a child, so maybe this is all good practice.

30th January - Website Access

Confirmed access to the website was granted today. This was the one that helps you search for children. I find it quite premature and bizarre as we still haven't been approved yet, but we are able to search for a child on the platform. Both Alex and I have said we will take it slowly looking at this stage because if we really like a child and don't get approved or it takes longer than we expect to be approved then it will be a huge disappointment to us both. We have decided that we may tentatively look at the site, but not actively for a child. It's more of an orientation if you like.

31st January - 2nd Home Session

In todays meeting we spoke about relationships and support networks. I went into this one wondering how this one would pan out for both Alex and I after the session really. I am a little bit of a jealous man (of course I don't tell Alex that) and I certainly didn't want to know about the details of his previous relationships to a level that made me uncomfortable and maybe he feels the same about mine. We certainly didn't speak about it beforehand. This all was of course assuming Patrick would go into silly amounts of detail just like he did in the first session. I was expecting him to go deep, but he didn't. I think we both pretty much shut the question down about previous relationships offering very little detail. To be fair though, for both of us our relationship was the only serious one we had both had.

Once he had got past the previous relationships, it was then he went into asking lots of questions about our relationship; *how did you meet? Do you trust each other? Have you had any surprises about each other's characters? What is it like living together? Do you argue? How do you resolve that? What is your physical relationship like?* etc etc. It was relentless for some time. It was also interesting to see how we both answered questions. I am sure Alex was surprised with some of my answers and vice versa, but we just kept rolling with it. We discussed a lot about why we wanted to adopt a child and how and when we started the conversations about it. There was nothing surprising to hear from either side as this is something we have been working towards for a number of years up until the point of planning our house move to this area for schools.

Patrick brought some Lego and asked us to build a bridge out of it. It felt like a corporate leadership task and was actually quite funny in hindsight. We both knew it was coming at some point (our friends told us they had to do it) and we were both super supportive and receptive to each others ideas. Normally when it comes to a task for getting something physical done, I am the one to do it; Alex does the admin side or tells me what to do. I think we both put on a bit of an act for this one.

Lastly, he wanted to discuss the support network around us and how we would potentially use it if we needed to. We had already sent back some answers to questions previously asked so it was a matter of talking over those and specifically explaining the people we would speak with and how they will support. For example we spoke about Alex's mum and dad and that they may help with child care in addition to moral support, where my mother due to her living 350 miles away, would be moral support and parental guidance.

We delved a lot into the relationships that we have locally and a big relationship we have is with the guys next door. They have a little boy who is 2 years old and he's a little cutie. We have chatted a lot (over beers and fire-pit nights) about parenting, their challenges, their frustrations but also the things they love the most about being parents. He made lots of positive and approving noises.

Overall, I guess the questions were all to ascertain how strong and stable our relationship is and how we deal with the good times and the inevitable times of conflict. I think it was also an opportunity to draw out our characters, understand how we may parent a child and maybe even to try and identify what roles are likely to be taken.

A bit of a side note from todays meeting, I have been looking on the website and playing with the settings and our own profile. We created a profile for ourselves so social workers can connect directly with us should they have a child that suits our requirements. The profile lets us filter what we would like from a child. God, it sounds like a shopping list.

6th February - 3rd Home Session

Today I had my 'solo session' with Patrick. It was quite an open session and based heavily around why I personally wanted to adopt a child, our relationship, and a lot more questions aimed at understanding my history with my father. It was clear that Patrick was also trying to gather my understanding about Alex's beliefs, reasons to want to adopt and of his family dynamics.

Patrick started with lots of open questions about Alex and I, and ones targeted at who instigated the conversations about adoption and why. I think we both had spoken about it at various points, but I would probably say that I was the one that led the conversations towards the start. I don't think it took too much for Alex to also confirm that this is what he wanted also. He possesses that paternal instinct. I have always personally wanted children, so it was always going to be on my agenda at some point in my life.

When Patrick was satisfied with the answer he moved onto our relationship, asking how it was, how we resolve arguments and disagreements, whether I knew any reason Alex shouldn't have children and whether I wanted to tell him anything *'in confidence'*. I can see the reasoning behind these questions and opportunity to ask me alone, but it still felt uncomfortable.

He then went over more details about my 'father' as he clearly had a number of questions that were unanswered from the first session. It was a full therapy session and quite frankly one that I really didn't want to have or think about again. I am aware of the bigger picture regarding the adoption process and his need to satisfy that I am not going to be triggered by something down the line. I had to suck it up. And just answer the questions, whether I liked it or not. I have come to learn that this personal experience may serve me well down the line as the social worker mentioned that many children who have been adopted show similar feelings towards their birth parents. He used the words 'trauma' a lot for both myself and what we are likely to encounter with an adopted child. It was all quite emotive, so I was delighted when the session ended. I was starting to grow in frustration and anger at his desire and need to keep delving deeper. If it would have gone on much longer, I think I would have exploded through either emotion or anger. I was close to the edge when he called time.

I really don't like my 'father' and I really don't want to have to keep going over this, so I hope I have satisfied Patrick's intrigue to understand the dynamics of our non-relationship. At points I could have said I wanted to drown my father and that I wish a slow and painful death for what he has done, but I don't think that would help our adoption application. Of course, I don't wish such actions on anyone, but I am 100% on my mother's team.

15th February - 4th Home Session

As this was Alex's solo session, I have no idea what he asked. I would assume similar questions to my solo session with the intention to see if we both answered in a similar way.

Alex and I had a chat about it when he finished, and he collaborated my thoughts about what I assumed he would be asked. He said he found it a strange and uncomfortable session being alone and that he was very cautious when trying to answer some questions . He said that he felt that Patrick may be looking to catch us out or look for inconsistencies. Luckily for us though, we had chatted about what he asked me and it was a good guide for this session, plus I would like to believe we are both on the same page, Alex and I.
Overall, there was nothing to worry about… I think. It just seemed as though Patrick wanted to make sure our views were not so far apart, and we matched intentions regarding adoption and the reasons we wanted to pursue it.

21st February - 5th Home Session

Another home session and today's topic was delving deeper into our financial situation and household setup. I am lucky that Alex runs this part of our ship because he likes to be in control of the finances and how we run our home, so I was merely a passenger in this session; that suited me fine. To be fair, half of the questions I wouldn't have been able to answer due to being so blasé about it all.

Patrick started off asking about our decision to move to this specific house, which was easy as the intention was due to the fact we wanted to adopt a child. We have been lucky to find a home that is in a great area, local to lots of children's activities and very importantly fro us, it has great schools locally. We also spent some time looking around the house so Patrick can see how we perceive our setup regarding the safety of a child. He then talked us through any potential hazards that we should be aware that we hadn't pointed out in the first instance. For example, any sharp edges, where we store such things like bleach and even down to the way we have our TV's hung on the walls. Most of it was common sense but he had to tick the boxes and make sure a child would be safe.

Once he was satisfied with the house, Patrick went into a very detailed review of our finances, but luckily Alex is a whizz on the budget spreadsheet and so that was quite an easy task for him; even easier for me on the side-lines with my cup of coffee. I think I learned some things about our finances to be fair. The level of detail was quite deep. We got to a point of detail where we discussed how many haircuts we had per month and how much that cost us. A message we took away from this session was that we should consider lots of additional expenses with a child. To name a few... nappies/pull ups, clothes, toothpaste, bedding, additional energy in the house, school meals, after school clubs, swimming lessons, more food etc. The list was exhaustive and it seems we need to put some more money aside and pay off that bloody credit card.

22nd February - Christian and Steve - Dinner

We went to see our friends for dinner today. Christian and Steve are part of our friendship group from training, it was really nice to see them outside of the formal setting and not via text. They are great guys and quite similar to us in regard to their personality and lifestyle. We spent most of the evening discussing how they have settled into the process, where they are up to and what challenges they have found so far. They are further ahead than us, so to know what is coming up is great. I think it's good that we (hopefully) won't get surprised by a topic. We also laughed about some of the details; like *'what do you do for adult time and how do you think having a child, or children, will affect it'*. I made the same joke as I normally do when this topic comes up about not getting any adult time anyway. Alex as usual just sighed and pulled a face at me; his usual response.

It was a lovely night and one that I really valued. I hope we remain friends and form an even stronger bond than we already have. I think it would be very beneficial to have two guys as friends and a soundboard who are in the same position as ourselves. This is especially relevant as we grow into being parents. I hope we can add value to their lives by being part of their support network. Only time will tell.

27th February - 6th Home Session

This session felt pretty quick and was more of an information dump on us. We also had a discussion specifically aimed at drawing out our 'care plan' for when we adopt a child. Patrick asked a lot of questions regarding our current routines, health, lifestyle, habits, exercise, family medical history and so on. Patrick then veered off at one point asking whether my brother and I ever used to argue and then how did we sort it out. Of course we argued and of course we did we fight, shout, fall out and make up. He often asks questions out of the blue and not related to the session we are in. Maybe he is trying to catch us off guard with the change of tack? He isn't a psychologist (or I don't think he is), yet he often acts like one.

The session fizzled out after a while and became pretty flat. I think we answered all of his questions but he wanted to fill a bit of time.

28th February - More information

There seems to be so much information and checks needed. It feels like a full-time job filling out forms and confirming things. Tonight both Alex and I have been working on our financial plan, family trees and safe care plan.

The financial plan was a ball-ache, but Alex's trusty spreadsheet massively helped. Patrick also needed 12 months of bank statements for each of us (we both have our own bank accounts), 12 months of the credit card statements and the details of Alex's student loan. Then there were the payslips from work too.

The 'safe care plan' was a funny one to work through together as we had to put ourselves into the mindset of having a child and what actions or changes we would have to put in play. We ended up with this.

Part 1 – Family Routine

Mornings

- *Beds are made by the last person getting out of bed*
- *During the week we get dressed before going downstairs but during weekends we may have breakfast downstairs or in bed before getting ready*
- *Usually Alex uses the bathroom first*
- *Bathroom use can be shared in the mornings (one using the sink, one showering)*
- *Bathroom doors are never locked*
- *Alex uses a bathrobe, Joe does not*
- *We both tend to get dressed in the bedroom*
- *Privacy is given when using the toilet*

Medication

- *It is not currently locked away*

Smoking & Drinking

- *Both of us do not smoke*
- *Drinking of alcohol - we are both occasional alcohol drinkers*
- *Alcohol is currently stored above the oven or in the fridge*
- *We are fully aware of the effects of children drinking and do not expect ours to because of this*

Visitors/friends

- *Hello and goodbyes with friends and family are usually with hugs and cheek kisses*
- *We spend lots of time with our friends and family*
- *We do things like dinner parties, meals out, going for walks etc.*

Internet & telephone

- *We both have access*
- *We use this for browsing, shopping, watching tv etc.*

- *We currently do not have blocking devices but will use if necessary, along with limiting usage for a child but to also lead by example*

Mobile Phones

- *We both have a mobile that we both have access to*

Car

- *We both drive – 2 car household*
- *Both cars are serviced annually*
- *Both of us have full driving licences and insurance*
- *We both use seatbelts and will ensure we use the correct car seats required*

Bedtime routines

- *We both say goodnight with a kiss*
- *Undressing takes place in the bedroom just before going to bed*
- *We both sleep in underwear*
- *We both have bedtime drinks*
- *Lights are all off and doors are left open*

Sex

- *We are both comfortable showing suitable levels of affection with other people*
- *Privacy is currently maintained as only the 2 of us live together*

Part 2 – Rules we would apply

- *Bedroom/bed will not be out of bounds to children*
- *Bedtime stories will most likely take place in the child's bed*
- *There is a tv in our bedroom. If a tv is to go into a child's bedroom, safety locks will be used if required*
- *A child may have access to IT in their room when age appropriate. Camera/ webcams will be monitored or disabled if required*
- *Appropriate clothing at all times*
- *Tickling and wrestling will only be used if appropriate*

- *A sexually abused child will not a share a bedroom*
- *Children will know all house rules*
- *No playing behind closed doors*
- *Diary kept to promote safety*
- *Clear and age-appropriate sex education*
- *Feelings and needs can be expressed which will be listened to, respected and valued*
- *Clear family boundaries*
- *A nurturing environment that cannot be misinterpreted*
- *Consider frightening environments for abused children*
- *Use nonaggressive ways of resolving conflict*

Finally, we compiled and sent a family tree. Mine was so bloody big that it took ages and yet Alex had only him plus 6 people on it. He has a really small family. It quite enjoyed doing this as it made me think about my family.

6th March - 7th Home Session

Today we discussed our adult lives. We discussed our past career history and current roles, the impact of me leaving the Navy and the loss of identity, our support network, our health and some other avenues that came up naturally, like thoughts on religion and beliefs.

The religion and beliefs conversation was interesting and I was never sure on what I could say on the off chance my beliefs are different to Patricks and it caused personal conflict. I didn't want any unconscious bias on our applications, although I am a very open book and open to many beliefs. I believe I am quite receptive to many ways of thinking and don't judge others for what they believe. I may have opinions as to whether I agree with someone regarding their beliefs, however I certainly wouldn't dismiss or judge them for it. An example being 'God'. I don't believe in God, but I certainly don't discourage others from believing. In fact, I quite like that people have something or someone that offers them purpose and value; it's just not for me.

The other talking point that made me laugh was based around health and most notably my BMI. I am not fat, but I am also not thin either. I would describe myself as relatively healthy and comfortable, yet Patrick had advised there was a concern regarding my weight. I don't think I have any form of body dysmorphia, but I don't see the issue really. I have a small beer belly and a couple of chins. I made a light-hearted joke to Patrick regarding my weight and he was quite deadpan with his answer advising that being overweight can have lots of 'health implications' and 'we want to minimise the risk of further trauma to a child'. In other words, he doesn't want me dying of a heart attack or stroke and frankly neither do I. I would also like to be able to run around with my child and not be breathing from places I shouldn't.

Other than politely being called fat, the session was pretty easy. Work has been tough recently too, so I am happy that it was an easy session. I couldn't handle another 'dad' and 'psychotherapy' session.

Away from the home visit, today we also received an email regarding 'foster to adoption'. A bit of a follow-up to what Patrick had told us in previous meetings, however we still don't think that this is a route for us. The fear we have with this is the scenario where we got a child to foster and then after 12 months (or whatever time) when we were fully invested and in love, that we would have to hand the child back because the birth parents' home scenario had changed to a state where they were fit and able to be safe parents again. The other part that jumped out was that birth parents often see the children throughout foster placement whilst they receive support and/or training to get them back to previous mentioned state. We wouldn't want that either.

We have friends who have fostered first and then adopted their little boy. They have said the risk was minimal for them to have to relinquish the boy back to the birth family but still they had a number of fears and significant anxiety regarding the unknown. This continued all the way through to when the adoption order came through. They said the whole scenario was very stressful and one they would have preferred to have avoided in hindsight.

7th March - More Questions

I received an email from Patrick today with some questions that to me seemed pretty irrelevant, but I am sure they are asked for a reason? *Is my middle name the same as my grandfather for a reason? Do my half siblings speak about our father/have contact with him? Why was I called Joe at birth?*

I was pretty short and quite curt with my answers to be honest. I was tired and embittered by the 'father' question, again. The others were fine and simple. I was unsure about my middle name and also why my mother called me Joe. I recall her once telling me she used our names as they were not overly popular at the time and wanted something a little different from the norm. In regard to the question about my father (I still hate calling him that), that was also tough as I don't really speak to my half siblings. It's an unconscious thing as I associate them with him, so therefore not part of my family. I have no love, yet similarly no ill feelings towards them. I simply answered with the only thing I knew about their situation and that was that they don't like or speak to him because he was violent toward their mother also. A coward and someone who I have never looked to aspire to be anything like and someone I aspire to completely the opposite of. I *will* be a better father to a child. To be fair the benchmark he set is low.

8th March - More Father Questions.

Another few questions sent over from Patrick. Yes, I know, some more! They were simple ones to clarify addresses but also some weird and super detailed ones asking such things like our birth weight and some (more) family dynamic based questions. I have found myself wondering why they need to know how much I weighed when I was a baby? I mean, why does that have any effect on how I can parent? I simply don't understand some of this process.

Oh and some more questions about my 'Dad'. This asking about when my brother (next one up) and I met him when we were 13 and 14. This got me thinking about it and actually quite emotional. Even writing this diary now is distressing.

My mother had never said a bad word about him as she has always maintained that we should make up our own minds when we were old enough to do so about what we think of him. I think she received a letter from a solicitor (or someone) to ask about us and to meet up with him. I remember she asked us both if we wanted to meet him and after some careful and teenage deliberation, we both decided to meet him and see for ourselves what we thought of him. I wonder how much that hurt my mother's feelings now? If it did, she never showed it. It must have been tough for her and I often regret that we put her through it.

On the day we got in the car I remember being very nervous and even apprehensive to meet him. I bet the emotions must have been a hundred times worse for my mother and possibly quite scary; after all he was a violent man. Mum dropped us off a little down the road and we knocked on the door to his house. I was cowering behind my big brother, who I really looked up to. The door opened and his wife answered and welcomed us in. She was lovely. The house was a terrace with a front room and a second TV room. He (I can't say it) was in the front room, dressed in scruffy jeans and t-shirt and talking on the phone. I vividly remember his wife showing us into the room that he was in and then telling him that my brother and I were there to meet him. He didn't even stop his phone call, where he was discussing football with his friend, to greet us. He bloody carried on; he f**king carried on his call. That should have been the biggest red flag there. His wife was massively embarrassed and showed us into the front room and offered us a drink and sat us down. I remember being so nervous and in hindsight, I now know that a lot of that was driven through embarrassment and the subconscious thought of betrayal to my mother.

From that moment on we both knew it was going to be a disaster, but I guess we wanted to try. Fast forward a few weeks later and with lots of visits to the pub where we somehow had no money when we left (due to him using our pocket money to buy his beer) and with him slagging off our mother, we quite frankly and quickly stopped seeing him. We saw his true colours and decided that we can't be around such a negative figure in our life.

I still often wonder how my mother feels about the whole situation, but never want to broach the subject as I don't want to bring up any negative emotions for her. I have no love , affection or feelings for that man. Even to the extent where we were told he had a blood disorder a few years ago where he could possibly have a shorter life; I didn't flinch. I didn't and still don't care. Even though I am a very kind and loving character, I wouldn't be bothered by his passing.

I feel a sense of relief writing this, yet emotional thinking about how he was a bastard to my mother. If I can take away anything from this, it is not to be anything like him as a role model or pathetic excuse of a father.

I want to be a parent just like my amazing mother. I always say that if I can, I will have done a good job.

15th March - 8th Home Session

Today seemed to be a summary of the sessions that we have already completed, yet it somehow navigated its way back to the relationship with my father, again. Patrick has clearly picked up on the hatred and lack of desire to chat about him over the past few weeks and he consistently keeps trying to draw out my inner darkest feelings and how I process them all. He's done this so many times now, that I have asked him directly why he wants to delve into the subject so much. His answer suggested that he wants me to use my experiences and methods of working through it when we have a child. He is aiming to turn my experience into a positive one in regard to adoption and suggests that it is likely that an adopted child will have a very similar experience to mine, so he believes this is a positive life experience for me, but only if I can see it that way. I can see he is trying to turn this into that positive he talks about, but I still want him to just let me re-bury it in the deepest darkest part of my brain where I believe it belongs. I fortunately see his point of view on it too, so I am receptive enough (just) to talk about it and swallow my feelings surrounding it.

We also spoke about family finding and more specifically 'activity days'. Patrick talked us through what an activity day is and also how tough it can be emotionally. He said that the activity days are where adoptive parents go to a play centre and interact with children that need to find a forever home (I like that term). When you arrive you are filtered into a room where the children are playing and you simply go and interact with them and see if you have any connection. With the child will be their foster carer and social worker, so you can also ask questions about the child should you want to. If you then decide you would like to explore further detail about the child then you can 'express an interest' where you can give them your PAR (Prospective Adoption Report). The PAR will be created by Patrick via all the sessions and information we have sent over these last few months.

We are intrigued about the activity day and having discussed it with Alex we think that we will go and gain some experience. We will still digest the idea and speak more about it before making the final decision.

21st March - Interest in Us?

We have interest in us! Patrick emailed to discuss an 'expression of interest' from a social worker in regard to our profile on the children's family finding and search portal. We are pretty far through stage 2, but we certainly weren't expecting any interest directed our way just yet. We are not mentally ready for it either.

He has advised that a social worker had expressed an interest in us for us to consider two little girls that she is working with. We had been online after his email and seen the message and profile. It was difficult to articulate back to Patrick why we said no to them. These two adorable little girls simply want a forever home and need someone to love them. Just looking at their profile picture drew us in enough to make it hard to say that we were not interested. We had to be strong and just go with our gut feeling about the girls. Our friends once said that from their experience we will instinctively know when we want a specific child. I hope that's the case because I don't think I can say no many more times. I hope they don't take it personally or that Patrick doesn't change his views on us.

Patrick also sent us the invite he previously mentioned to attend an adoption picnic and to meet some children and their foster carers/social workers. We are still thinking about whether we want to go. Imagine if we found a child we fell in love with and we didn't get approved.

22nd March - After Adoption Closing.

We have just received alarming and sad news that the agency we are with, After Adoption, have gone into administration and are closing with immediate effect. We had hundreds of questions, but the main one was what would happen to our application because we were so far into the process with them. Thankfully they would be transferring it to another agency. We just hope that they have the same after care and supporting ethos as After Adoption. Patrick said he would let us know in due course which agency would pick up our case. We didn't know what would be happening to him either.

Frustratingly and significantly our panel date in a couple of weeks has been cancelled, slowing the process down. Rescheduling this is unknown at the moment due to the agency changing and them requiring a new date.

How bloody annoying and inconvenient it all is.

26th March - New Agency

We will be transferred over to Barnardos. Patrick called me when I was at work to advise that our application and case would be transferred over to them and significantly that he would also be continuing with us on our journey due to him being moved to the same agency. On a personal note, I am happy that he is OK on the job front (I have grown to like him) but I am also happy that we have some continuity with someone who knows us.

Patrick can't offer any dates for the rescheduled panel yet and so we will have to wait until there has been integrations with their work transfers. It's a small bump in the road and one easily overcome with patience.

30th March - Discussions

Alex and I have been speaking quite a lot about the adoption picnic and we have changed our minds on a number of occasions. I am more pro-going where Alex isn't so much due to the timescale of the process and where we are in it. I get it but I am completely intrigued by it all. I am sure I am getting ahead of myself, but I have always wanted a child, so it feels like a good step to psychologically feel we are moving forward. At present we are still waiting for a new panel date after the change in agency.

After lots of consideration, we have (I have probably ground Alex down so much) decided to attend to 'see what it's all about and gain some experience' because this may be a route we explore when we are really moving on with the search... if we make it that far.

6th April - Adoption Picnic

I was super nervous this morning. I didn't eat breakfast, which is completely unlike me according to my BMI and Patricks comments previously. I was awake most of the night thinking about the 'what-if's' and different scenarios that could happen today. What if we found a child that was perfect for us, yet we haven't been approved so could miss out. What if we hated it?

We got in the car and made our way to the centre where the picnic was to take place. When we arrived we both were still hyped up and were talking about absolute rubbish generated from that nervous energy you get. We got ushered into a room with another 15 or so potential adoptive families of all different structures; same sex, opposite sex, different backgrounds, single parents (male and female) and a disabled woman. Nobody spoke to anyone else and the room felt pretty tense and weirdly competitive. The room was set out in a theatre style with a speaker at the front who proceeded to walk us through a brief of the events that we were about to join in with.

The social worker, who was soothingly welcoming, explained that we would be introduced into a room next door where the children were playing (we could hear them) and we were then to interact and not *'hog a child if you like them and let others have an opportunity to interact too'*. She encouraged us to take some time to meet as many children as possible and speak to the social workers to discuss the child and their needs in further detail; issues with a polite warning to be mindful of the child being within earshot. We were given what effectively was a brochure of all of the children waiting next door. It was surreal to see the profile of children in a catalogue like this with a full description describing their character and some of their needs, should they have any, which they all did. It felt we were purchasing a product and not looking for a child to give a forever home to. At that point I knew it was going to be a tough day.

After the brief we were asked in small groups to walk around the building to another entrance to where the children were playing and having fun. The process of walking into a room full of children playing that didn't understand the reason for us adults to be there was daunting. Alex gave me a little dig in the ribs as he was feeling it too and wanted some attention and most importantly, some reassurance that we would be OK. I wasn't too sure because I think I was emotionally invested in the whole process and wanted to be a father in quick time. Maybe I need to reassess my mind and pull away a little.

Once we were in the room, we kind of shuffled over to a little girl who had nobody playing with her. It seemed as though many - if not all - of the other children had somebody there with them and interacting. We didn't head toward her out of pity, more so as she was the closest and it was an easy option for us. I think we were battling with our own emotions rather than thinking about the children at this point. The little girl looked up from her play-doh as we approached and offered the most amazing and beaming smile. I felt like a complete fraud. We knew that we wouldn't be looking to further our interest in a child today, but more so a little girl of her age. I think she was 4. I wonder what she was thinking when we approached her. What had she been told today about why people were meeting her and why was there a big party arranged? What if her foster carer had told her that they were looking for a family. I felt so bad at that point and my fraudulent emotions only increased.

We spent about 15 minutes with her. She was absolutely gorgeous and she seemed to be very outgoing, engaging and *normal*. As we were preparing to move on, her foster carer told us about how she was a child that struggled with learning difficulties, had emotional problems and had attachment concerns, to the point of over-attachment and familiarity. She just seemed *normal* to Alex and me. I couldn't believe all the additional information we were given. It was a stark reminder that face value wasn't all that had to be considered. Information was key.

After this we moved around some of the other children with caution - for them and us - and generally just interacted at a very basic level. I felt very uncomfortable throughout. There were so many children that just wanted some attention and there were so many adults crowding around some that seemed to be the more popular ones. At points it looked quite awkward as some adults were trying to interact with a child knowing their 'competition' was next to them trying to do the same. It came across as a popularity contest with the child.

One little boy did stand out to me. He was about 6 and that in itself was a surprise as we had always envisioned wanting a younger child. If I could have taken him home there and then, I think I would have. He was polite, well-mannered and generally presented himself as a really nice boy. Something just made me connect with him and I have absolutely no idea what that was. Looking back a little too, I just couldn't understand why he was in that position and why anyone would want to put this little boy (and all the others) through such a tough time. It really hit me and pulled on my heart strings. None of them deserved it.

I couldn't wait to leave. I was mentally struggling, A LOT.

In the corner of our eye we also saw our social worker Patrick there. We knew he was going to be there so it wasn't too much of a surprise when he did wave at us. He eventually came over and asked how we were getting on and finding the experience. He genuinely cared about our emotions here and did say we could leave if we wanted to. There was only a few minutes left anyway so we stuck it out until we were ushered back to the room where we started.

The social worker who started it all off, finished it too. She closed up with the details on how to express interest in a child using some forms that you are asked to fill in that were piled up at the front of the room. They were then placed in a box specifically for the child. It was such a basic process for such a huge action. We didn't go forward to show interest, as we knew from the start we wouldn't, but it was encouraging to see so many others that did. I am glad that some (I hope all) of those children had some form of interest from someone; they all deserved it. I really hope the little girl found a family today!

When we had finally finished, we headed back to the car. My brain was emotionally crushed, and I felt as though I had run a marathon, backwards. All of my energy was drained from my body. I was overwhelmed and I think coming out of the building signalled to my body that it was time to let the barriers back down and release any emotion. I felt like crying. I still do hours later. As I look back on today, I felt various amounts of different emotions. The one that hurt the most, for me, was the guilt towards the children. The feeling that I couldn't do anything for them and that just being there may have given them false hope of finding a family was just heart-breaking.

The next thirty minutes as we drove home were pretty much silent. We were both internalising what had just happened and processing our feelings. When we got home, I had to go and read my book. It is my way of dealing with emotions that I am unsure how to process. I fell asleep and stayed there until late. My mind and body were shattered. I could have stayed there for a good 24 hours I reckon.

I really need to switch off now. It's been a tough day for me, but nowhere near as tough for the kids. It has been a super emotional day.

7th April - Picnic Follow Up

Patrick called this morning to see how we were feeling about yesterday after being able to digest the day. I am still quite overwhelmed about it all and I am sure this will stay with me for some time. Both Alex and I really struggled in the knowledge these events are often billed as the last chance for many kids and that hurts. Personally, I feel pretty guilty that we weren't able to help one of those children, but when I was explaining it all to my mother, she was right to say that *'at least there were lots of children that had interest shown in them so take comfort that there will be someone there to show them lots of love and keep them safe'.* She was correct of course. They also have the love and safety of their foster carer too.

I actually can't really remember what I said to Patrick but I know it was pretty flat and quick. There wasn't much more to say about the session other than expressing the feelings that we experienced. Alex and I are not sure that is the route we want to go down when we are actively looking for a child. I think we would rather keep it via the online platform and through the social worker matching direct support.

20th April - Panel Date Given

There has been a bit of silence recently as Patrick is putting together our PAR (Potential Adopters Report) and in the meantime we have just been sitting tight and waiting it out. We have now been given an approval panel date of the 17th July. It feels like ages away and we have lost so much time. I'll be dead by the time this process finishes... well, maybe not dead but fatter, grey and less mobile. Oh, well, at least it is a confirmed date to look forward to.

I am very happy we have a date yet still rather flat about the speed.

23rd April - Questions, Questions, Questions

Patrick has asked a lot of questions recently. It must mean that he is putting the PAR (Potential Adopters Report) together and he has some holes and gaps to fill in. It is all basic stuff and thankfully no more questions based around the relationship with my father.

He has asked for more on the eco-map of our support network, some pen pictures (pictures of us) that he can use as our 'profile picture' and some more detail around our home life. Additionally, DOB's of my mother and Alex's parents and a 'random one' as he called it asking whether we had middle names. All simple and easy to answer, so only a quick one.

His reply was then setting the scene around the next contact, likely being when the PAR has been completed and now that the date was the 17th July for the panel, he had plenty of time to have it done. In other words, we shouldn't expect to see the PAR soon. Keep waiting.

5th June - Sibling Training.

We got an invite to 'sibling training' today should we be considering more than one child. Patrick is trying his hardest for us to consider more than one child, yet we have been quite clear that we will not be going to the training as we don't have the desire to have more than one. It's becoming a running joke now that he is trying his hardest, and he even told us that the agency is often asked to encourage siblings where possible as they are harder to place, and they need adopters for them.

25th June - PAR Report

Today we received our PAR (Prospective Adopters Report) from Patrick asking us to read through and check for any errors or comments that we may not agree with. The PAR is a detailed account of our lives from birth all the way until the present day. This was made up from the discussions, questionnaires, home sessions, training, phone calls and any other contact that we have had with the social workers. All the details have been pulled together to help paint a picture of who we are in readiness for the adoption approval panel and also for the social workers of the child we express some interest in (if and when we get to that stage).

When reading through the amount of detail regarding our lives and how we have lived until this stage is staggering. It's quite bizarre to have all of our intimate past to all be summarised in one 46 page document, however on the first page was the most important statement of all;

'I recommend that Joe and Alex are suitable to adopt...'

After so long in this process, it is great to know that the social workers believe we are suitable to be able to offer a child a forever and loving home. When we finished reading the document, we sent back a couple of small amendments, however on the whole we were satisfied with the summary. We were encouraged to make changes should we feel anything be incorrect or misleading as this is effectively our 'sales pitch' to any social workers that may find interest in us for the children they are representing.

As this is our 'sales pitch,' we really hope Patrick has got it right.

APPROVAL PANEL

17th July - Adoption Approval Panel

Today is a big day and may decide our future. Alex and I were up early this morning to head off to Yorkshire for our approval panel. This is the panel that will decide whether we are suitable adopters, so we were bloody nervous. Patrick has tried to reassure us by advising us that he hasn't seen anyone get to the panel and not be approved. We know that's not true as we have seen rejections when we have been researching, but he was doing his best to calm us down. He called us as we were driving and told us that he would meet us there. He was already there waiting in a small room when we arrived. The room was very bland, and the walls were covered with adoption, fostering and childcare posters. I must have read them a hundred times, not really taking in the information. I was so hyped up and trying to prepare some answers for things I thought they may ask. Patrick tried to make small talk about the drive and to be calm, but again we just wanted to get it over with. He was doing his best and it helped ease away some of the worries through the minor distraction. Finally, we got called into the conference suite where there were 8 people sitting on the panel across a large wooden table that had been crammed into another small room. They looked a little uncomfortable. The lady who was chairing the meeting was very nice and welcoming, asking a few small talk questions to try to calm us down. She must have known we were flapping because after all, the people in that room had the power to change our lives for the good or not depending on the decisions they were about to make.

After those basic ice breaker questions, we got into it.

'What has made you want to adopt a child or children?'
'How do you feel about birth families knowing they may have hurt children, emotionally or physically?'
'How will having a child affect your lives?'
'What do you feel are the most important factors to being a parent?'
'How do you feel your past relationship with your father will affect or help you?'

I don't remember how we answered these but both Alex and I were stumbling as to who was to answer and I know we both took over from each other a couple of times when we could see the other struggling or heading down a route where we began to waffle. The session must have lasted 45 minutes, but it felt like 5. We were then asked to head back to the meeting room with little indication of how we had fared. Patrick looked happy enough and reassured us that we did a good job. We spoke about the session for ten minutes until the chairlady came to the room and delivered the news. She said that *'overwhelmingly, the panel believed that you will be amazing adoptive parents one day and that we unanimously agreed that you should be approved'*. Wow, that knocked the socks off of us. It was such a positive response and we were both overwhelmed and so happy. Patrick was over the moon for us too. It's nice to know that we have him on our side.

The next step we have is for us to get the formal and signed off approval, which usually takes 10 working days. This will be done in the background and the recommendation as to the outcome will be from the panel that we had today. They said it is pretty much a foregone conclusion unless *'you commit a crime in the meantime'*. That now means we must cancel the international bank robbery we had planned.

We headed outside beaming from ear to ear and took a photo of us at the location to ensure we had the memory. It will be a superb memory of the day that could trigger the domino effect on the rest of our lives. We had done our part to be approved and now it's time for family finding.

We both called our parents in the car on the way home, and they were so pleased for us both. Alex's mum summed it up with *'it's about bloody time'*. She was just as relieved as we are and expressed it with her emotion. It was nice to hear the relief in her voice as it completely echoes the rest of our families' sentiments. Everyone is onboard and itching for a little one.

18th July - Expression of Interest.

OK, we have been a little bit eager to move on with the adoption, so we have been looking online and have expressed an interest in a lovely little boy. This was done on the website and to Patrick. Reading the minimal information, he tentatively fits the bill for us regarding the amount of additional needs he has; or more-so the lack of additional needs. He has just turned 3 years old, which surprised us a little because this was our top bracket and our least favourable age. We simply haven't seen any other child that we have been drawn to. It was a good sign that we had both been drawn to this little boy. We have made a rule that should we like a child, then we would add the child to the 'favourites'. We could both then check that folder and if we both agree then we would discuss the prospect of expressing interest in them. If one of us is not 100% on a child, then regardless of how much the other likes them, we do not proceed. Not even 99%, it must be all in. We don't want any friction around the child being favoured by one of us and the other not being so sure. It just wouldn't be fair to the other person, but most importantly it wouldn't be fair to the child.

I think the rule is a good one to adhere to. We had heard of other couples where one had been interested and 'sold' the prospect to the other party. Further down the line the one that wasn't 100% invested had ended leaving the relationship and family due to the child having some troubles that she didn't *'want in the first place'*. To me that seems as though the emotional investment was never there, so it should never have been pursued in the first place. In our case, if our child is struggling or has troubles, then at least we had both 100% agreed and there is absolutely no blame from one of us to the other.

Anyway, this little boy… he's a cutie, so we hope we get some positive feedback giving us the chance to learn a lot more about him from his CPR (child permanence report). Fingers crossed.

19th July - Nothing

Come on, this is taking ages. Well, not really as it's only one day, but it feels like ages, No news…but then again, they say no news is good news? We must be patient.

25th July - Follow up

There is patient and then there is just taking too long. It's a child's future we are taking about here, so you would assume they would be quick to view a possible match. I sent Patrick an email today to see if he has heard anything from our expression of interest. We have learned that he has direct access to the child's social worker, so can at least ask for an answer. I am impatient enough as it is. He has told us that he will chase for an answer because he believes we are a strong option for the little boy.

6th August - News

We have received some direct feedback from the social worker of the little boy and due to the answer, a follow up call from Patrick. Both Alex and I are very frustrated as we have been rejected in regard to pursuing interest for this little boy for some shocking reasons. We were told that they want to keep the little boy *'in the region due so they can keep the funding local and we are concerned about 1 hour travelling time over the course of introductions should it reach that stage'*. I don't know how to react here. This little boy has been 'online' for quite some time and they have not been able to find a match for him, so why the hell would they deny the opportunity for him to find a loving home. There is no 'child centric' (what we have always been told is priority number one) reason for the interest to be rejected.

I've just sent Patrick an email. One that is quite blunt as I am raging, but I now also feel that our relationship warrants the candour around our thoughts and experience, and frankly he has taken it all very well and been very supportive over what is a tough and, in my opinion, an unjust outcome.

Email that I sent to Patrick....

> *Thanks for today. I appreciate the call and the feedback. As you may be able to tell from the tone of my voice and my candid replies, I am a little aggrieved / frustrated / unsure by the process and the reply from the child's social worker seems too much like a cop out especially if the process is meant to be in the interest of the needs of a child.*

They have rejected us because they have 'an aim to keep 80% of children in-house' screams 'funding' to me as opposed to the 'best interest of the child'. You even said this yourself.

We absolutely don't understand the decision and reasoning and I am taken aback by the insular attitude from the local authority. Is this normal? Is this a scenario we are going to have to get used to and will we need to amend our strategy to find a child? i.e...look locally only?

Frankly some of the comments also don't add up. Travel time? This is done so infrequently that surely it's negligible enough to not warrant the long term goal? We will only travel to meet the support bubble and the child, and then after that it will be for introductions. It seems like a feeble excuse to me. Is there something that we are not being made aware of?

Please can you offer some guidance on this and some reassurance regarding the process. I'm emotionally shocked.

I hope you take this email as it is intended. You know I am candid. We are very frustrated and we don't want to be getting such rejection in the future for such a poor reason. If we need to change the way we are looking for a child, then please guide us on it.

Thanks Patrick. We really do appreciate the support and guidance.

STAGE 3 - FAMILY FINDING

7th August - Stage 3

Patrick replied with quite an arbitrary *'sorry it didn't work out email'* not really addressing our concerns . I think we said all we needed to in the previous phone discussion and email, so he knows how we feel. I am sure that when we meet up face to face next time, he will go into more detail to address the issues raised. It's not his fault in any way, however he is our social worker and expert, so it's unfortunately him that gets the brunt of our frustrations (and I am sure later, happiness).

10th August - Progress Reports

Recently, we have had quite a lot of people in our friends and family bubble asking how we are getting on in the process. I am always happy to discuss where we are up to and the learnings that we have had so far because I know people are genuinely curious about how the whole adoption process works. In a way, it also helps me understand the process more when I talk it through with other people as it kind of forces me to answer questions that don't come up with Alex. It makes me think about what I have learned too.

Some of the questions are great, and some are questionable. I am learning how to navigate the silly ones.

28th August - Expression of Interest

Alex and I were online on Link Maker (the search site) last night and have agreed to send across another expression of interest for a lovely little boy. His profile suggests all the ideal criteria that we are looking for and we feel we can meet his needs. People say don't be drawn in by the pictures and read the profile first, but his eyes just got us. It was as if he was looking at us directly. It is so hard not to look at the pictures first and I can honestly say, I have been put off by some of the profiles of children because of the photos that have. It's a travesty to think that the pictures are part of the 'sell' of the profile and yet some are just so poor. Surely you would expect that whoever is taking them, to get the best they can and not some shocking picture that looks as though it was taken on a brick.

Anyway, I sent Patrick an email to advise that we have sent across the expression of interest. I think he is on leave, so we will have to wait for a reply.

Later tonight we received an email back from Patrick - he wasn't on leave - acknowledging our interest and he advised he *'hopes you (we) get some positive news from the family finder or social workers and will keep us informed'*. I guess he can't really add much more assurance unless they express interest back.

29th August - Activity Day Notification

Patrick also followed up today noting that *'I've seen that there is an activity day on 12th October in Liverpool. Would that be something that you are interested in?'*.

No thank you! It was a simple and easy answer from both of us. The last one was so emotionally draining, that we didn't feel we could do it again and at least we can keep some distance via the online platform, Link Maker.

I still think about the last one we attended and that little girl we spent some time talking to. The feeling of guilt always comes over me when I do think about her and that day. I hope she found a family that can fulfil her needs and love her.

Later today… (from Patrick)

'Dear Alex and Joe,

Just a note to confirm that the family finder for L has opened a discussion on Link Maker, sharing that your profile has been forwarded onto the social worker for review. It is noted that there has been a lot of interest in L, which I would expect there to be for any child as cute and with such a low level of additional need'

Well, that's some fantastic news, but let's not get ahead of ourselves. As Patrick said in his email there is an abundance of interest in this child, so we may not get anywhere yet. Maybe our last experience has helped him think about setting our expectations early.
Our PAR (potential adopters report) has now been sent over to the social work of the little boy. Fingers crossed for a positive outcome and some good news.

30th August - Stand Out

Patrick has followed up and suggested that we should try and stand out from the rest of the other profiles and people who have expressed interest in this little boy. I was once told by an old boss of mine to do something that others won't and to make myself (in this case *ourselves*) the obvious choice. We have decided to write an additional note to the social worker and family finder for Patrick to send on to her, on our behalf. This is what we have sent across:

'Hi Jessica

Thank you very much for considering both of us when searching for a forever family for L. We just wanted to follow up to solidify and firm up our interest to be considered to move forward and show how interested we are. We are taking the search very seriously and this is only our second expression of interest.

We are only expressing interest based on how we feel we can meet the needs of a child and in this case we feel this beautiful young boy is certainly one we can meet and exceed them for.

The first thing that jumped out to us was that 'L is an affectionate little boy who thrives on attention and being active'. We certainly feel that we can meet these needs as affectionate and active people ourselves. In fact, there are huge synergies here with our needs too.

Additionally, you mention L loves to play out in the garden. We have recently had our garden 'child proofed' making it a great and year-round area to use. Our neighbours have a 2 year old who loves to play in their garden and also ours when they come around, so much so we have left a few sections of the fence down so both children can interact when they want to and safely. I am sure they would make superb playmates.

We've also been pre-warned by the neighbours to love Peppa Pig and all sorts of other weird and wonderful kids TV. We're still kids at heart, so I'm sure we will take this in our stride.

From L's profile, he seems like a superb little boy who is progressing well with his foster carers. We would love to explore the opportunity to find out more detail and information regarding L so we can really make a complete and informed decision on whether we should pursue our interest and vice versa and all for the greater interest of him.

Thank you again for considering us. We massively appreciate it.'

Let's hope this puts us ahead of the 'competition'.

5th September - Fantastic News

Fantastic news! We have been shortlisted in regard to little L. It is now just a matter of waiting, again. It is all in the hands of L's family finder and social workers.

10th September - No News

We have chased Patrick today regarding L and we were told that it is out of our hands - and his - and that it is just a waiting game. He did promise that he would send a polite email to chase up the family finder. Maybe chasing them up will show how interested we are.

26th September - No News… Still

Any chance? We still have no news regarding L and the next steps… I am learning that the system takes so bloody long. Come on, this is the life of a child in the balance and surely they should want to find a family for them as soon as possible.

15th October - FASD

Still no bloody news, however we have had lots of assurances that Patrick is chasing L's social workers. We have also read through the CPR report (child permanence report) and have sent some questions back about L and his family history. One of them was about the drinking of his mother during pregnancy and how that could affect L as he grows up. Patrick sent us a follow up email with information on FASD (foetal alcohol spectrum disorder) but did caveat very quickly that it was by no means a sign that L has got signs of FASD. He has to be clear about the possibilities as this could be the situation in the future. It is unknown at this age.

It is a hard thing to consider as it sounds like a gamble. This gamble isn't one where I can lose a tenner on football, but one that can change the whole course of our lives. Alex and I have chatted about this already and for us to make an informed decision we need more information. We will keep asking questions; we always do.

17th October - We Have News.

We have some news! The family finder and social worker from L want to meet us on the 30th and see if we fit the criteria of the family they feel would suit and meet the needs of L. The agenda will be to meet us, ask us lots of questions about why and how we feel we can meet the needs of L, and finally have a look around our house to be sure it is safe for him. They will be travelling from Bristol, so that means they must be very interested in us. It's looking good. We, of course, have accepted for them to come.

Today we have also asked a lot more questions regarding L as there seems to be some information that isn't clear and could even suggest he may have autism, which unfortunately is a game changer for us. We are trying to reach in-between the lines of the information of that is being sent over and it has been a bit of a curve ball for us. Patrick has asked the questions and the family finder and social worker for L have advised us that L is too young to have that diagnosis, however the notes and previous medical history don't suggest this could be a concern. The issue here is that L has not had any updated notes for nearly a year due to his social workers changing over.

We really need to fill in some gaps.

This is what Patrick had to say...

> 'To follow on from the below and telephone call. In relation to having a meeting with the social workers, at that point you would be under no pressure to make a final decision and no one would expect you to do so as you have not had all the information in regard to the medical assessment. This would be a continuation to the information sharing and we could gain assessment information when speaking with the medical advisor at a later date. At which point if this brought any concerns up, we could still close the interest. In short, what I am saying is that there is no pressure on the meeting to make a decision there and then'

This is welcomed reassurance from Patrick and we hope the sincerity behind it is there. Alex and I don't want to muck up our chances with the social workers. We know of course, their role is to find adopters for children, so I am sure being candid will not ruin the relationship and good work we have done so far.

We simply don't have enough information yet to make a full decision anyway, so the meeting will be a superb opportunity to ask direct questions and gain some answers that we don't currently have. We hope they can provide answers beforehand however, otherwise I am sure they will have the Spanish inquisition upon them; after all this decision will be for life. We want to get it right for L and for us.

30th October - Home Visit

We never got the answers to the question we had and so we decided to go ahead with the meeting so we can ask. The social worker and family finder for L came this afternoon, just after lunch. This could be a day that changes our lives and I must have had about 5 nervous wee's before they finally pressed the doorbell. Patrick was with us as well and it all felt formal. L's social worker and family finder were both softly spoken and 'nice mum' type people which immediately put us at ease. They were easy to speak to, yet we both remained guarded. Both Alex and I were very anxious about the whole scenario and the visit. Patrick was on one side of us and L's social worker and family finder on the other. It was a bit like watching tennis when they were talking to each other.

Patrick got the meeting underway and then quickly the two visiting ladies took over asking a million questions; all were quite simple and based around the needs of L and how we feel we can meet his needs. We answered to the best of our knowledge and what we thought we would do and be able to offer. Additionally, there were plenty of questions about the local area, schools, activity centres, medical facilities, our financial status etc. These were the easiest to answer as they are very factual. It was pretty much going through the PAR again, but this time in person.

When they had finally finished their many questions we got the chance to ask some of ours. Many of them are based around the development of L and the lack of supporting and most importantly, up to date information. Everything was so outdated that it was hard to really understand the full profile and needs of L. Of the information that we had additionally received outside of the CPR prior to today, both Alex and I had lots of questions that we were told would be answered at this meeting. We asked a myriad of questions about L and it was clear that the social worker and the family finder had spent a very limited amount of time with him and didn't fully know about his personality, character and current needs. A lot of their information was from the old CPR. Something doesn't stack up about it all.

Finally, we asked about autism as that was something that from our interactions with them that kept offering more and more evidence each and every time we had contact. Nobody had, nor would say that L has autism, but the information we have is showing signs that it could be something we need to explore more and consider a possibility.

The social worker and family finder both said, *'there is no evidence or doctor's notes to suggest he has autism'*. We are taking this at face value as frankly our gut instinct (and I have a bit of a gut) seems to be that something is amiss.

The ladies left and I actually felt quite deflated because we didn't get the answers we wanted. Emotionally this has been very hard for Alex and I as we are invested, even though we are trying not to be at this stage. It has been hard to not think about L being part of the family and the things we might do together; something as simple as going to play centres together or having dinner. However, we still feel like there are so many questions left unanswered. It is clear that L is a lovely little boy, but they don't know enough about him regarding the actual needs he has. We need more updated information, mainly around the autism part. I find it so difficult to get my head around the lack of knowledge when they are representing a child's life, but I also understand they are both new to him. It is a job for them and people move within their careers.

How bloody frustrating. Arghhhhhh

31st October - Happy Birthday

The social workers for L has said that they would like to proceed with Alex and I as a potential match for L. That is amazing news and a great confidence booster to us both. It's my birthday today too, so its a lovely birthday gift.

3rd November - More Hoops

L's social workers have asked a few questions based around our finances. We are in a very good position, luckily, and the detail shows this, however they still want some detail on how we will pay off the credit card. We used it to pay for the garden renovation so it looks a bit hefty at the minute but will be paid off in good time should we continue at the rate we have been. I don't see any issue at all.

I have to bite my lip sometimes. Even more so when I know the level of detail that Alex sent Patrick over in the first instance. I know they are just completing their due diligence and they are completely correct to do that, but still they could just look at the detail sent for Christ's sake.

We have also asked for some more pictures and most importantly videos of L. We have told Patrick it is so we can paint a picture of him, but in truth it is so we can make our own judgements on whether we can see any signs of autism. We have also asked for an updated medical report; again to politely highlight that the ones we have at present are so outdated that we can't be confident that it still represents L.

We are so invested in him, however we can't just skip past this hurdle even though most people on his side suggest there *'is not evidence to suggest he has autism'*. In other words, nobody has the balls to give us a formal answer or they simply just don't know.

6th November - Old Medical Reports

Patrick sent us an email and he has quite descriptively titled the report *'Old medical report'*. The clue is in the title as to what he sent us, yet once again I just don't understand how that adds any more value to what we already know. Patrick is very sympathetic to what we are asking and what our reservations are and has been pushing for more information and L's health visitor to give a formal assessment of him to us. I can't fathom how a social system like this can't get an updated version of a medical assessment report for a child who is in the adoption system. This could be - quite literally - a deal breaker for him and us. I guess the worst scenario is that we (or another family) don't get this level of detail and it comes out later causing a breakdown in the adoption.

Patrick keeps reassuring us that we haven't made any formal decisions yet and still don't have to (and we won't), but it is still hard not to be emotionally invested. I wish someone would just pull their finger out; it is a child's livelihood at stake here!

8th November - Photos

This morning we received some photos of L. He is such a cute and beautiful little boy. The photographs were of him playing with toys and he looks like a happy boy. Taking away the heavily emotional part, this still doesn't really give us much insight into him as a character and that all required questions based around autism. We wanted videos to check in on his interactions and social cues, but nothing.

Alex and I are struggling to remove our emotions from this, but we have to. We need to make the best decision for our future family. We will keep asking the questions. We have in fact gone back to Patrick with the same concerns, still. We need more information.

11th November - Video

Finally, we got the bloody video! Without sounding like a broken record, we didn't get much from this one either. He was once again playing with toys and wasn't interacting with anyone, so it was not possible to answer our questions from them. We have still not moved forward.

Oh, well. Smile and wave.

15th November - Life Appreciation Day

We have been approached by Patrick to see if we want to visit L, his foster carers and social workers to conduct what they call the Life Appreciation Day. This day - or days in this case - will give us the opportunity to speak to the people around L that have interactions and care for him. This means the health advisors and likely the doctors too which would give us the answers we are looking for and have so desperately been needing.

He lives 3 hours away and we would certainly need to be there for 2 days to get through all of the information and people surrounding him. We believe it would start with a session where we would watch L from a distance in a public place - we are told is called a 'bump into' meeting - then spend some time with the foster carers. On day two we would meet the doctor (if they can book it!) and then his nursery and maybe his old social worker. The agenda may change.

We have expressed our reluctance and advised that we would think about the Life Appreciation Days, however Patrick continued to express that we could use this time to draw out the answers that we are craving for and make decisions based on this. He also reminded us that nobody had still even suggested that L may have autism, so there is limited reason to suspect it.

It's such a hard decision. We need to talk and think about it. We may end up going and completely falling in love with this little boy and that would make it so difficult to make calculated and non-emotional decisions. That wouldn't be fair on him… or us.

We need to think and pretty quickly too.

28th November - Confirmation of Dates

Over the last couple of weeks we have been back and forth with Patrick regarding the dates and times for the Life Appreciation. It seems that a date can't be found with the medical people, surprise, surprise. Sods law as they are the people we deem to be the most important at this stage too. The dates have been confirmed for 18th and 19th December. It will be a long month waiting, but one we hope we can get some more detail and fuller answers before then.

Both Alex and I have had so many conversations surrounding the pros and cons of us going to meet L's support network. The conclusion that we have come to, is that if we don't go we will never find out the answers that we want and that we may miss the opportunity to fulfil our life-goal of adopting a little boy. We just need to go there in the knowledge that we could get further and more emotionally involved and attached, yet the outcome could be a tough one. We will have to work it out as we go along; I mean that has been my life philosophy anyway, so why change anything now.

I am still feeling emotionally vulnerable at this point and I don't like not being in control of my own emotions. I am doing more reading than ever, and this usually means I am feeling anxious or frustrated by something. It's usually my release of tension or it makes me fall asleep, then the next day is a new day so I can move forward and forget it. Some people would call it compartmentalising emotions, I just call it cracking on. Going down to Bristol could be the best or worst decision we have made yet, but as my mother always maintains *'everything happens for a reason'*.

Still so many questions lie unanswered.

29th November - Medical Booked

Just as we had emotionally accepted we wouldn't get a chance to speak to the doctors or health workers, Patrick surprised us by advising us that an appointment had been booked for the day after we were due down there. This is the major session that we want and actually one we would prefer to be first, or even before we go all the way down there. A three hour drive, work holidays, hotel costs and food are all at our expense so it will be a waste of all of those to go belly up. Our gut instincts are still not good here;

that's from both of us too, however we can't refuse to go as there is a chance that all could be perfect.

So far I think the biggest frustration with all of this process is the lack of information. Our friends have suggested that this hasn't been the case for them and that they got as much information as they needed and all in good time. Maybe the lack of information is due to the change in the social workers; but that doesn't change my views on the fact that this is a child's life and they should be moving heaven and earth to help him get a forever home.

Patrick is trying his best to help us get the information and keep us posted, but there always seems to be quite a few days delay as we ask him a question, he then in-turn asks them and then the return process the other way. It's very laborious and frustrating.

5th December - Speech and Language Report

A speech and language report was received today for L. It was something that we had asked for as this often can give a big indication as to whether a person has a likelihood of being on the autism spectrum (if that's the correct term). The report offered information advising of delays and causes for concern, so in turn we again raised the same questions as we have previously, only to be met with the same answer regarding L's likelihood of him having autism. We have even questioned Patrick as to whether they are withholding information. We are getting nowhere! I just don't understand why nobody can offer a bloody answer. Alex made a good point around nobody wanting to take account for putting the label on such a young boy and maybe being the person that stopped the process.

It is all so tough because we are certainly emotionally invested in L. It is very hard not to create internal pictures about the future and how you may be as a family. I am trying not to get ahead of myself. Still. I am really trying to be realistic. It's a really hard position to be in because I really want to be thinking about this as a strong family possibility and should I not be thinking that way would be counter productive and maybe even adverse for the future.

7th December - Hotel Booked.

We have booked a hotel for two nights on the 17-19th December. It is our way of confirming and making a concrete decision to go down and meet the significant people around L. It is the only way that we can really find out. I am not going to lie, I am pretty nervous now, but I am also energised by the idea that this could be a positive move forward in our life goal.

11th December - Good Advice

We received the below email from Patrick regarding our challenge around the withholding of information and also the couple of days down there.

> *'As I talked about, the key information will be seeing him and how he interacts with people and his surroundings. The medical report may give lots of information and may lead you thinking a certain way, but when you see him moving around, playing, communicating, seeking out comfort, relating to adults and peers this could paint a different picture. I am in no way saying that we ignore what the reports are saying, but if we use the reports as a foundation to build our own observations I think this would paint a more balanced and varied view point.*
>
> *Please be reassured that all the information is being shared and although the information can appear conflicting there is no one trying to cover up information or push L into a family. The conflicts are around different people's views, which I fully understand is unhelpful. The more people that are involved the greater the number of views.'*

17th December - Travelling

We are travelling down to Bristol later on this morning. I am actually very nervous about what might happen over the next couple of days. I am also excited at the prospect of this being our first meeting, but I really am trying to curb those thoughts even though I am emotionally involved and deep down wanting this to work out well for us all. It has been a little tense in this house so far today, hence me coming to the office to write some bits and get away from Alex. We need some space before we set off to gather our thoughts.

Christ, that was a long drive! The hotel AirBnB isn't that great either but to be fair it's only 2 nights of laying our head on a pillow and I have certainly slept in or on worse when I was in the Navy. Whilst we had our evening meal, Alex and I just talked through what we thought may happen over the coming days and even had a drink to calm the nerves. The content of the conversation was based around hypothetical scenarios and was really just fuelled by nervous energy. When we got back to the room, we started over-thinking. We questioned what kind of clothes we should wear because we wanted to make a good impression with L's social workers and the other people we will be meeting. After about 30 minutes of not making much progress, we eventually came to the conclusion of just being us and dressing how we wanted. We are smart and clean, so that's all that matters.

It's only 9.30pm and we are off to bed. Our brains are exhausted. We have to meet Patrick at 9am for a quick brief on the day's agenda and then on to meet L's social worker at the garden centre where we would conduct the 'bump into meeting' and watch L from afar. That's going to be a weird thing. Three guys and a lady sat ten meters away watching a little kid. I wonder what others around us would think if they spotted it.

18th December - Life Appreciation - Day 1

Today has been a shocking, tiring and overwhelming day. I am exhausted and emotional.

As the day began we were a bundle of mixed emotions as you can probably imagine. I think we were both well awake before the alarm clock, but we were deep in our own thoughts and not speaking to each other. I know how much we want this to work out well as we are both wanting a forever family.

When we finally pulled ourselves together and after having little for breakfast - it was a self-catering cereal thing - we made our way across to the hotel where Patrick was staying and grabbed a coffee. He was already there waiting for us and looked very relaxed; of course he was, he has done this a hundred times. I wish we were as relaxed as him. For the next twenty minutes he discussed the next two days, what we should expect and the agenda. The agenda had been amended a little, but nothing major. We were to head straight to the nursery where we would get a report from the staff and his primary contact there. Then onto a local garden centre where we were to watch L interacting with his foster carers. At that point we could have lunch. Then in the afternoon we will have the opportunity to meet his foster carers which would give us a chance to ask lots of questions and really get the full picture. The following day (tomorrow) we will meet the doctor and then onto a meeting in the early afternoon where we would meet other people who had interactions within his life. After that it was a long drive home.

When we had finished our coffee, we headed to the nursery. I can't ever remember being in a nursery before so it was quite a sensory overload walking in. L was not there that day as he was with his foster carers, so that was both positive in the manner that we didn't have to be sneaky, but also a missed opportunity to see him interact with other children. Once through the security door we got ushered into a room that was designed to only fit in 2-3 people but there were 4 of us. It was quite a squeeze. After a few ice breaker questions about the drive and breakfast, we discussed L in quite some detail. It was clear from the start that the nursery believed he had some social issues and often would seek out a 'comforting face'. His speech and language was put into question as was his learning and development; they weren't progressing as much as they would have liked. It was so nice to see how much the nursery nurse gushed over L and she kept saying how he was such a lovely child, but it did feel a little like she was conscious of us wanting to adopt him, so she may have felt she had to be super positive and 'sell' the fact he is a nice child. I couldn't blame her for that.

Once she had finished going through his paperwork, pupil plan and her 'sales' pitch, I had a feeling in my gut that there was something missing. Something didn't feel right. I asked her directly if she thought he had autism, and she kind of swerved it by advising that she isn't able to diagnose something like this, but she did say that she does see some similarities to children that she worked with in the past... *'but that doesn't mean he has it'*
We said our thanks and then left to head over to the garden centre. It was a good 15 minutes of discussion time between Alex and I. Alex said he felt something wasn't right too. We were both thinking it in our own rights. We really wanted to give the situation the benefit of the doubt, so went to the new meeting as open minded as we can.

When we arrived at the garden centre we found a spot to park. Patrick spotted L's social worker in the car park, so it was quite natural to meet up with her and walk in together. What we didn't expect was the foster carers to come in at that exact time, open the car window and then make conversation with the social workers. It put us in the position of meeting the foster carers straight away and we then somehow ended up walking into the garden centre together as a group and more notably with L there too. So, instead of us watching from a few tables away, we ended up at the same table as L and his foster carers. I do have to say he was beautiful but had very little awareness of his surroundings. While they settled at the table, we went to get some lunch from the cafe and then returned to the table. For the first 15 minutes or so, we just watched L at the same time as eating lunch. We tried to hone in on how he interacted whilst answering some small talk questions. L was all over Patrick, climbing on him and squashing the butter packets that had come with my potato; of which Patrick encouraged as 'messy play'. After that we started interacting with L ourselves. He would run up and down the cafe and we eventually ended up chasing him down and bringing him back to the table. That made us hold his hand or even at stages pick him up. When I picked him up, he would cuddle into my shoulder and just stay there. It was also clear that he wouldn't respond to verbal cues. You could say his name and he would not react in the slightest. The only time he reacted to a sound was when a dog barked and made everyone jump. It was getting to the point of certainty that something was amiss and it was more and more likely that it was autism. It was so mentally tough for Alex and I because he was such a cute little boy and one that clearly gave attention to the person he was with. That was really nice in a safe environment, but also worrying that for someone he had never met (us) he was so comfortable to instigate affection. I found myself drawn to him but I had that nagging feeling that it wouldn't work out well.

We left the garden centre with more questions than answers. We hoped the afternoon with the foster carers would be a good opportunity to dig into the details and ask direct questions about his character and how he presents himself on a day-to-day basis.

In the meantime, and before the meeting with the foster carers, we went and had a coffee. It was another opportunity to talk through and digest the situation we are in. All this coffee and caffeine probably wasn't helping the nerves and jitters. Anyway, Alex, Patrick and I had a good chat and of course Patrick kept reiterating that we should have an open mind and to keep asking questions about L. *'Keep painting the picture'*. Balancing the emotions for him which we have gained over time (and because we are so invested in wanting a forever family) and accepting the reality is very difficult. It is something that we need to continue to step back and take stock of. We need to be careful not to be caught up in the moment and miss vital information.

Later this afternoon we headed off to a small pub close to where the foster carers live. This was our opportunity to ask direct questions to the people who interact with him on a daily basis. When we got there, it felt like a test as to whether we should get a coffee or a beer; I went for a beer and so did Alex. We were stressed enough as it was, and a drink was just what was needed. Balls to being judged, we were just being us.

We moved around to the quieter part of the pub and sat at a table out of earshot of the other daytime punters. It was only polite to do so for L's sake. The foster carers then proceeded to tell us all about L and his personality at home, how he behaves and all the things he likes and dislikes (like TV, food etc). It was heart-warming and really drew me in. However, the most interesting part was when I asked a question about this morning and his lack of acknowledgement when anyone said his name. Automatically, both foster carers went into quite a defensive mode on behalf of L. They were clearly highly invested in him and loved him to bits, but I would say the signs were there that they knew something was amiss with him. I don't think that they could accept it themselves. *'There is nothing wrong with him, he is just a child and needs some time'.* We must have heard that three or four times. The whole situation felt similar to this morning in the nursery. It was as if they wanted to make sure he got his forever home and were doing their best to ensure he did; I can completely understand why too. They only want the best for him, but to do that they need to be clear and honest about all and sundry.

Both foster carers were lovely people and it was nice to see how much they love him, but I also think it has clouded their views of him. Leaving the meeting we had to (and still do) decipher what is true and what is emotionally driven. I can't begin to describe how my mind is racing right now. It is going crazy. We have another full day tomorrow and it starts with the doctor at 10am. We are still very open minded. We are still very emotionally involved and I say it again, subconsciously we really want this to work as we want a forever family.

19th December - Life Appreciation - Day 2

I am awake early this morning, again. I really could do with some more sleep, but my mind is in overdrive. There is so much to try and contemplate about this whole situation and whatever decisions we make are going to affect the rest of our lives and how we then live it. I must get up and have one of these rubbish breakfasts. I hope today goes well; I really do.

Let's do this!

23th December - Chipsticks and mindless TV.

I have been on the sofa for the last few days eating Chipsticks and mindlessly watching rubbish on TV. I am so upset and devastated about the whole situation. Alex has been with his parents and I think that has helped him release some emotions. I feel like he has taken this much better than I have. I wanted to be left alone to deal with it and maybe even grieve a little. His mum is probably more receptive than I am right now to talking through it all. I am just angry and emotionally exhausted. I now realise how much I actually wanted this little boy to work out. My heart hurts!

On the morning of the 19th we made our way over to the doctors and true to form, we had to wait a lifetime to get into the meeting room where we would meet the doctor representing L, joined by his social worker and Patrick. It probably wasn't as long as we thought, but it felt like we were about to get a life changing medical decision and the anticipation was high. I had three nervous wee's.

When we finally got called, the doctor who was a middle aged lady with her glasses half way down her nose, led us upstairs and took us to a meeting room, which had already been booked by someone else. We then got ushered into another room that happened to be free. She looked bored and tired and it wasn't starting well. Under her arm was a large blue folder with L's name on the side. It was big and clearly had a lot of information in it. We all settled around a small table with her on one side and the other four of us facing her. She then proceeded to tell us all about L's history from birth, starting with the day he was born, his weight and then all illnesses and health checks since his birth; with a lot more detail when he was added into the care system, but not masses in the last 12 months. She went through every finite detail and when she had finished on illness and updates (about 40 minutes later) she moved onto his speech and language report. This is where I perked up a little and sat up like a little boy in school who was doing his best to listen. This was the part that could potentially tell us the answers to the big question. Patrick and the other social worker were just writing notes and throwing in an odd question here and there. Finally, when she had finished we didn't feel we had learned any more about L and the question that was the most important to us had to be asked; so I did.

'Do you think L has autism?'

'Yes, and I believe we can sign him off now as high dependency so you can get the support you will need for him'

OK, pardon? Say that again! Could someone not have confirmed this weeks, or even months ago? How can she have said that with so much confidence now, yet it couldn't have been said before this stage? My heart and arse just fell out. My heart beat rose to well above heart attack level. My blood was pumping.

She wrapped up the meeting and both Alex and I zombied out. Patrick looking at his watch, ushered us downstairs and in the cars to the next meeting. As we were walking to the cars I told him that we needed to chat, but he was too busy and preoccupied thinking about the next meeting. He was in timekeeping mode and not thinking about us and what had just been said. He was fully aware that this was a deal breaker and significantly, he had not acknowledged what had just been said by the doctor; either that or he chose to ignore it. I hope it was the first and an accident.

We had to follow him to the next meeting. In the 15 minutes that we were driving both Alex and I had come to our conclusion. When we arrived we chased him across the car park.

'We have to talk Patrick'

'We need to get to the next meeting; we can chat after it'

'No, (stern face), we NEED to talk, NOW'

'Oh'.

The social worker for L clicked what I was trying to say and found a side room that was empty. We went in and I just told him that we would not be going ahead with this match due to what the doctor had just told us. I am not really sure what happened then as it was just a blur. I think he tried to reason with us, but we were clear that we would not move on. I am so angry that Patrick has completely missed the point and the major concern that we have. We have been labouring the point and issues that we could have with him on a near-daily basis.

We walked across the car park and as I sat in the car ready to start the engine, I just burst into tears. We didn't leave for a long 10 minutes which felt like an eternity. Alex did his best to comfort me, but I couldn't help it. I had emotionally invested more than I probably should have and I was just so upset. Eventually, I managed to compose myself and have vision through my teary eyes so we set off on the longest and quietest three hour journey home ever. I just wanted to lie in bed, on my own and cry… hence the Chipsticks and sofa.

The whole situation is horrendous! I feel overwhelmingly guilty and have cried so many times about how I believe I have let that little boy down and have not been able to offer him a stable, caring forever home. I have been brave in front of Alex and not cried. I am sure he knows though. Overall, I know we shouldn't feel guilty; if we didn't make the hard decisions now and just went with it, the likelihood of the adoption breaking down or us having mental breakdowns would be much higher than going into this under the correct and accepted circumstances.

We have done the right thing, but I am still very angry that Patrick completely missed it.

6th January - Reflection Session

> *'As agreed prior to the Christmas break it would be good for me to come over and have a feedback / reflection session, where you could share your views on the link with L.'*

Was it not obvious? A bloody reflection session! I am still raging and had to let Alex reply to this message. I really had to try hard as there seems to be very little acceptance that he missed the most obvious issue at the meeting with L's doctor and I am struggling to manage my emotions so as to not reply too negatively.

Alex has agreed that he will be coming to the house in a few days to talk it out. We settled on the 13th January which still gives me time to calm down.

In the meantime, Alex and I had chatted with family over Christmas about what happened, and it certainly doesn't make things much easier. I am not great with sympathy and constant chat about something that is now dead in the water. I just want to move on.

FAMILY FINDING - JACOB

13th January - Home Visit and Profile

Patrick arrived for his visit today and we had a very candid conversation with him surrounding the circumstances and how we feel that we had been let down by not only the system, but mostly him. He seemed to take it very well or he didn't really care; I am not sure which. What was still very noticeable was that there is still no apology for the oversight and that he was *'just in work mode, so missed it whilst taking notes'*. Throughout the meeting I had to take some deep breaths to calm down. Alex was great in the meeting and was very methodical and constructive with his feedback. I am glad he did most of the talking.

Right at the very end and just as he was about to leave, Patrick asked if we had been back online and looking at profiles for other children. We had, and told him that we were both discussing a little boy called Jacob who was 3 years old. We also told him that we are taking it very slowly and thinking hard on the next move as we don't want to be caught in the same situation again or move forward showing interest in a child to their social worker whilst we are at the height of emotion still. I think I am also feeling very stand-offish and protecting myself. I don't want to be emotionally caught out again, so we need to be 100% set and ready for the next one.

After we poured our hearts out, told him all about the little boy and why we had chosen to look at his profile and maybe pursue interest, Patrick pulled out of his little backpack a set of printed documents. He had a weird smile on his face and told us that he had also been speaking to a social worker he knew over the last few days through the course of placing another child with her. They had somehow moved on to speak about us (I think it was due to the major balls up before Christmas) and she had told Patrick that she was working to find a family for a little boy. That little boy was called Jacob and as luck would have it the printed profile Patrick had brought with us was for him.

Patrick then handed over the profile - which I knew inside out already but didn't want to tell him or Alex that - and we discussed him from birth. We also got an insight into the needs of Jacob and frankly there were very few, other than some 'possibilities' due to either unknown information or due to the knowledge of his birth mother. His birth father was out of the picture and had zero interest in Jacob.

Some dominoes in my head were falling into place. I really liked this boy, but I wanted to be cautious. We would think about it and discuss it when Patrick left, which we did, a lot.

17th January - More Information Required

Alex and I have asked for some videos of Jacob as we want to paint a better picture of him from the start. Patrick has said he will reach out to Jacob's social worker and in turn she will request them from the foster carers. Knowing how long things took previously, I am not confident that we will get them for a number of weeks, so in a funny way, it gives us more time to re-warm ourselves back into the whole adoption process and family finding.

28th January - We were right…

We were right, it is going to take weeks. Alex has chased Patrick for those pictures and videos of Jacob.

29th January - Holding message

Patrick has sent us a holding message. He has chased the social worker on his side, blah blah blah. Nothing to report. I am still struggling with him.

31st January - Video and Pictures

Awwwww. He is so cute and has a lovely little personality. Finally we got some sent over. The videos we got showed Jacob playing with the foster carers dog and having so much fun. We also got to see him dancing around the front room and even hoovering up helping his foster carer. He seems to be such a happy little boy and the videos are very good at getting that across. It has also shown that he has some social skills, which makes us feel a lot more confident about us being able to meet his needs. I think my heart just missed a beat. I really am starting to like this little boy and I feel a bigger desire to be his father and 'gut feeling' than I did with L.

We don't want to be burnt again. We are looking at everything. We want to get more information regarding his full background.

1st February - Accepted and PAR

We have now been introduced to Julie, the social worker for Jacob. She has read our PAR (potential parents report) and has accepted that we would likely be good for him subject to a few questions and a meeting. That also depends on us too and the level of interest we have. To help with really understanding his background, we have now got his CPR (child's permanence report) which details everything about him, all the way from birth. It also states a lot of information on his reasons for being in the care system. We will read it tonight and then send some questions back, should we have any. I am sure we will after the last time. We want as much information as possible so we can make the most informed decision. I am excited to read it, but I don't want to know the bad things that have happened to him.

14th February - Answers

We sent over a lot of questions, and we got some very in-depth answers. That in itself was a great sign as Julie clearly has lots of knowledge of Jacob and most importantly the answers she has given shows an abundance of experience, integrity and care for Jacob's future. Patrick has previously expressed the level of respect she commands because of her work, from her colleagues.

The answers were all very thorough. Due to the level of information and depth of answers, we had no further questions and from these answers we were able to get a very clear understanding and insightful set of information about Jacob that helped us continue to paint a vivid picture of him; a picture that was getting more colourful by the day.

We asked about his health, development, nursery, foster placement and one thing that had caused a little worry, was the plan for the birth parents and the 'contact' plan post a placement. At present Jacob sees his birth mother once a month. It was suggested by Julie that this would stop after placement but that we should meet her for the best of both her, Jacob and of course us both too. We would be happy to meet her as long as it is in a safe environment.

Finally, it was a nice note in the email from Julie to see that the foster carers are helping him and preparing him to move to a forever family. They have been *'giving him permission to move to a forever family, helping him understand his next phase of life'*.

The end of the email was asking to meet us in the next few weeks. That would give her and us a massive opportunity to ask questions to each other. I am still apprehensive because of the last issue we had, but I am really starting to like this little boy. Alex and I have had a few conversations and have been clear that we need to not fall into the trap of wanting a family so much that it becomes a detriment to our decision making. After lots of thought, we are clear that Jacob is the little boy for us at this stage of knowledge and that we want to meet the social worker.

We have agreed to meet on the 24th February.

LINKING - JACOB

24th February - Linking Meeting

Julie is due later on tonight and I am pretty nervous. I am heading to work in a few minutes and I don't think I will be able to concentrate that much. I am lucky I have the afternoon off for this meeting. It has been a pain to get the time off and I have had to use my annual leave. Work hasn't been so accommodating for today and frankly they weren't last time either.

After Julie left this afternoon both Alex and I were over the moon with the conversation. She stayed for about an hour and we must have offered her about 30 cups of coffee through nervous energy and wanting to portray that we are nice people. It felt similar to when you take an exam that is very important. The good news was that Julie expressed that she thought we could make fantastic parents to Jacob and that was very reassuring for us both. We are ecstatic that she feels this way because we really do like him based on all the things we are hearing. He sounds like a great fit for us and it seems we could reciprocate that as parents too.

She was lovely. A very assured person, who was articulate and measured with her questions and answers. This woman clearly knows her stuff and the confidence levels it has given us after the experience with L, is fantastic. She is worlds apart from the last social worker. I am sure Patrick was very much in awe of her too. She is that good.

Throughout the meeting Julie discussed Jacob's development in the foster placement and went over the details of his medical (I bet Patrick had briefed her on the importance of knowledge here for us). There was an old medical report, but she had requested another and more up to date one to ensure the detail was relevant. She was quite apologetic that the system is so slow on some occasions.

She asked a lot of questions about us and how we feel we could offer a loving and safe life for Jacob. We went into detail about the local area, schools, our support network and more. It was pretty much the summary of our PAR that Patrick had created, but in 60 minutes.

Finally, and just before she left, she had a walk around the house to ensure it is child-safe, and offered a couple of recommendations on how we could safeguard it for Jacob.

The way she was talking and the terminology was suggestive that this was going to go ahead. It was very presumptive and *'when Jacob comes....'* Thinking about the terminology and language used, it made us subconsciously place Jacob in our home already. We were talking about which room would be Jacob's, where would he sit at the table and so on.

It's certainly become real very quickly… but I like it. I have *the* feeling.

25th February - Medical Report and Firm Interest

Very pleasingly and incidentally after the day we met Julie, we received the medical report for Jacob and it all seems very good. He has asthma and eczema, but that's not a concern for us in the slightest. There was a mention of him not being able to manage his emotions very well at present, but from what I have read and what the training suggests, that's common with children who haven't had much interaction at a younger age. Julie is confident with the right level of care he should be able to learn to manage them. She suggests that she has no concerns regarding his health and is very pleased with his progress since he moved to foster care.

Patrick also called following the meeting yesterday and it was confirmed that Julie wants to pursue Alex and I as potential parents for Jacob. Wow, just writing that has made me have happy tears. How bloody amazing! The next steps will be for us to go to see him in a bump into meeting and the people around him. An agenda will be sent in the next couple of days *'if you feel the same way'*.

We 100% feel the same way and really want to meet him and pursue this 'link' and balls to the mental barriers now. We really like this boy and we need to fully focus on him and throw a little caution to the wind.

All in all, this is looking absolutely amazing and is all very exciting. We can't wait to get the agenda.

LIFE APPRECIATION

28th February - Life Appreciation Day Agenda.

The below email came through while it was at work this morning, forwarded from Patrick but written to him, from Julie.

'Hi Patrick,

I have spoken to various people and can confirm the following:

Meeting with foster carers at their home on Tuesday 10th March at 10.00 am – address is X. This meeting will last no more than 1 hour.

Jacob will be at nursery and when the meeting is finished the foster carers will collect him and meet us in the community – hoping to go to a local park/café – the foster carers will confirm the venue and address with me in due course and I will let you know. This will be the 'bump into' meeting with Jacob and will last for approx. 1 hour, depending on weather and how Jacob is.

Please note I cannot arrange the mini life appreciation day for 16th as key professionals are not available. I have arranged it for 20.3.20 at X as follows:

- 1.00 pm adopters and yourself to attend.
- 1.15 pm nursery worker, Joanne to attend
- 2.00 pm health visitor, Linda to attend

> - 2.30 pm contact worker, Jessica to attend
>
> *If Alex and Joe would like the foster carers to be part of this afternoon, they are also happy to attend, just let me know.*
>
> *I will arrange for a telephone consultation between Alex and Joe and the medical advisor, Dr Smith after the above have taken place.*
>
> *If you could kindly confirm you, Alex and Joe are happy with the above I would be grateful*
>
> *Thank you, Julie'*

Yes, yes of course we are happy to go. It was a simple email reply frankly. I was straight on the phone to Alex to make sure we had both booked off our time at work. My work has actually started to warm to it all now as I am thinking they realise that they legally have to. It's quite clear that this is not a process that the HR team have had to deal with yet. Alex's workplace has a guy in HR that has adopted, so they are pretty well versed and ready to support. In fact he has been offering advice, via Alex, to me to support our HR team.

Ohhhh this is all real and very exciting now, but it is still a month away.

3rd March - COVID-19

COVID-19 has kicked off and nobody really knows what this is fully yet and how it is affecting life in general. Let's hope that this doesn't affect meeting Jacob and the foster carers. Let's hope this blows over soon.

14th March - COVID-19

This COVID-19 seems to be worse than we thought. There are talks of lockdowns here in the UK. Spain has just gone into a partial lockdown and just watching it on the news is pretty grim viewing. With people not being able to leave the house, unless for food or medical reasons. I hope this doesn't happen here.

16th March - UK, COVID-19 Update

Well, I spoke too soon on the last update in the diary. The Prime Minister has advised that all non-essential contact and travel must be stopped. We have no idea if this means we can't travel to meet Jacob. Is the social care sector part of essential travel and contact? Patrick and Julie are not sure as they haven't received the guidance yet from anyone further up the chain. At this point, we are still to continue as we have planned, but there will be some things that may have to change at the life appreciation day. The social workers are flapping as much as we are. We can tell how invested Julie is in regard to Jacob's future. I love how she is really wanting to get a placement for him, all for his benefit.

20th March - Life Appreciation Day

Thank God it went ahead today. I am absolutely drained, but I have a heart that is so full of love right now. I know it's not love-love, but I am smitten with him. Alex is the same. All the way home we couldn't stop smiling and talking about what a wonderful little boy he is.

We were up pretty early this morning and it felt like we were waiting forever to set off, however before we were to set off, we had a call from Jacob's nursery nurse as he isn't in nursery at present. He has asthma and the recommendation from the government is for people with conditions like this to be classed as higher risk, so they should have limited contact with other people. We have been isolating enough to know we are safe from the virus. I haven't spoken to anyone face to face for days. When the nursery nurse called she pretty much gushed about how amazing, attentive and loving Jacob is and you could hear in her voice how much he is adored. Additionally, she spoke about his development. His speech and language is progressing OK, but with some work still to do, plus his creative play seems to be going well. He is a social butterfly and very caring to other children with no concerns over sharing. The focus points that are being worked on are his fine motor skills and concentration on tasks. He can be easily distracted and has a big desire to ensure whatever task he is doing has to be completed. It was so nice to hear he is doing well and progressing, though catching up on some areas where he previously was struggling, which frankly is to be expected based on the background and past. Overall, the nursery nurse showed very little concern over his development. At the end she wished him well and *'hopes Jacob finds a very loving, playful and caring family in you'*. I read into this a little that she has been told he is coming to us.

Both Alex and I were very happy with that call. It went very well and was a very strong start to this amazing day.

The agenda had changed away from the original plan. Due to the limited amount of contact allowed, we were to now only meet the foster carers, social workers (ours and Jacobs) and of course we were to 'bump into Jacob' at a play centre.

The car drive was pretty quiet but luckily only about an hour away. I think the nerves got to us, but as we have spoken so much in depth about Jacob that there wasn't much more to say. We just had to enjoy the day and process as much information as we could that would help us come to the correct decision for both Jacob and us. We had set off early enough to make sure we got there on time, and after a couple of drive-pasts we found the foster carers house. We parked up and walked up the drive each hoping the other would knock. Eventually, I did and immediately heard the dog bark indicating they were in. Those couple of seconds felt like an age as the door opened to be greeted by an absolutely lovely and welcoming woman, his foster carer. She welcomed us in and immediately offered us a drink. It was a quick ice breaker and gave us a couple of seconds just to settle on the sofa and take in our new surroundings. When she came back in with the coffee, Julie and Patrick arrived at that same point so we had familiar faces to help steer us through the next hour or so. It was actually a very organic conversation with the foster carer walking us through Jacob's life in the foster placement and giving us lots of first-hand detail about his character, likes, dislikes and triggers. The best part for me was that she told us about the bad or developmental things which demonstrated to us that she wants us to make the right decision for us and him. To be fair there isn't much that was a concern frankly, but for a couple of minor points. He was scared of using the bathroom, so didn't tell anyone causing a few accidents and when something like the TV was on he would completely zone into that and nothing else. At this point he wouldn't communicate with you unless you brought him out of the 'zone'. They believe it could be something to do with his past and him removing the background noise. Overall, these things are not game changers (of course) and things we can work on and be cognisant of the future should we move onwards (which is looking nailed on right now). The foster carer also discussed how her family have helped other children move on in the past and talked through the strategy of how they consistently give permission to the child to find a forever family and that they will make sure it is a safe place.

We certainly felt very confident in the way the foster carer went about her job and the amount of candid information she shared was very important to us. Both Patrick and Julie were relatively passive but threw in the odd questions and filled in some gaps where the foster carer was unsure. It was all very easy and relaxed and all very natural. I felt good.

We left with Patrick whilst Julie and the foster carer had a debrief. In the meantime, the foster carer's husband went to pick up Jacob in readiness to meet her and Julie at the little play centre and cafe. We went for a quick coffee elsewhere and had our own little debrief. We went over the details from the meeting and we are very happy with what we have heard so far. We really wanted to continue and couldn't wait to 'bump into' Jacob. We set off to meet him shortly after our coffee. It was quite a bizarre feeling thinking we could be meeting the little boy that we would potentially spend the rest of our lives with.

When we arrived at the centre, Julie and the foster carers were there with Jacob. We approached them at the table they had sat at and Julie got up and we played the game of *'fancy seeing you here'* to try and put Jacob off the scent of who we really were. In hindsight he definitely knew who we could be as he was very attentive to the 'foster carers friends' that he had just met. He had seen these types of meetings with other children, so it is fair to think he is on the right track. Both Alex and I couldn't keep our eyes off of him. We just wanted to watch him and interact with him and it was kind of left for us to do just that. He came with me to get some drinks and he was eyeing up the cakes, so I asked if I could buy him one. He picked the chocolate one, so I did too. His manners, even at 3 years old, were amazing. He said both *please* and *thank you*. I could have taken him home there and then. He is so cute.

After a cake and some small talk, Jacob went and played in the play centre with one of the foster carers to give us a little bit of time. We ended up discussing Jacob's plans to stop seeing his birth mother and with all the emotions flying around Alex was overwhelmed and got upset. He told us when he returned from the bathroom that it was because he felt a little bit guilty for taking a child from his birth mother and I can completely resonate with him on it, however Julie was very clear that he should not feel guilty, but some empathy towards her and to try and understand why Jacob was in the process he was. We were encouraged to think about his future in a safe and loving home; something he may not have got should he not be adopted. It made sense, but it's still hard to not have some feelings for the birth mother, especially as we know that the cycle she was in as a child and someone growing up was not great. Luckily we were saved by Jacob coming back and changing the tone of the conversation. He asked for one of us to go and play with him in the play centre and with a quick nod of confirmation from Julie that it was OK for us to do that, Alex went and joined him first and had loads of fun chasing him. One thing we did notice was when you were not engaging in him, he would fall over on purpose just to check that you were watching him and most importantly, his foster carers said that it was so he knew that someone would pick him up or show him some attention. We were encouraged to do so by Julie to ensure we created a nice bond. Once Alex got tired, I got the chance to go and play with him too. I loved it. I felt like a kid again. I also loved how much Jacob wanted to interact with me. At one point he gave me a big cuddle and I just melted and that's where my emotion got the better of me. I had a couple of tears as he then ran off to go back down the slide for the hundredth time. Luckily the others didn't see me as I was in the middle of the soft play.

We eventually had to leave and Jacob had to go home. We said our goodbyes and he cuddled us and waved us off. It was a great feeling and I already couldn't wait to see him again. Alex expressed the same feeling. We were both on an adrenaline high this afternoon. We will follow up with the social worker over the next couple of days, but we will talk it out when the initial emotions subside and we can talk about it rationally.

I am absolutely shattered now however and can't wait to get in bed. It's only 6pm.

21st March - Jacob is the ONE.

Jacob is the one for us and that is irrefutable from both of us. We have discussed it a lot overnight (I never got my early night) and both of us 100% are committed to this little boy. He ticks all the boxes that we want to tick and more. We want him to be part of our forever family. It's all in on the emotions now.

Luckily when we spoke to Patrick and Julie this morning too and it was conclusive that after our meeting that we would make *'great parents to Jacob'* (from Julie). That is music to our ears and we are very pleased. Julie said things could now move pretty quickly and for the sake of Jacob meeting us and continuity, we should send over some videos asking if we could be his daddies and also a teddy bear that he can use as an anchor and memory of us.

We will get on with that later in the day. We just need to think about what and how to say it. Maybe we shouldn't over think it, but you can't help but want to make a good impression.

Additionally Julie has already been exploring matching panels. This is the panel specifically for Jacob and us to be granted a match, formally which means he can come and live with us as a 'placement' and in readiness for when a full adoption order is granted. This is after the application which we can make after a minimum of 10 weeks into placement; however speaking to our friends that have already adopted, that's going to take some time longer than the 10 weeks due to the speed of paper and subject to no objections.

Now all parties are pretty happy that this will go ahead, it seems all go. Julie has got a lot of ducks in a row prior today; either that or she works very quickly.

22nd March - Video and Teddy

We have sent over the video that we did in the front room of Jacob's new forever home and Alex and I went to buy a teddy together today. I sent it from work over lunch. It should arrive tomorrow. How very exciting is this?

25th March - Questions, questions, questions…

We have been exchanging messages with the social workers and as a result we have asked a bunch of questions.

We asked if Jacob had received the teddy and message and wanted to know if there was any recognition as to who we are and maybe - although he may not be old enough just yet - did he understand what it meant when we said we wanted to be his daddies.

Additionally, as we are now in a lockdown due to COVID, we have asked if we can get some videos and photos of Jacob. Also due to lockdown we wanted to understand their key-worker status and whether the panel and introductions could go ahead as normal or would we have to do some of it via video. There is so much up in the air due to this bloody virus.

Ideally we should complete the matching panel and then move onto introductions. Matching panels haven't been done online before, so this will be trailblazing. The introductions clearly can't be done online as the end goal is for placement and Jacob to be living in his new forever family home.

So much depends on the virus.

MATCHING

27th March - Adoption Placement Report (APR) - Sign Off

Patrick has sent over an APR - so many acronyms - which is the 'Adoption Placement Report'. This report details what has happened in regard to interactions to date, but also the reason that the social workers believe we would be a good match for Jacob. We were asked to approve what the social workers had written about us and the whole situation. Some of the comments were lovely and we very much believe we can offer Jacob a very loving and safe home. It was quite a simple document with very factual statements, however there were a number of errors from the beginning. For example, the date was incorrect, Alex was classed as an only child (he isn't) and also single, which he isn't unless he hasn't told me something. It was quite surprising that there were so many mistakes though; a bit of copy and paste maybe. We changed them and sent back the changes we thought should be amended. Additionally, we filled out the answers to a number of questions asking about such things like our views regarding birth parents, childcare experience, household circumstance and finances and so on. It was a very small version of all the questions that Patrick asked when he did our home visits, so it was just repeating our past answers, really.

30th March - Matching Panel Date

On the 21st April we will have our matching panel for Jacob. It's amazing news and I can't wait. Alex was very excited when we chatted about it at lunch. I was at work and so was he, but he was over the moon. Hopefully the panel agrees with what Julie and Patrick feel regarding our suitability as parents for Jacob.

How very exciting!

2nd April - Adoption Support Plan

Julie has sent across the adoption support plan for Jacob. This is a 21 page document that has given us notification on such things as general health, educational and behavioural development, family and social relationships, school relationships, self care, contact, financial and more. It's all very in depth and I believe it is due to be part of the adoption panel to offer them full guidance on the proposed plans. It also confirms to us the expectations we need to uphold with regard to such things like 'contact' with birth parents. In this case we are to write a letter annually.

7th April - Adoption Placement Report (APR) - Amendments

Patrick has sent us back the report to confirm the amendments have been made and to sign. We have completed this and retuned it. I am still baffled how many mistakes there were in it. It must be super tough though as I am sure his and all the other social workers have a massive workload. There is no secret that they are overworked.

11th April - Connection with Foster Carers - WhatsApp

Julie has connected the foster careers and us via WhatsApp so we can have direct contact with them and so we can ask any questions about Jacob and continue to paint the picture of him and also what we need to prepare. Once we connected we sent over a message just to thank them for being so accommodating and open to help us on our journey. We are still not sure the level of detail we can get into as we haven't been formally matched yet, but we did get a very positive message that was letting us know that *'Jacob really enjoyed meeting you'*. That certainly was amazing to get back, but I am pretty sure it was the foster carer just being nice. We will take it regardless.

14th April - Risk Assessment & Family Book

More flipping paperwork! We completed a risk assessment of our home today. There was nothing to really do with it other than confirm that we are safe. The hard part was getting the certificates for the electricity and gas. Luckily we have a new build so we kept it all.

Additionally, we have been asked to create a book introducing our home. The idea behind this is to show Jacob what his forever home will look like going into depth by showing his room, the kitchen, the garden, local area and so on. Julie advised to use a teddy in each picture and send both the book and teddy to him. It should give Jacob a sense of connection to the new home. What it will also do is help his social worker talk about moving on too. She can use language that tells him about '*your new room, where you will eat at dinner time*' and so on. Ideally it will break the ice when he moves so he doesn't feel like he is in a completely new environment and causing a shock to the system.

We have been working on the book and pictures and having some fun doing it. Let's hope he likes his potential new home. It's getting very close and we are feeling excited and overwhelmed.

That has got me thinking about what we will need to buy for him too. Oh god!

INTRODUCTIONS & MATCHING PANEL

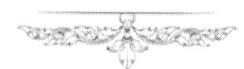

18th April - Video Calls

Having spoken with Julie, she has decided that we can have video calls with Jacob and the first one is tonight. Normally video calls are not something that is done, however due to the COVID-19 restrictions and 'lock-down' we are not able to complete the introductions should the matching panel go to plan on the 21st. Julie must be confident enough in the outcome for her to allow the first call tonight. I can't wait to speak to Jacob and the foster carer later.

We have just finished the call and we got a really good insight into Jacob's evening routine and his character in a homely setting. He was the typical child on a call putting the camera facing up his nose and in his eyes, laughing at the silliness of it all. He came across as such a loving little boy towards his foster carer, who he clearly loves and adores. She showed lots of protective and attentive behaviour back towards him. We also tried to have a direct conversation with him too, but as he is only 3 it was tough to get much from him but when we did, we had some troubles understanding what he was actually trying to say. We had already been told this could be something that might happen, so the foster carer filled in when we looked confused. Jacob just had a glint in his eye full well knowing something is different in his life. We think he has connected the dots somewhere.

Other than us trying to interact and laughing at him being silly, we just watched and enjoyed seeing him happy. He certainly looks like a very happy character. In between interactions his foster carer continued to ask us questions and tell us about what toys he likes to play, what he likes on TV and lots of little bits so that we could build up our bank of knowledge regarding him. We want to ensure that when (hopefully) he comes to his forever home, we can keep as many consistent routines as possible so it doesn't completely throw him off course. He will have enough change as it is.

As we signed off he blew some kisses and said goodbye to us both. We told him that we were really looking forward to seeing him again very soon on video. We hope that on the next call, which is after the matching panel, we can tell him a little more about who we are… his Daddies.

His Daddies. That sounds bizarre.

21st April - Matching Panel

Today was the matching panel. It was at 10am and we had to do it via conference video call. We were only on for about 5 minutes asking very basic questions. We were expecting lots of in-depth questions, but it was very underwhelming, bar the outcome. We got a call just after from Patrick and Julie letting us know that the match had been successful and approved. I wanted to cry with happiness, but before I could we moved straight onto the next piece of the puzzle. We discussed the next stages and Julie was to go away and look at 'introductions'

24th April - Official

Over the past few days we have exchanged some messages with the foster carers in regard to us being approved as a match for Jacob and how she should tell him and introduce us as his new Daddies. Julie has suggested that she tell Jacob so we can have plenty of time to work on the new relationship and also in readiness for the call tomorrow. We can then speak using the correct terminology. In the meantime the foster carer has sent us a lot of pictures and a few videos of Jacob working on some homework from nursery. In every picture he is smiling or laughing. We are told he loves dressing up and playing games. One of the messages of him was dressed up as a pirate and was signed off *'Pirate Jacob for Daddy Alex and Joe. He is in a lovely mood and he's really excited'*. I can't tell you how excited we are too. The terminology has changed so much and so subtly that the barriers are down and I am now visualising our life fully with Jacob.

We have also had some email exchanges with Patrick. We have a million things we feel we need answering. The pressure is building and I am feeling it. We have asked a lot of questions to Patrick about registering for school, doctors, dental and more. He said that we can't do any of that until he is actually placed. I am glad I have got Alex who takes care of most of that type of admin. We already know which school we would like Jacob to go to and as he is classed as a 'Looked After Child (LAC)' we are able to jump the queue and pretty much place him in whatever school we would like. That takes one stress away, thankfully.

25th April - Video Call.

'Night, night Daddy Alex and Daddy Joe'. (blows kisses)

That got me in the feels. My heart melted and from the noises and face Alex pulled, I could tell that it got him too. That was the first time we had heard Jacob say our names with the Daddy prefix. He wasn't even prompted to use the term by the foster carer. It was so cute and amazing that I have been riding that amazing adrenaline wave for the last hour or so.

The rest of the call was again trying to interact with him and ask him some questions about what he likes and enjoys. We know he loves tomato ketchup and chocolate now. These are small bits of information, but they are really helping us understand him and what we can do to engage with him.

He hasn't seen the book and teddy yet as they are to be dropped off by Patrick at some stage this week. On our next call, next week, we can go through it with him.

28th April - Family Book

Just before lunch we received a set of pictures from the foster carer. The pictures were of Jacob reading through the family book we had sent with help of course. He also had the bear in his arms cuddling it whilst pointing to the pictures showing where he found the bear. Julie told us that this will really help him engage in what was in the picture and help him put the meaning of the words together. *'Bear is sleeping in your bed'.* My favourite picture was of Jacob pointing to the 3 stick-men I drew of us three holding hands. The foster carer said that Jacob had said *'that is me, Daddy Alex and Daddy Joe'.*

There was something in my eye again. After lunch I walked around work with a massive spring in my step and a huge grin. How could I not?

We have another call set in for tomorrow. We were given some ideas regarding starting to set some boundaries just like parents would. Just some small things like asking him to stop doing something or to listen to what we were saying. I am sure some opportunities will come up organically to do it, so maybe we shouldn't over think that. We also thought that we should maybe show him the house on video so we can keep the calls engaging. We don't want them going stale just asking him what he likes to eat and play with. That will become tougher to do over time.

29th April - Video Call

It was a really great call tonight as we got to go through his book together. That took about twenty minutes of the thirty we have set aside before his bedtime. We didn't get time to show him the house on the video at that point so we will do it on the next one.

When we spoke about the pictures with Jacob he used the terminology of *'my bedroom'* or *'my bathroom'* and *'my forever family'.* The foster carer has been clearly reading him the book a lot over the last few days as he seems to know it inside out. He didn't seem to have any hesitation to moving and seems to have taken it in his stride, even asking to be able to use the local park. I am not sure if he fully understands the whole situation. He is three after all, so I am sure there is and will be some confusion in his mind.

I am so happy. Things seem to be going very well and in the right direction. We are really getting to know him well. Not only that we are getting on so well with the foster carers which clearly is a massive help. She has been very receptive to us asking questions adhoc and has always replied with lovely messages about how we are doing too. I can certainly say it helps with the confidence.

We also got a lovely message from the foster carer telling us we were doing a great job in becoming his daddies and asserting ourselves in a way where he has boundaries and feels safe. She has said this is the most important factor for him, feeling safe. It is music to our ears to hear that we are doing the correct things and organically.

3rd May - Videos, Pictures and Questions

Over the course of this week we have asked a bundle of questions to the foster carers. Everything down to the size of the car seat we should get. I can't believe how expensive things are. I think we need another mortgage, and I am glad that the local authority will contribute £150 to support the essential purchases.

We have also received lots of pictures and videos of Jacob just being him. Lots of playing, creating things and of course eating. He is adorable and I can't wait to be his daddy in person. Each and every interaction we receive confirms that we are completely besotted with this little boy.

We have also started preparing the house. I have painted his room and created a pattern that's like a mountain range with snow on the peaks. It looks really cool actually and I am impressed with myself. Additionally, we have been adding stick-on blackboards in the kitchen. We draw Jacob's name and lots of love hearts on. It just came out and to me that's showing the subconscious way we view him.

Both Julie and Patrick have been checking in too. It is easy to forget about them both now we have the foster carers as a direct link. They are pushing to give us as much information as possible regarding the physical introductions and move, but at present with the COVID-19 lockdown, there has to be a number of risk assessments completed. I am not sure it will be anytime soon. We massively want to get on with it, however re-framing the situation, it gives us more time to prepare and build our relationship with Jacob over the calls.

5th May - Video Call

Tonight we got unprompted kisses and cuddles from Jacob on our call. He was so attentive to us. His foster carer has said that he has been so happy all week and has been asking for *'the book'* to be read to him a number of times and at points pointing out *'my bed'* and other things that are his. He is clearly starting to understand the situation and what it actually means for him. Even on the call, the foster carer is using such good language with Jacob, that will massively help him understand what is happening. It is all *'when you move to your forever home'* and *'your daddies'* etc. Subconsciously he is taking all this onboard and it's not going to be a shock to the system of us just turning up one day for the start of introductions. He will be warmed up to us when it finally is arranged.

Tonight we also showed him some of the rooms that he has seen in the book. It was mainly his bedroom. We stayed in there for most of the call and we could see he was looking and taking in as much as possible. We tried to ask a lot of presumptive questions too. *'What toys will you put on this shelf?'* and *'Which side of the bed will you put your pillows on?'* and so on. We wanted him to think about all of this and hopefully get him excited about his move. Speaking of that I can't fathom how he must be feeling about moving as this is such a massive life event for him.

The call seemed to go so quickly tonight. I wanted to stay on. I just love watching him do pretty much nothing. He is amazing and he must be such a strong character. I am in awe of how strong he is, or at least presenting himself.

Alex said he could have stayed online too. He really has engaged with Jacob and I am so pleased that we all have a connection. At some points we found ourselves wanting to ask Jacob questions and so we were speaking over one another. I think it was starting to frustrate us both at points because we gave each other a few side glances. Maybe it's the subconscious fight for attention from Jacob, that we both clearly crave, that caused it. I guess that's normal in these first stages. We certainly didn't mean to do it to each other.

We have got lucky with this foster carer, Jacob's social worker and of course this beautiful and happy little boy.

6th May - Child Maintenance

Alex being Alex has already got his admin together and is working on the child maintenance forms. We think we are eligible for it, so we are going to apply for it and if so, we will put the money into an account specifically for Jacob when he is 18.

I still don't understand how someone can be so organised. That's Alex for you though and I am glad I don't have to do all of that stuff. I did very well marrying him.

10th May - Toys

Today, we asked some questions to the foster carer about some of the toys and other things that he brought with him from his birth family. We want to make sure that he always has a connection to them as they are part of his identity, but of course our new instincts are to protect him and his emotions. We don't want anything that will cause him to emotionally struggle. I am sure he has enough to think about already.

He has a toy box and some toys that have come with him. The foster carer says when he plays with some of the toys he can have emotional reactions to some of them. She thinks they may bring up some memories.

11th May - Update on Introductions

Alex reached out to Julie today to see if we can get some more information regarding the formal and in-person introductions. The lockdown is completely slowing everything down and it is getting very frustrating. We want to get on with it and form our forever family.

13th May - Video Call

When the video connected, Jacob had such a massive smile. He genuinely looked pleased to see us (which is a relief). His voice was full of delight saying hello to us. I don't think I will be tired of him calling us *'Daddy Alex and Daddy Joe'*. I can let him say it all day to me. It just warms my heart so much. Similarly, I love it when he says it to Alex too.

Jacob showed us some pictures that both he and the foster carer had been drawing over the course of the day. They were pictures of the three of us and the words 'family' on them. It's another method of helping him understand who we are. She has been so clever using all of the tools to help him understand his future. I am in awe of the skills she shows.

Most of the remainder of the call was Jacob showing us things. It was very basic children and adult interaction again. One thing that we did see today that we haven't seen before is a meltdown. His foster carer had a sore foot and was messing around knocking her, by accident, but it was hurting. She then gave him a bit of a telling off, rightly so, and he then went off on one. That ended the call pretty quickly as she needed to take control of the situation. We received a message afterwards explaining what happened and that he didn't like getting told off. Jacob likes to be in control and she said that he struggles to regulate his feelings and because of this he is still working out what they all mean and how to deal with them.

In a complete coincidence we bought a book today about recognising emotions as we have heard it is quite common with children who are looked after to not understand how to recognise and self regulate their emotion.

15th May - Risk Assessment

We have been back and forth on email with Patrick as he has been asking for more information to see if we can get the introductions started. There seems to have been some movement in the local authority to move adoption journeys forward. If they continue to hold everything it will surely put a massive burden on the system and most importantly the children. On a selfish note, we just want to get on with it soon because we have the feeling that Jacob might start to think we are pulling his leg about being his forever family. We don't want to lose his confidence.

We have sent back lots of details to confirm that we will do what they want us to do. Luckily, I am furloughed from work and I have lots of flexibility to do as I need to, to ensure we cover every base to maximise the chances of bringing the dates forward.

We are ready to bring him home.

18th May - Introductions - Update

Both Julie and the foster carer have been looking at how we can conduct the introductions. It has been suggested that we self-isolate for the recommended 14 days so we can do them properly. There will of course be some differences to the 'normal' process. For example, there will be no social workers there. Frankly, we think this is a good thing as we don't want any distractions and want to just get on with it.

Everything is in the hands of this bloody COVID-19 and the local authorities' risk management team. Let's hope they can find a safe solution for us and anyone else adopting.

There was also a question regarding 'final contact' with his birth mum. This actually upsets me as this is his birth mother, but on the other hand I am angry at her for what he went through. Due to the virus risk, there is no option for it to happen before he comes home, and we have confirmed that we are comfortable for it to happen after his placement date. I think I still want to meet her myself. I am curious to know about her as a person, and I think candidly it's for my benefit just as much as Jacobs in the future.

20th May - Video Call

Although we absolutely love speaking with Jacob, we are now starting to struggle with the content as we have shown him the house a few times, read numerous stories and feel like we know his routines inside out.

Today was mostly speaking to the foster carer as Jacob wasn't massively engaged and candidly it helped us a little because we didn't have anything new to discuss with him. It was really a tough call. We mainly spoke about the past week and how home-schooling had progressed. We got some interaction from him when he heard us talking about his writing. At this point he had to show us. He was so proud of his work.

When we signed off, both Alex and I felt very deflated due to the call. We need to get this moving forward and we are going to send a big email to Patrick with our frustrations.

Alex wrote this…I think it portrays how frustrated we are. It has been building for a while now.

Hi Patrick,

We are incredibly frustrated and disappointed to read that we remain in the same position as we have been for several weeks since being approved to adopt Jacob. **We would like to outline our frustrations and work on outcomes or solutions.**

It feels like several call review meetings take place with managers with no real outcome or action plan of what can be done to overcome the situation. The area of conflict seems to be delaying Jacob being moved to us vs the impact of him having final contact with the birth mum several months down the line when in placement with ourselves. Everyone has been aware of this conflict for some time, yet no decisions have been made, or relative progress, on what can be done to overcome this, apart from to wait and have more calls and reviews.

We appreciate the situation is very difficult and appreciate all the work that is done by yourself and Julie, however, we feel that the message remains the same in that it is being under constant review and risks are being assessed. Due to the severity of the situation we kindly ask that we are now involved with management calls or to be provided with minutes if this is not possible. This is just so we have a full understanding of what is coming out of these meetings and perhaps express our concerns and frustrations first hand. We are unhappy that no real progress has been made over the last 4 weeks since being approved.

Final contact with the birth mum (which we fully support) was due at the end of March so we would like to see in detail the work that has been done by the LA over the last 2 months. The reason for this is that it has always been understood that final contact had not happened, and this was a requirement before Jacob is moved to us; so, this should have been the highest priority to resolve. As virtual contact is not possible, has self-isolation been considered as an option? It is also now possible for anyone to request a test to see if they have or have had coronavirus so could this be used to move things long to arrange final contact?

Our biggest concern is that we have been doing video calls with Jacob for over 6 weeks and these have been weekly since he was told we are his new daddies. It does feel that because Jacob is presenting well, there is no immediate concern with moving him on and unless his behaviour deteriorates rapidly, he will not be moved onto ourselves.

Although the calls are going well, they are increasingly becoming a challenge as we have now shown him each room and garden, shared pictures regularly and read stories back and forth a lot. It is a lot to ask of a child of his age to give his full attention on these calls and we are concerned what internal impact this is having on Jacob being repeatedly told we are his daddies but no sign of him moving in with us. Has anything come out of your calls with Julie regarding what can be done differently to keep the calls "alive". Have our suggestions of routines being videoed been discussed too?

Apologies for the long email but we are incredibly frustrated and feel that no real progress is being made. It seems to be just discussions and reviews taking place but no clear action plan or decisions are being made. We are even more concerned about the impact this is having on Jacob's wellbeing now and potentially in the long term. We urge that the Local Authority make a decision and consider other avenues to arrange final contact - maybe through self-isolation or COVID tests being taken, now that they are available to all.

We simply want some tangible actions and outcomes as opposed to the current 'reviewing' that keep taking place.

Many Thanks

Alex and Joe.

20th May - Reply

We got a reply back relatively quickly and it was appreciated. We knew the answers we were likely to get before we sent the email and they pretty much mirrored them. Everyone on this side, social workers included, really want to move this forward, but are at the mercy of the unprecedented COVID-19 and the restrictions that it has caused. At least they all know of formal views and it is down on paper.

I guess there is some more bloody waiting to do.

23rd May - Video Sent

We have loads of messages on WhatsApp with videos, messages and Jacob talking to us. It is so frustrating that we can't just get these introductions completed. I am struggling mentally at the moment and I have had some pretty low and upsetting days. It's been tough.

27th May - Video Call

Again today was another call that was hard. Lots of small talk about the week but we just all want it to come to a head now. Even the foster carer said she was struggling with the time it has taken. She said she is struggling mentally not knowing the outcomes for Jacob. She can't mentally set herself up for him leaving her without knowing some dates. It must be so tough for them on that side too.

2nd June - I Can't Feel My Legs

I woke up this morning and I couldn't feel my legs! Ohhh sh**

I have been in hospital all day and I am now waiting to go to surgery to fix my spine. Two of my discs have dislodged again. The surgeon said that the last time it had been worked on in surgery 4 years ago, they had missed a few bits on it and it had not healed well at all. The lack of follow up had also been a major factor. He has been prodding and poking me a lot and I just can't feel anything still. It is such a bizarre sensation. I just hope I don't need the toilet as I wouldn't know! The doctor has also told me that if he can't fix it and my nerves are too damaged, then I could be wearing a colostomy bag. My first thoughts were about Jacob and the process we are hoping to move on with. Will this change anything?

Alex isn't allowed to come and see me due to the hospital's COVID-19 visitor policy. I am feeling pretty lonely and my head is spinning. Luckily, I packed a bag with some things that may be needed like my book and phone.

I have come around from surgery and I am groggy. I feel pants. To make things better (or worse), we have just received an email from Patrick regarding the proposed dates and schedule with Jacob. We are due to start introductions on the 17th June. I am in complete mixed emotions as I am not sure we can go ahead right now. I just need to sleep and let Alex deal with that.

3rd June - Upset

I just want to cry. I have seen the draft plan and we just won't be able to do that as I am advised I will be here for another week at least because of the nerve function and I am to have a 6 week stay at home plan doing very little, recovering. We just can't wait that long. It is not fair on Jacob either. I spoke to Alex at about 8pm about this specifically and I have told him that we should try and do the dates.

This is the draft plan.

> *Draft introduction plan in respect of Jacob and his adopters, Alex and Joe.*
>
> *The adopters have met Jacob via 'bump into' meeting and this was positive. Jacob has been looking at their 'about us' book, listening to their voices and watching a video of them for the last 6 weeks. In addition, Jacob has been having weekly face-time video contact with his adopters where they have been able to observe him, speak with him and interact with him through play. More recently the foster carers have shared video clips of Jacob's various routines with the adopters in order to familiarise them with these and provide the opportunity for the adopters to ask questions. Hence, the adopters already have a wealth of knowledge about Jacob and have formed an emotional connection with him. The foster carers, in particular, have also had the opportunity to form a positive relationship with the adopters on which to base the introductions moving forward.*
>
> *Jacob's behaviour has been up and down since he has been told that he will be moving to a new family, which is to be expected. The adopters are fully aware of this and have had the opportunity to discuss his behaviour with their social worker, Jacob's social worker and the foster carers in order to prepare and support them as much as possible.*

Date and Time	Location	Detail
17th June 10.00 am – 3.00 pm	Foster placement	Alex and Joe to spend the day with Jacob. To assist in his lunchtime routine. They can go out with Jacob for a walk for ½ hr on this day.
18th June 7.00 am – 2.00 pm	Foster Placement	Alex and Joe to spend time in the placement with Jacob. To assist with his early morning routine and undertake his lunchtime routine. Foster Carer will encourage Alex and Joe to spend parts of the day alone with Jacob in order for them to take the lead in caring for him, but will be on hand for support and advice in order to encourage their confidence. They are able to take Jacob out for a walk for up to 1 hr on this day.

19th June **9.00 am video-call by social worker to Jacob / foster carer** **Both social workers to review how things are going this morning at 10.00 am** 11.00 am – 7.30 pm *please note there are lots of open spaces to visit safely in the local area Jacob will be involved in packing some of his belongings to take to his new home tomorrow. Eg some of his toys, teddies and clothes	Foster placement	Alex and Joe to spend the day with Jacob and to assist with his teatime, bath time and bedtime routine. They are able to take Jacob out for a picnic lunch in the community * between 11.30 am and return by 2.00 pm at the latest (subject to weather). If they are unable to go out, the foster carer will go out to enable them to have time on their own with Jacob.

20th June Foster carer and Jacob to go to the adoptive home for 11.00 am. They will stay until 2.00 – 3.00 pm, depending on how Jacob is. Jacob to be involved in taking his belongings to his new home from this day onwards.	Adoptive home	Foster Carer to take Jacob to his new home. Both of them to spend time in his home, stay for lunch and help Jacob to begin to settle. **Jacob will have a goodbye tea/ celebration of him moving to his new family with his foster family this evening.**
21st June 10.30 am – 6.30 pm	Adoptive home	The adopters will collect Jacob at 10.30 am and take him to their home. Jacob will spend the day there, have lunch and if he remains settled, tea. Jacob will return to his foster placement by 6.30 pm. Alex and Joe to undertake Jacob's bedtime routine in the foster placement. Jacob not to be taken out of his adoptive home today.

22nd June 10.30 am – 6.30 pm	Adoptive home	The adopters will collect Jacob at 10.30 am and take him to their home. Jacob will spend the day there, have lunch and tea and if he is settled enough, Jacob to have his bath and get into his PJ's in his new home. Jacob will return to his foster placement by 6.30 pm. Alex and Joe to undertake Jacobs bedtime routine in the foster placement. Jacob can be taken out today with Alex and Joe (only to a local park).

23rd June 10.30 am Jacob to be collected by Alex and Joe **Jacob will not be returning to his foster placement – although placement day will not be until Thursday so we can see how Jacob is settling, review the plan and decide if the plan needs extending**	Adoptive home	Jacob to be collected by Alex and Joe and taken to his new home. Jacob will move into his adoptive home on a permanent basis today and will be staying overnight. Jacob to have a short video-call with foster carer at some point in the afternoon in order to reassure him that she has not completely disappeared, is well and for her to give him permission to move on (this is because Jacob has had too many sudden endings in his life and can be very vigilant as to what is going on)
24th June **9.00 am video-call by social worker to Jacob/adopters**	Adoptive home	Depending on how Jacob is, he will have a short video-call with foster carers at some point in the afternoon in order to reassure him that she has not completely disappeared, as well and for her to give him permission to move on. This will be the last planned video-call.

25th June Review of Introductions between all parties. All being well this will be placement day for Jacob.		

5th June - I'm Home

Finally I am home. Alex picked me up and we went straight to McDonalds for a late dinner. I have had a really tough few days mentally. I just lost the will for anything including talking to Alex about things. I just tried to sleep so I wasn't thinking. My mind has been racing to the worst-case scenario regarding the adoption and introductions when I was awake. In the meantime, Alex has been great and has been speaking with Patrick about changing the dates. I have given a little input, but I am determined not to change the dates backwards too much. Last time I had surgery I was walking the day after and I am walking pretty well now. I will just have to manage what I can do.

We will be fine. I know we will.

10th June - Update

We are on! We have been given the 24th June as the new date. That is fantastic news and I am overjoyed. It's not much of a change; only a week, so I am hoping my dodgy spine strengthens up as quickly as possible. It feels OK, although I am walking with a limp. My brain isn't talking to my muscles due to the nerve damage. There is one positive, the co-codamol is strong.

I have really been struggling mentally due to the nerve damage and possible long-term effects, so this is a welcome distraction.

I also have a one-to-one call with Jacob tonight. Alex did one whilst I was in hospital, so I will do one today. Jacob hasn't been made aware of me being in hospital. We were told that this may trigger some memories. After the call we need to work out how we are going to tell Jacob about the date that he will be coming over to start introductions. We, of course, need to word it better than that.

I have not long finished the call with Jacob and it was lovely to spend some dedicated time alone with him. I told Jacob that Daddy Alex had gone to the shops. To be fair it may be good to see us individually as we won't always be together. It's a small step so Jacob knows it is OK for us to be apart.

We chatted about absolute nonsense and played a game pulling faces. I really enjoyed acting like a child. Alex always says that's my mental age.

It was also nice to not have to jostle for talk-time with Alex. It just felt more relaxed and natural too.

11th June - Spinal Pain

I am struggling with the pain today. I am scared something will happen again and we won't be able to continue as planned. I need to get out of my own head.

We are also now in isolation too, so we can barely do anything to take our minds off things. The waiting is hard enough so compound that with the pain…

12th June - Our 1st Family Shop

Alex has messaged the foster carer to get some more details on what we need to get for Jacob. We have a massive list of foods and drinks, plus we now know the nappy sizes for bedtime.

13th June - Video Call

We still haven't told Jacob about the date yet. We will try and do it about 7 days out so we can do a countdown. On the calls he is so confident calling us Daddy Alex and

Daddy Joe. I am really hoping he understands what it means for him. I know the foster carers are doing a lot of work with him to make sure he does. The call today was us playing lots of games because from the last call we know it engages him pretty well. We got quite a good amount of time with him engaging. I have also noticed that the foster carer is spending less and less time on each call. I didn't really notice it until today. I guess it is her way of letting us engage with Jacob as much as possible and maybe even a way of her pulling away a little?

17th June - Countdown Calendar

We have been back and forth with the foster carers on WhatsApp with final preparation details. Small things that we haven't really thought about too much but are important. Most of being around having the right things to help with his transitions. Things like washing powder (we were told to use the same), bedding, tablet, games, nappies, cutlery, PJ's, new clothes etc etc. There is an endless list of things that you need. Luckily, everything is so accessible that if we need it, we know we can just go out and get it.

We have also agreed to send a video each night showing a little countdown calendar to when we will be with Jacob. We have 7 days on it, so it started tonight. Alex did the first video whilst I filmed. It was actually quite funny watching him speaking to the phone (video) as if he was talking to a three-year-old. We had to do a few takes to get it right as we were laughing.

The foster carer messaged to say it went down really well with him. Jacob enjoyed counting the numbers and interacted well with it. She also said he came across very happy that we are only 7 days from coming to see him and creating our forever family. It will be interesting to see how he reacts in the next few days as the foster carer continues to embed the actual event that is happening. I am not sure that Jacob has understood that he will be leaving the foster carer home or if he has, I am not sure he has understood the huge amount of change about to happen. Only time will tell.

The foster carer has also been going through the family book in more detail with language that has a timescale. An example being *'in 10 days you will be sleeping in that bed'* and so on. She said his reactions are positive.

19th June - Countdown Calendar

We received a video of Jacob tonight doing his own countdown calendar. The video itself was absolutely gorgeous. He was counting down the days and crossing off 7 and 6. Then he counted the remaining 5 and said *'then I will see Daddy Alex and Daddy Joe'*. He then told us he wanted to draw himself. He is gorgeous. I can't wait until the 24th.

Just as he was getting in bed his foster carer sent us another video. She asked him to blow some kisses to us and then unpromted (you could tell by the way the foster carer reacted) he said *'save them in your hearts'*. I am sure both of us melted and had a happy tear welling up.

20th June - Video Call

We did the video call from Jacob's room tonight and then went down to the kitchen to do the countdown calendar together. It was so nice to be able to speak about coming to see him and how excited we are about it on the 24th. The tone of the conversation tonight was more in the excitement zone instead of the practical stuff. When we did the calendar he got super excited when we got to the day of seeing him.

Jesus, it's close now. I am going to be a dad and responsible for a child. That's quite overwhelming to think about. Patrick - who we are due to have a chat with tomorrow actually - has said these thoughts are completely normal and he says we should take it one day at a time. My mother said the same too.

22nd June - Patrick's Call

We spoke to Patrick yesterday and it was a positive call. There was no agenda from him. He just wanted to talk through our feelings and if we had any questions. We didn't have any for him really as they are all being answered by the foster carer. She is our primary contact at the moment. Patrick has done a really good job getting us here. It now sounds as though he just becomes the soundboard for us should we need support. Most of the actions will be completed by us, the foster carer and Jacob's social worker, Julie.

Finally, we went over the plans for introductions. They are expectedly slightly different to 'normal' due to the fact that COVID-19 restrictions are in place. I think I've said before, I would rather do this without a social worker over my shoulder.

My back is also feeling good too. It is hurting, but good. I am confident that I will be fine as long as I don't need to pick Jacob up or any other heavy things. Alex will have to up his game on that front.

PHYSICAL INTRODUCTIONS

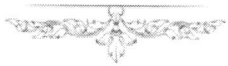

23rd June - The Night Before Introductions Start.

It's all very real today. I found it really hard to sleep last night – which is unusual for me. I can sleep anywhere and anytime. Ex-Navy et al. *If there is a lull in battle, eat or sleep.* I've felt very anxious too, but again I am told that's very normal from our adoption group friends. It's great that we have their experience and feelings to draw from. Alex has been the same too. You can tell with Alex as he has cleaned every square inch of the house to within an inch of its life. We have been pretty quiet towards each other, choosing to internalise our thoughts, but what has been expressed are those thoughts in statement form.

'God, we are going to be parents in two days' or *'what if Jacob doesn't like us at all? Have we got all the things we need for when he gets here, food, car stuff, clothes, toys etc'* and other things to that effect. The most harrowing one I guess was us questioning if we are doing the right thing. We are of course being silly and over-thinking (a common occurrence on this journey). We were told by our friends that these are all normal thoughts as they had many of them too plus lots of other doubts.

We arrange an unscheduled ad-hoc call to speak to Jacob. It was to tell him that we will be there in the morning to see him and to finish off our countdown with him together. When we called he was all smiles and lovely greetings of *'Hello Daddy Alex and Daddy Joe'.* He seems in a good place, which is superb. It makes me feel warm inside. After the greeting he just wanted to get straight into the countdown. His foster carer has clearly done a fantastic job. They are superb and we will be forever grateful to them.

Alex asks Jacob who he wants to cross off the last day on the board, our-side. Many of the questions on the call so far have been mainly from Alex and I feel a little left behind. I am sure it's been the other way and Alex may have felt left out on other calls too, so I just need to suck it up and get on with it. Jacob wanted Daddy Alex to do the countdown, so feeling like I need to get in on the act, I ask the colour he wants to use. Small wins, I guess.

As the camera is being turned around to selfie-mode, Jacob is ahead of the game already shouting down the camera in his little high pitched excited voice. *'It's one sleep left, one, one, one. Do it'.*
It melts my heart that he is super excited about tomorrow and I can see it's the same for Daddy Alex. We exchange looks together, knowingly. We just hope he really understands what it all means.

We are on the call longer than we originally planned, but we are learning he (and kids in general) are a master at distraction and buying time. We made to say *goodnight* and *see you in the morning* but he asks questions and tells us he doesn't want us to go just yet, but we tell him we have to go so we can see him quicker. Hugs and kisses are finally exchanged and we tell Jacob that we can't wait to see him. The foster carer just let the call be so organic; she's letting us take on the parents role naturally. We've noticed an intentional reduction in her involvement. We are so glad we got such a superb family of foster carers this time around after the last ones…

A big sigh and breath of relief from us both. It went as well as it could have. I need something to calm me down and hopefully help me sleep and also to have some food.

24th June - 1st Day of Introductions

I managed to get to sleep straight away last night, but was awake so many times, with a final wake up at 5am; my alarm was set for 8am. I had some pretty weird dreams too.

Through my nerves, my shower, shave and hair were done as if I were meeting the queen. I was so anxious to make a good impression. I may even have put a bit of aftershave on too.

Jacob probably won't even notice and I could turn up in my pyjamas and he would have been fine with it. I am conscious of how I am portraying myself around Alex as I am worried about him too. I don't want to compound his anxieties and I am sure the same is reciprocated. This morning is quite a weird atmosphere. I'm putting on a brave face and I need to be conscious of not shrugging things off as 'normal' when Alex and I are discussing today. I have a tendency to do that for my internal self to deal with whatever it is. It may come across as flippant and that's not helpful.

I headed downstairs to make breakfast. I am super nervous as to whether Jacob will like us or not. Or even just one of us… or me. I buggered up the first two of Alex's eggs. I don't often make breakfast, but it must still be my way of dealing with the nerves. I need to preoccupy my mind.

Just as we are finishing up, our social worker calls for some moral support. Patrick can talk for England usually but today he is very reassuring; to the point and that is how I prefer things. He also asks for an evening update too when we have finished the day. Patrick has always been on our side and tried to do his best by us, despite the major failure that happened. In hindsight this happened for the best outcome in the end. We are over the moon with Jacob and would have been devastated to not have him as our son (that still sounds weird and unnatural to say). Jacob is absolutely perfect for us. I wouldn't change a thing.

We jumped in the car and I fear it's going to be an awkward silence all the way there with us both internalising our thoughts. Luckily, or not, it sounds like something is wrong with the wheels on the new car that we had bought specially for Jacob (5 door). It gave us something to discuss in the silence.

Then out of the blue… *'wow, today we become real Daddies'*. It clearly hit Alex there and then. I am sure I had a wobble of the steering wheel as it hit me too.

Thirty minutes later, we turned into the foster carers street my Apple watch buzzed asking me if I was having a workout. I know I am not in the best shape of my life but my heart rate was raised so much it thought I was halfway through a marathon. I was very nervous, but really trying not to show it. I didn't want to compound Alex's nerves either, still.

We walked up the drive, looked at each other subconsciously as if to say *it's all going to be OK*, then pressed the doorbell. The door unlocked after what seemed like a second and the foster carer greeted us in a super welcoming way. We certainly needed that smile from her. Jacob had followed the foster carer to the door, so was also quick to give us a cuddle; our attention had switched very quickly to him as opposed to greeting his foster carer, naturally.

We said later on the drive home that at the point of meeting him as his *Daddies* today that we both instinctively knew we had made a great decision with Jacob. I was close to welling up when he cuddled Daddy Alex. It was just like such a happy moment for Jacob, Alex and myself too. It was just a wonderful feeling to finally be starting the introduction to our child. *Our child. Our child.* That will take some getting used to.

Our emotions were everywhere. If I can give a tip to anyone at this point, be prepared for any emotion. I wanted to cry with happiness, laugh, leave, cuddle Jacob for hours and wondered what the hell we have got ourselves into, but the overwhelming thought and feeling was one of pure happiness and joy. We have found a perfect match and everything just felt right.

Anyway, we'd had a bet on how long it would take the foster carer to offer us a cup of tea. She was a superb host – which continued throughout the day – and has been since our 'bump into' meeting. I'd barely taken my shoes off and she had asked. I won the bet that she would ask before our shoes were off, so it was my choice of dinner on the way home. We had Chinese food.

In hindsight, I also think this was a subconscious tool for her to semi-control a situation as this meant she had to leave Jacob with us and let us interact as his new daddies. It worked a treat as Jacob was focussed on us and engaged really well. I don't doubt that if we hadn't had the opportunity to do the video calls beforehand, then this would have made this time a hell of a lot harder for all parties. He knew who we were, trusted us and felt comfortable with us. His foster carer had done so much work with him about having a forever family and relating his story to other children that had been under the family's care when Jacob had been there. Plus she had used our forever family book too.

When we made it to the front room, we knew he was comfortable with us as the first thing Jacob went to and wanted to show us was his bike. We had been pre-warned that this would be out in the front room and that it had come from his birth family. He said he was *'bringing this to my forever home'*. That was the first time in person we had heard that, so my emotional roller coaster continued. The foster carer is really pro-us teaching him to ride it so we can have a first. It was very thoughtful of her.

It felt pretty awkward – that's the only way to describe it – as we **are** his Daddies, yet we are still in the foster carers home and we didn't know what line there was in regard to how we can act, but mostly, whether we should parent and start setting our boundaries from day one. There has been no guidance, just to let it go as naturally as possible. We are certainly glad that we didn't have the social workers looking over our shoulders, so actually COVID19 restrictions have been a bit of a blessing. We can be natural and not subconsciously forced parents.

We ended up asking (a lot) if he was allowed to do certain things – like playing with certain toys or getting out different things – as we just didn't know and we may have done things slightly differently at our home. The foster carer is so understanding and has been very clear that we should now set our boundaries as Jacob is now our son, however as much as she says it, it's very weird to do this because we are still in her house and Jacob will still be living here when we leave later. Due to the uncertainty, we just tried to roll with it and do what we thought was right. It was quite a bumbled effort to be frank. It may be down to the nerves of not wanting to get things wrong?

It just felt abnormal and weird. On many occasions both Alex and I shared little glances toward each other looking for reassurance. We must remember there is no script for parenting. As long as we meet Jacobs' needs and he is happy, then we are doing enough.

Alex came across as very natural when playing. I was over the moon to see this as I know it will do his confidence a world of good. I thought I did a good job too. I was very nervous as I really wanted Jacob to connect and respond to me well. Maybe that was quite a selfish thought, but I have to be honest that I was having it. I wanted both Jacob and Alex to have a strong connection too; we are BOTH his parents after all.

We spent lunch there too today. The foster carer cooked the meal and then left us to eat it. In hindsight, we would have preferred her to have stayed so we could watch and then model how they normally do it. It was just a bumble through again but it went well and Jacob displayed superb manners; something that I am very pleased with. Table manners are something I feel are very important for a foundation on general manners. Internally I did have a little laugh as I could just hear my mum's voice *'Please don't speak with your mouth full'*. It's one of our pet hates; especially the disgusting noise it creates. I politely tell Alex's mum off for it constantly and it's now become a family joke.

At 1pm we got back to the plan that the social workers have presented to us and we had the chance to take Jacob for a walk, alone. We walked down to a little piece of grass near the shops that we had seen in some of the videos that the foster carer had sent us. It was a strange sensation as we were now the parents of Jacob and there to protect him with everything we have; it feels different to walking down the street with someone else's child. I felt hyper vigilant. The main thing for us here, I think, was to make sure he knew he would feel safe with us and show him how safe he is with us. Instinctively, I held Jacob's hand as we left the house and I could have just picked him up and cuddled him for hours (had it not been for the spinal surgery). It just felt completely amazing and a little overwhelming for us to have the physical connection. He just looked happy and that smile... He's going to get anything he wants if he looks at me like that again.

I wanted Jacob and Alex to interact, so I suggested they hold hands on the way home.

Playing on the grass we had to set out our first boundaries and rules for things like staying on the grass or balancing on the wall (one brick high). It felt a little unwieldy enforcing them, but I felt we acclimatised pretty well and relatively quickly; to be fair we had to. The first one to set a boundary was Alex – I'm still struggling with my back so can't have any small jolts – and I really felt it was a big step to overcome for Alex. His confidence will have taken a good jump as he was now 'parenting'. I bet it was a good step for Jacob too because he knows that we are there to keep him safe. We used lots of terms and figures of speech that the foster carer used too. We want to keep as much familiarity as possible for him so he feels the transition isn't forced or too much of a change.

We also managed to get a lot of photos. Lots of moments we can treasure and some photos that we can use to put at eye level in the house for when he comes here. We need to ensure he feels at home in his new forever home straight away.

When we got back to the foster carers, it was close to the end of our day with Jacob, so we told him so. He announced very quickly that he didn't want us to leave, and I could see his shoulders drop and his eyes looked sad. He tried a few tricks like asking if we had seen his toy or if we could read a book to him. It was hard for us to say no and continue with leaving. What we did and were very clear about though, was that we are coming back tomorrow. That brightened him up a little. Maybe he thought coming from previous experiences was that he wouldn't see us again for months. We just really needed to reassure him so we got massive cuddles and lots of kisses before we left. It did feel a little like we were leaving him behind.

The drive home was a little cagey, I think. My emotions were everywhere and I am sure Alex's were also. We both had some tears of joy and some of anxiety being released. We are still very anxious about whether we have the capability to be good parents. In truth I'm, well, shi**ing my pants. My heart is pounding right now, I sincerely hope it's not a heart attack about to come on; it would be just my luck after my spinal surgery.

We've spoken to some of the people who know about today, like my mother and Alex's parents. Both of our parents are so excited about Jacob and meeting him, that we really just need to slow them down. It's hard processing their excitement along with our own, plus adding to the mix our nerves and anxieties, it can be a struggle. Managing their expectations was something I think I took too lightly.

Before bed we had some decompression with our friends and neighbours. I am so glad that we have them as an outlet and people to talk over our day with. Without an outlet it would have been pretty tough to process all of this. I don't think they realise how much of a support they have been by just being friends and there for us. I am also very happy that they have an active interest in Jacob and our journey too. They have a little boy a little younger and I think they are super excited for him to have a friend. We certainly are for Jacob.

I can't wait to see him tomorrow. It's a 05.30am start and the foster carers are making breakfast and hopefully lots of coffee. All in all, it's been a very emotionally charged day, but I am sure it will get easier as we learn to manage these emotions, or not!

25th June - 2nd Day of Introductions

We were both awake before the alarm went off at 05.30am as neither of us had slept much last night. It probably didn't help with the heatwave we are experiencing too, plus the major anxiety going through me right now. I am so desperate to get it 'right' whatever that is, plus I still find myself worried Jacob may not connect with us. I keep telling myself that he will, and all will be fine. I have just heard stories of children not connecting well with their new parents.

We got in the car, coffee in hand, in near silence and stuck in our own thoughts. We've already checked the plans from the social workers about three times each to make sure we know the schedule for today. It just seems a little bit of a forced (COVID 19) scenario where we are pretty much left to our own devices. We get the reason for it though and to be fair, I would prefer the social worker to not be breathing down our necks. We can be a bit more organic.

We are unsure whether to text the foster carer to confirm we are on time. We didn't in the end as we agreed to last night we would be there at that time. More overthinking! I don't think I have done so much worrying about things in my whole bloody life. It's silly.

Knocking on the door was much easier today too as we were more mentally prepared for the day.

Once again the foster carer greeted us both with a welcoming smile and we had a coffee offered before we had taken off our shoes. The plan this morning was to wake Jacob up and get him out of bed. It was now approximately 07.15am but I was wide awake with excitement and adrenaline. I couldn't wait to get upstairs and open the door to see his beautiful face. Speaking of opening the door, the foster carers are not allowed to have their looked after children in their bedrooms and have to close the door of the children too. All for safeguarding reasons. That meant that Jacob would be in his room and his door closed.

Approaching the door, we were unsure as to whether we should knock or walk straight in. I went for the latter, one to just make the decision and two as I just wanted to see him. Daddy Alex was right behind me.

Jacob was already awake, and his big blue eyes engaged mine straight away. The joy in his face to see us both was one I will keep with me for a long time. I remember just feeling and thinking *'how could anyone be so cruel to this child to get him into a position of him being here?'*. I knew selfishly though, that we would give Jacob a much better home than he could have with his birth family. A really selfish and horrible thought, but one we believed true. We are unsure why his backstory had happened but it did and we had to accept that. We just have to give him every ounce of love and offer as much safety as we possibly could.

He sprung out of bed and as I can't bend down too well he was hugging my leg and said *'Good morning Daddy Joe'.* He moves on and does the same to Daddy Alex. He knows who we are and seems to understand the significance of us being there. I'm also sure he is super happy that we kept to our promise of being there for him. It is something we need to be conscious of every time we say we will be there. The foster carer has been superb with Jacob keeping him learning about us and setting him up to understand that we are his *forever family*. It was an amazing start to our day.

After heading downstairs – massive smiles on all of our faces – his foster carer had already got his clothes ready. I was faced with the first task that was our first intimate and personal one and I was genuinely worried about it; it was taking his night nappy off, cleaning him up with wipes and getting his daytime clothes on. It wasn't the fact that he was naked that bothered me, it was the idea of him feeling really uncomfortable around me and not trusting me when he felt vulnerable. I want him to feel safe, as that is a primary emotion that he needs to have when moving to us. Alex was really encouraging too. He likes me to do things first, so he can see and learn from it. In turn that makes me feel like I need to be confident as I want Alex to feel that too. Luckily (and thankfully), Jacob seems to feel comfortable enough. He laughs and tells us he calls his bits, his 'trunk'. That's a new one for us!

Once he had his underwear on we learned about his routine of creams as he has eczema and also his inhalers as he also has asthma. By doing this routine correctly we are reassuring Jacob that we can look after him and keep him safe; at least that is what the foster carer had said. We also hope that subconsciously it's helping Jacob understand our roles as his parents too.

Our first breakfast together and we had our first push back. *'I'm not hungry.'* Let's see how we can deal with this one. To be fair we can understand why he wasn't feeling hungry; neither were we as the adrenaline was high. Alex jumped in and explained that Jacob will need his energy for today and food was there to help give energy. That seemed to work. Simple things? We all sat at the dining table and were left to it from the foster carer. We felt a little uneasy in her kitchen as we didn't know where anything was but with best guesses and some persistence I managed to find the breakfast things whilst Alex chatted to Jacob.

Jacob wanted chocolate hoops; more things for the ever-growing shopping list. It seems never ending and we thought we had everything. My advice is not to underestimate the amount of things you will need before a child comes home. Both Alex and I continued stumbling over each other trying to converse with Jacob. I am sure we both didn't mean to do it, but we both just wanted to speak to him and gain confidence. I can see a pattern that this is starting to become commonplace, and we need to chat soon about this so we don't continue with two voices and potentially confuse Jacob. We had a chat post breakfast which was great as we had agreed beforehand that if we had anything that may concern either of us, to speak up and not be afraid to offend each other. I am very glad that we did set that 'rule' up before introductions started. It means we can be very candid with each other.

We were also told he has some issues with going to the toilet and telling someone that he needs to go. It certainly didn't seem like it as he asked me to go with him and have a wee. I thought that was a really good sign that he is comfortable in our presence.

After breakfast we had been allocated an hour to take Jacob out in the local area. I was genuinely worried about bumping into someone who knew him from his birth family. They had been informed that Jacob had been allocated a new family of two dads and they also know where the foster carers live too. We had been told by Jacob's social worker that his birth mum had been happy that there wasn't a new 'mother' in placement as she felt we weren't taking her role away from her. Anyway, as they knew that we were on introduction week and as they knew where the foster carers house was, I was convinced that they would be looking for him. I am sure that is a completely stupid thought, however something in my mind has convinced me that could be a possibility and to be vigilant of our surrounding.

We opted for a local park a little further away than yesterday, so that means we needed to drive the car to get there. It has a grass verge and also some pathways as we are taking the bike to try out. I've also packed a small football because I've had dreams of playing football with my boy for many years. Something I missed out on as a child; dads and lads. Packing things to go out was a lesson learnt, right there! You need to ensure there is a good 15 minute grace for everything due to the sheer amount of faffing about.

It seemed like it took an age just to get some shoes on and then there was gathering all of the other things we needed to take with us. Inhaler, sun cream, helmet, football, drinks for all, spare trousers in case of an accident…

Finally we managed to get out of the house. Getting Jacob into the car seat was fun too. We must have checked about 15 times to ensure he was in correctly and the seatbelt was secure. It is a bizarre feeling to know that the safety of a child was completely in our own hands. Alex was driving today so he had the responsibility of driving with our child in the car for the first time. Selfishly I was happy it was him and not me. I know I am going to be nervous the first time and if Alex was nervous himself then he wasn't showing it.

When we arrived at the park area, we climbed out of the car, got the bike out and helmet on. '*Safety first'* was something the foster carers always tells Jacob. Finally we got Jacob on his bike ready to go. He had never ridden his bike before and so it was a very slow circuit for the first time. What I did learn was that we needed to be patient, very patient. I couldn't get my head around the fact that we would have to show Jacob how to pedal and then he would do it for a few minutes and then somehow forget again. It was so frustrating for myself as an adult. How can you forget so quickly when you have just been doing it? Maybe he wanted our attention, I'm not sure. Alex eventually had to push him and take control as I couldn't due to my surgery. I think at some point Alex told Jacob to use his *big, strong legs.* That again seemed to work for a while and we nearly got a full lap out of him. In hindsight, we probably gave way too much encouragement as we are trying to win him over and partly because we know he has been through hell of a lot in his short life. I can only imagine what we looked like from the outside looking in. We had only managed about 200 metres in 25 minutes and I was mentally tired, constantly watching and flinching at every sign of him wobbling. Silly really as he has stabilisers and goes about 2mph. The inert need to want to protect him was instinctive.

A little later and out came the football next and wow, what a ball of energy he is. Selfishly I really want him to enjoy playing football and also be good at it. I would love him to play in a football team later on in life, however if he prefers to do something else I will be happy so long as he is. I feel like he needs to do team sports for his confidence, social interaction and the skills learned whilst working as a collective team; but again that is way further on from today. Jacob really seemed to enjoy football. He was running around making lots of delightful sounds and it was so nice to see a happy little boy just enjoying an activity and playing with us both. He does need some work on his balance because he managed to fall over a good 10 times in 15 minutes, each time asking for kisses to *make it better*. Some of the falling over was on purpose too. We have been told that he will often do this as a subconscious way of checking that he is safe with us and being looked after. We made a deal of each fall and the giving him a kiss better so that he knows he is safe and loved.

He had a mini-meltdown and was finding his boundaries with us when we asked him to stop and have a drink. I have to say that I am impressed with the way we handled it. Both Alex and I did what came naturally to us and what we think we would do as parents. We both also did the same thing too which will help him with consistency. We talked Jacob through the reasons why we asked him to drink and stuck to our guns about him having a drink, stopping playing until he did. I am really happy with that response and it was a nice learning for us both.

When we got back to the foster carers, we had lots of playing with his toys and we gave and received lots of attention. I certainly enjoyed the attention and cuddles! Jacob is such a loving child and it also makes my heart melt when I see Jacob cuddle Alex too. It is everything we've wanted for the last 2 ½ years or so.

After an uneventful lunch, we told Jacob we would be heading home soon. The foster carer left us some bits (toys and clothes) to take home with us because we had agreed to start moving some things over from there to here. There is a lot that would need to come with him and we wouldn't be able to do it in one car journey. Jacob saw us taking his scooter and this made him a little bit emotional. He didn't want us to take it, but then again he didn't understand that it's only going to his new forever home and would be with him here too.

We eventually had to leave and the goodbye was really tough and arduous again. He broke down and cried a lot and once again tried his diversion tactics. We had learned from yesterday and had to be quite direct in the intention of leaving, yet still be very reassuring that we would be back again tomorrow. It's super important that he knows we are coming back tomorrow so we made a big deal of that too. We also got a little nugget of information from our social worker to give Jacob a transitional toy to help and so we took across a shark teddy bear. It was one we had used in our video calls and it was certainly something he recognised when we gave it to him to look after for the night. We told him to give it lots of cuddles as we have filled him up with lots for the night time until we see Jacob in the morning. Jacob held it and just cuddled it with a massive smile on his face. It was so cute.

When we were in the car it was again quiet on the trip home, with both of us acknowledging that we needed some time to mentally come down from the day. Personally, I was thinking about the foster carers and how they may be feeling. I have a lot of empathy for them as it feels a little like we are taking the child they have looked after for over 15 months away from them. The other side of me knows that this is a job for them. This is our journey with Jacob and they are aware and supportive of that too.

When we did break the silence, Alex and I spoke in some detail about Jacob and how we think we should parent him. We have very similar values in that respect so I am pleased about that. Both of our parents have good values so we have them instilled in us too; let's hope we pass them on.

My mother always maintains that all of her five children would never let her down when going out and that she would often say that *'I could take you anywhere and I knew you would all be polite and well-mannered'*. I sincerely hope we introduce these values and manners to our boy.

It is now time for an early bedtime. I've needed the sleep over these last two days.

26th June - 3rd Day of Introductions

It's the 3rd day today of seeing Jacob and it's the last one where we will see him at the foster carers home. It was an 11.00 start this morning, so we had some time to gather our thoughts, pack our picnic as we are due to have one for lunch and take our time on the drive.

Today we need to learn more about his likes and dislikes regarding the broad spectrum of a childs daily life and routine. We still don't know what toys he likes, what food he eats, what food he hasn't tried, what clothes he likes to wear... what football team he likes (please say Blackburn Rovers) etc. We feel like we know very little about him other than his past (which still upsets me). When he comes to his forever home, we know that there will be a lot of stumbling through parenthood and asking him if he has ever done something before or whether he likes something. I am sure we will need to be very patient with him and we will need to check our attitudes, egos and how we present ourselves.

Going in today we parked on the drive as one of the foster carers is still shielding so wasn't in the house. We nicked his spot. It feels like it is getting easier going to their house now because we feel more comfortable with the boundaries between the foster carers and ourselves.

Aside from likes and dislikes, our other main task was to learn about the night-time routines including bath time. We got left to our own devices again today because the foster carer took her dog for a long walk and got on with some housework. That was OK for us, but I also think there may be some subconscience distancing happening. I am sure she will be doing that to protect her own feelings; I know I would be.

Sharkey (the shark teddy as he had now been named) was a genius idea. Jacob just wanted to tell us how much he had looked after Sharkey and that he had fed him, took him to the bathroom and had lots and lots of cuddles. It was very cute of him to want to tell us all of this. His foster carer had said he had responded really well to having a 'transitional toy' and it had helped drive home that we would be there in the morning for him to make sure he had looked after him. That really hit home for me today. He needs to constantly be aware and told that we are going to be there for him for not only the long term, but tomorrow too. Children don't understand the concept of time and so tomorrow is a big deal for them. We need to think how we embed in his conscious and subconscious mind that we will **always** be there. That's certainly a question we need to ask the social workers again. They mentioned using both short and long term language but also using props. Examples being growing plants and using height charts. I want some more ideas to help though.

After the Sharkey story from Jacob, it was quite an uneventful first hour or two. It was nice just being in each others company. The attention was still all on him, which he completely thrived on, but it was more about presence rather than constant playing and interaction. Jacob did ask for us to take him to the toilet and that was great news because he has been having troubles with the number two's. He hasn't had a poo since we have been there and it's been a big problem of his over the last few months. The foster care thinks it may be due to him knowing something was changing in his life, but he was unsure what. Luckily enough he asked to go for a poo which I am glad about as he has clearly been holding it in. He has that smell of a child who's holding one inside yet can't control the gas that is still coming out. To be fair, he stinks. I got a lucky escape as he asked Alex to go in with him.

Alex came back with a grin but a look to tell me that I had got lucky. He told me that he found it really uncomfortable to watch a child have a poo. He has never seen me even sitting on the toilet, but he knows things will need to change. The amount of times we have been told from our friends who are parents that *'you will never go to the toilet in peace again'* may be about to ring true. We had discussed that whoever was the first to see him poo needed to see if it was a hard or soft stool. This is so we can work out why he may be struggling? Alex said it was like a rock and that Jacob was visibly shaking and straining a lot to get it out. We will need to talk about that later out of earshot of the foster carer and Jacob. We don't want to offend or question how she has been looking after him – which we are 100% sure is amazing - and we don't want Jacob to hear us talking about him and possible solutions.

After his poo we had the picnic but we had to have it in the living room due to the weather. It still went down really well though. Jacob absolutely loved it and even asked us *'when we get to our forever home, can we have lots of picnics?'.* I just wanted to tell him that he is super cute and can have whatever he wants; but the simple answer was that *yes,* we can have lots of picnics. I bet Alex is on Amazon later getting a picnic bag.

Jacob nailed quite a few ham, cheese and *'mato'* sauce wraps. It's been interesting to listen to his shortcomings with regard to his speech and language. But then again, we don't have any 3 year olds to offer any markers regarding his development and milestones. There were some concerns over his speech and language on his last review. I haven't heard much of it frankly but maybe that is because we have spent quite a few hours on the video calls to him. We will have to keep an eye on it all but I don't think there is much to be concerned about.

The afternoon consisted of doing lots of playing and asking lots of direct questions to Jacob about what he likes and doesn't. The standard response seems to have carried over from the calls. *'All of them'.* That hasn't been of much help to be honest, and it seems like he is looking for a way to please. He doesn't want to say he doesn't like things for the fear of losing it. It's been pretty frustrating for us to not be getting the answers as we just want to know this information so we can ensure to give him the most perfect start. We certainly need to accept that this will not be the case. When I called my mother yesterday she was very good with her guidance and to be fair she always is. She said to us that as long as we can offer him love, a warm safe home and food, then we can work on the rest as we go along. That's very true!

Later in the day we went down to feed the ducks that was a small car trip away. I can't describe how much fun we had by doing something so simple. Just watching Jacob throw bread and chase ducks (yes, I know letting him do that is bad parenting, but he was being cute as he was trying to feed ducks bread directly) was lovely knowing how free he is. He has such a good spirit. Once we ran out of bread we headed off down to the local beach front. We sang lots of children's songs in the car and I felt great being young. Fifteen minutes of them as our inner child was well and truly enjoying itself. It is amazing how children songs can either cheer you up or be repetitive. He looked so happy in his car seat bopping and singing away. When we arrived at the beach we navigated our way to the shops to get some photographs printed for his foster carer; she has mentioned that she keeps photographs of the children. It was a strange event as it felt a little like we were receiving the baton, as such.

We went down to the sea front too and spent some time being overly cautious parents. It was the first time there, so when he was close to the water the instinct told us to stop him or when he wanted to walk on the low wall, we would again say no. In hindsight it was quite silly really. We need to let him (and us) learn and explore his own boundaries of what he can and can't do, both physically and mentally.

After a couple of superb hours and Jacob both eating and wearing ice cream, we headed back. When we arrived back at the foster carers we gave Jacob the photographs to give to them and it instantly hit them. Maybe a little bit of reality was creeping in. They were in tears when they got the photo and both Alex and I got quite emotional about it too.

Later on in the evening, we did bath time and bed time. Bath time was about us learning the routine and how he does it. We want to replicate as much as we can to help the transition. Jacob also has eczema so we need to make sure that we get as much information as we can to stop flare ups. There is also a concern from both of us about him feeling comfortable when he is naked and vulnerable. We want him to feel safe and comfortable around us both. We told him that it was time for a bath and his clothes were off before we knew it and he was laughing and joking with us wanting raspberries on his tummy.

Running the bath we must have checked the water temperature about five hundred times each because we were unsure how it should be. We had been told he hadn't had many warm baths in his past life before coming into care and that really makes me angry and really sad. How can someone do that? When we were all happy with the temperature – we asked the foster carer to check – he got in the bath and spent 20 minutes playing and splashing and just being a happy child. Alex will have a fit if he splashes this much in our bathroom. He had so much fun and I did too until my back started to really hurt whilst being sat on the bathroom floor. I have clearly still got some restrictions that I need to work out. I had pretty much forgotten about it today.

When he was out of the bath, I got him in the towel and dried him. I felt a little uneasy for the first time doing this and to make things worse once we got downstairs I had the worst experience yet. I've been really upset about this since being home and I've had quite a few tears about this. Jacob was getting dry and we had started putting his cream on. He started messing around with his willy as boys do. Of course, I told him to stop which in turn just made him do it more. He then starts laughing and shouting that his *'trunk is getting big'*. I laughed at it because I thought he was just being silly and doing what lads do but his foster carer gave me a bollocking for that. When Jacob was in bed she explained why she told me not to do it and I guess it's all part of their training. She told me that a fair share of children come into care and have experienced some sort of sexual abuse. This causes such behaviour similar to what Jacob had just displayed. I just thought he was just being a little boy and doing what our friends had said their little boys had done in the past. Especially as there is no evidence to say Jacob has experienced such abuse. It has really upset me thinking I've laughed along with something that could be or have been serious. I don't know if I have misjudged the situation.

Once that situation happened, I just wanted to leave and get in the car and go home but Alex had taken him upstairs to read him his book and say good night. Internally I was in a state. I was so upset but didn't want to show it to the foster carer, Jacob or Alex.

When we got in the car I just let go. I cried. I felt so bad that I could laugh at something that Jacob could have experienced that nobody other than him knew about. I'm questioning myself so much right now and whether I can actually be a parent. I told Alex about the situation when I had composed myself and he was right, I am being irrational.

Alex's mother called again. She did so on day one and two of introductions. She is very keen to know how we are progressing and we love her completely for it, but right now we have a lot to take on board and we need some space to process it all without a 30 minute conversation. Alex is stressed as he feels like he has to call back or answer. I keep telling him to let her know he will call when he has some time to himself and is ready to.

27th June - 4th Day of Introductions

This is the first day Jacob comes to his new home. It's a huge day and I am really anxious as to whether he will love his new forever home. What happens if he hates it? I don't want to think about it. I am super nervous about it and I am sure Alex is as he is making himself as busy as he can cleaning up the whole house… again. I'm unsure if this is for the foster carer or for Jacob? It is just his way of working through his anxieties and having something to do.

I'm unsure how to describe the emotions we were experiencing in the 15 minutes before Jacob arrived. We both fidgeted, spoke nonsense to each other and had about 5 nervous bathroom stops each. What is he going to think? How will he act? Will he recognise the house from our Forever Family Book? It felt as though we had been waiting for some time and we were constantly looking through the blinds.

When he arrived with his foster carer, I was close to happy tears. Jesus, where have all these emotions come from lately. This time it was due to the realisation that this is where he will grow up. I can't describe how happy it is making me feel that we are giving this little boy a life that he likely wouldn't have had should he have stayed with his birth family. It's through little fault of their own that this is the case, it's all very situational after reading the backstory of Jacob's life. It is believed that they are in a cycle that means this may be the norm to them and their actions are learned.

Finally they arrived. Jacob was lifted out of the car and bounded up the drive shouting about his new forever home. He was straight into our arms for a massive cuddle and then he proceeded to take his shoes off. He knew that we did that from the Forever

Family Book, bless him. He was a whirlwind, as he was exploring his new home. What I found very endearing was that he was relating the house to the video calls and the book and recalling all the information on them. Just little things made me smile. '*this is where I will put my toys*' or '*look at the garden, is this where I can play with my toys and friends.* It was an amazing time. Overall, he has seemed to take it all in his stride and presented himself as very positive about the huge change in his life. He is so brave. What an amazing child!

I can't remember much more than us running around the house all day looking at the rooms and talking through them. We only had a couple of hours with him, so that took up the day. Before Jacob left we explained that we would be collecting him tomorrow and then bringing him home, before taking him back to the foster carers. I felt we had a language change here as this is now his home. We hadn't really verbalised our house as his home properly. It seemed to be very much about it *will* be his forever home.

As we said our goodbyes, Jacob gave us huge cuddles and kisses. He said that he couldn't wait to come back tomorrow. It was a voluntary remark too, so it was even better that he seems to understand.

When they got in the car and we had pretty much waved until our hands fell off. I felt drained and needed a long sit down. Luckily for us, our neighbours were out in the garden and had said for us to come over if we wanted to relax after he had been and then gone. We were there within half an hour and just talking through our day. Our neighbours have been an amazing support not only for talking through children 'things' but just being there as a bit of a decompression aid. I don't underestimate how much of a help they have been and continue to be.

At the end of the day, I sat on the bed and managed to reply back to our adoption friends who have been very interested in the last few days. They all wished us well on day one and reiterated that they are there for us if we need any guidance or have any questions. All of them have been great and we have been very appreciative of their support too.

28th June - 5th Day of Introductions

I was a little bit ropey this morning but only had 2 small beers. I felt guilty already as surely I shouldn't feel like this. I think Alex feels a little rough too. Maybe it's a mix of mental fatigue and a drink. Anyway, we headed off to the foster carers. This was going to be a strange day as we are collecting him from the foster carers and it will be the first day without them until we took him back. I am reluctant to call it *home* now, as here is his home; his forever home.

When we arrived, Jacob was waiting for us and all ready for us. His foster carer had been giving updates. He was very excited and nearly forgot to give her a cuddle until we reminded him, before we all got into the car. We had also packed some more of his things to bring over from the foster home. This was mainly toys, but a few clothes too. This was also our first longer journey with him in the car and we didn't know the protocol for whether we had to speak to him constantly, let him look out of the window or just give him a game; we were finding our feet and its silly to have to think about things like that, but we did. It should just be parental instinct. I was nervous, so I just kept talking about absolutely nothing. The amount of animals or blue cars I told him I could see was probably unbearable for him. I bet he just wanted me to shut up so he could look out of the window in peace.

Once we got home he took his shoes off again (good lad) and then straight up to his room to check it out again. It was as if he was checking it was still his confirming to himself that we were telling him the truth. He was then down to the living room and getting toys out to play. His body language was as if he had been here forever mixed with a bag load of excitement too. He had certainly made himself at home and that made us both very happy; it means that he feels comfortable, I think! He played with pretty much all of his toys and a couple of new ones we had bought. We had gone through the process of deciding whether to buy anything extra or not because we didn't want to add too many new things to his life in addition to moving house and families.

Jacob had his lunch and dinner with us too and it seemed a little too easy. It was as if he didn't push back or give us any challenges at all and was in complete 'pleasing mode'. I think we could have given him any food and he would have probably eaten it. It felt a little surreal. Jacob had such good manners at the table and throughout the rest of the day. One thing that was worth noting about the meals today was that we had been anxious as to what he would eat. I feel like we need a recipe book for 3 year old children. It's hard to think past some form of tomato based food (beans or spaghetti hoops) on toast, pizza or chicken nuggets. I might write a recipe book if I can ever work out what he would eat.

What I've also noticed today is that his language is mixed up. He refers a lot to his *'forever home'* which is our home and *'my home'* which is his foster carer's home. We are told by the social workers that his language will reveal a lot about what he is thinking so we should listen intently. Just that snippet gives me the realisation that he still isn't quite sure about the whole situation. We need to make sure we are listening and maybe reading between the lines a little.

Whilst here today he has had 2 bathroom accidents. He hasn't had these since we've been with him, so this is a new experience for us to deal with. His foster carer said that when he found out he had a new forever family, he had some regression in this area. She thinks it was linked to a change in his life and his mind processing all that is going on. It is life changing after all. We also didn't know what our response should be for this and are unsure whether to make a big deal of it or not. We need to check this out and ask the social workers and our friends for advice too.

To round off the day, Jacob had a bath and he loved it. Maybe it was because he was in his new bathroom. We had no issues at all and again we think he is in pleasing mode; overall though, he had a ball paying with the toy we had (another note - we need more!). Once he had finished and was clearly starting to tire we put him in his pyjamas and into the car to take him back to the foster carers. At this point I can't express how amazingly beautiful and happy I was to see our child fall asleep in the car. He is the cutest thing I've ever seen. I really feel like he is our boy now. That still is a bizarre thing to say *our child* and *our boy*. Technically he isn't and so there is a little bit of weirdness in saying it. In our minds though, he is a Young now and he is part of our family.

When we got back to the foster carers, we took him to bed and let him settle and sleep. Alex took him because I couldn't carry him and said he was a little upset when he left, but that was due to Jacob being in and out of sleep, bless him. We had a cup of tea with the foster carer and talked through our day and then left to get home. We had done some miles, some long days and were getting exhausted. I have used the term overthinking so much in the last few days, but that is exactly how I feel. With any other child, like a niece or nephew, I wouldn't think so much about what and why I was doing something or why they were. I would instinctively just get on with it. Not with Jacob!

What I also felt today, which Alex also said was the same, was that it was a less stressful day and much easier due to the likelihood of not feeling that we had the foster carers watching over us due to them not being here. We felt there was a weight off our shoulders and it was down to us to parent. The whole day felt more authentic, although it was clearly still a day of bundling through.

29th June 6th Day of Introductions

Today was a similar set up to yesterday regarding Jacob coming home, however we did have some licence to go out of the house and into our local area this time. When we arrived at the foster carers home again, it was a quick greeting and then a handover of a lot more of Jacob's things; he certainly has a lot of *stuff* to bring with him. Some of it, from his foster carers and some of it from his birth family. We are a little unsure who has bought what and who it's from, so we need to keep asking that question to the foster carer. There is also the notion of throwing some things away as, for example, they are too small or just broken. We have heard through some of the reports and comments that his birth mother used to give him broken toys (cars without wheels) and also she would re-wrap old toys. I'm not judging her for this, as she may have been doing her best with what means she had at that point, but it is just frustrating for me to know that Jacob may have been disappointed or upset about it. I do feel guilty that I am having thoughts about throwing some of his things away, but we have to move forward, yet be mindful of the important things.

The morning has been slow and relaxed. We have played in the house and sorted a couple of his things out, like packing away clothes and toys. We are still falling over each other trying to play with Jacob and gain his trust. We've also found we are likely giving mixed messages as I may ask Jacob to do something and Alex suggested the opposite (an example when Jacob asked to play with certain toys), or vice versa. I am glad we have both recognised that we are both doing this because we need to find a way to both head in the same direction with instructions, so not to confuse him. We will both settle and find our parenting boundaries.

We are also finding that we are telling Jacob that we are his Daddies quite a lot, that this is his forever home and that we are here to keep him safe. I think we are really trying hard (maybe too hard) to get the message over that he's here for *'ever and ever and ever'*. I'm pretty sure he doesn't really understand time frames and what 'forever' means. Our friends have said they did this a lot too and it was quite an involuntary response that just happened.

Alex and I have been thinking about the 'poo' and bathroom issues that have been discussed and how we can look to normalise using the toilet. We feel a little more comfortable in our own home speaking about it to him and even more so that we don't have a social worker or foster carer sitting with us, watching. I spoke to my mother and Alex did the same with his mother. Both said to just make light of it all and if possible into a game or fun thing.

Jacob was starting to do the wee dance and fidget a lot. He also smelt like he needed a poo. This was a new experience, so I was trusting my instincts. He was just emitting an unpleasant scent and it became clear he was holding in a poo. Plus he hasn't been to the bathroom here yet. *'Let's go and try for a wee'* I tried as we were going to head out for a walk. Surprisingly he went without any pushback. It was as if he was waiting for some form of permission. When we got to the bathroom he was straight on and had a wee straight away. I still find it a little weird to watch a child have a wee. He then sneaked a trump out and looked at me as if to assess whether it was OK for him to do it. Remembering my mothers comments, I just burst out laughing. Jacob exhaled as if it was a weight off his shoulders and then proceeded to have the biggest poo I have ever seen. The problem was that it was solid and he expressed he was *'scared and it hurts'*. This was a strong indicator that it may be an issue with constipation. We need to get some laxatives for him but I have absolutely no idea about what you can get for children. I was straight back on to WhatsApp to our friends. They had the answer.

Once finished we headed out for a walk and to explore the local area. We are lucky we are close to some woodland so headed out exploring and searching for friendly Trolls. We saw some diggers which he got very excited about and clearly loves (note to buy some toys of that nature). We also noticed while walking that he is a little clumsy and likely needs to work on his co-ordination and balance. I remember in our training that co-ordination and balance are often something children in care lack due to previous engagement or lack of development. We will ask the health visitor for some advice I think.

Later in the day after we got back home, we played in the garden. George the little boy from next door was outside too in his garden, but we have left the fence between our houses open purposely so both boys can get through to play with each other should they want to. George came around to play when he heard Jacobs' voice; to be fair you can't fail to hear it from some miles away! George is a confident little boy and loved playing but it was still quite a lot for both children to take in yet so we had to encourage them to interact and play. Having them both as best friends is something we have all talked about. Both boys were a little tentative and then when some toys got exchanged, they were off and running around like headless chickens as if they had known each other for some time. I am glad they both met as it gives us another permanence tool to be able to discuss with Jacob about how they will grow up together (long term tool) or even play tomorrow (short term tool).

Alex and I have been challenging each other about how we speak around Jacob today too. The tone is super important here and I know that as we are learning, we are tired and a little overwhelmed with the amount of attention and brain power you have to give a child. This has led to us telling each other (maybe spitefully) that one of us should 'be careful how you talk around Jacob' when referring to tonality of our voices.

Dinner was chicken wraps. I still maintain that there is definitely a place in the market for a 3 years old recipe book. We need some ideas and it is only week one. I'm going to Google some recipes and write some down. Again, he had such good manners at the dinner table and I am really pleased; I did however have to tell him about speaking with his mouth full, which he accepted immediately.

We did bath time again, which is becoming easier already, before taking him back to the foster carers where we completed the bedtime routine too. It is clear from yesterday and today that he loves playing in the bath and he has such a good little imagination. Once out of the bath (eventually!) it was time to put on his cream. Tonight we put the steroid cream on and he even tells us which spots are needing *'a little bit more, please'*. He is just so cute when he says little things like that. The foster carers have done a great job with his manners and nurturing his personality.

Finally, and once we had him in his pyjamas, we got him into the car and set off. It felt a little overwhelming for us as this would be his last night at the foster carers. I really struggled to keep my emotions in check due to empathy I shared for them. Alex and I had also discussed that maybe the foster carers should get to do the bedtime routine when we got back as this would be their last time. It would be a nice touch and I am sure something they would be grateful to be able to do for their closure. Alex was driving so I texted the foster carers and asked if they would like to put him to bed. We got a quick reply that was lovely. She was very pleased and appreciative that we had offered.

We did a pretty quick handover, assuring Jacob we will be there in the morning to pick him and Sharkie up. When we got back in the car, I got a little upset and had a number of emotions flowing through me. I felt so much happiness, so much guilt, sorry for more loss for Jacob. I also felt so sad for the foster carers too. I struggled a little. Alex was great at giving me the right amount of attention yet leaving me to get on with it. He is good and I appreciate him for it. It was also interesting that I was the one struggling and not him. He has been a little hard faced about it and managed his emotions differently than I have.

When we got home, we had more tears. This time it was from both of us (I spoke too soon). We've been given a Memory Box of all of Jacob's things that have come from his mother and birth family. As we were going through it we both found it was completely overwhelming. It was evident that his mother loves him and it must be such a tough scenario to go through on the *other* side. Alex went into full on cry mode; the one that is the ugly face type. I tried to leave him to have his time, so I went to put some clothes away. That set me off again! I am supposed to be this ex-military type guy who plays sports and drinks real ale, but I couldn't help it.

Half an hour later we managed to calm down and laugh it out with some comedy on TV. I am glad we put something funny on TV. It was a nice decompression.

FOREVER HOME

30th June - Final Day at Foster Carers

Today is *the* day. We pick up Jacob for the last time this morning and then that means he is in his new forever home and little contact with the foster carers bar a couple of video calls over the next few weeks. I'm personally exhausted and I can see the cues in Alex to recognise that he is exhausted too. It isn't the physical side that's making us so tired, but the mental side; this is a tough process and now that we are coming to a head with Jacob coming home, I feel this is going to be the big release. There seems to be something to think about all the time and that is using a lot of brain power. We are constantly worrying about whether we are doing things correctly and quite often overthinking each scenario where we would normally not. We just want to get it right for Jacob.

I knew today that I was going to be emotional, and I was correct. I don't know where all the tears are coming from lately. I am usually quite composed.

The drive to the foster carers provided us with a lot of silence and thinking space. We both just wanted to gather our thoughts, I guess. Later I found out that Alex had similar thoughts to me and ones that we didn't want either. There was some self doubt creeping in, again! I had thoughts of *'are we doing the right thing for Jacob?'* but also some very positive thoughts about the fantastic future he will provide us and also we will (hopefully) provide him. We can only do our best as my mother would say.

As we arrived, it was a bit of a strange atmosphere. I'd messaged the foster carer as we were driving there and we had agreed for a quick 'handover' because we didn't all want to be on the driveway in floods of tears and we also didn't want the experience to be a negative one for Jacob. We all felt it important for smiles and positivity so Jacob knew the move is a positive one for all parties.

When the door opened, Jacob was ready so Alex beckoned him forward to get the gift out of the car that we had bought for the foster carers. 'Jacob' (Alex and I) got some nice candles and we got her a bottle of Bacardi, as we knew she likes both through general conversations that we had previously had. We gave the alcohol separately, of course! In return we got the final things of Jacob's belongings to take home. It felt like final confirmation and we all had the wobbly bottom lip thing. We really tried hard to keep it in as this was a massively positive thing.

The foster carer had to close her door very quickly and I certainly couldn't blame her. I can't imagine how she must have felt with Jacob leaving after living there for 14 months. I felt highly impassioned thinking about how tough it would be for her as they all have been fantastic to us and most importantly, Jacob. I can't describe how thankful we are to them. They have done an amazing job with this little boy and now it is officially our job to continue and grow that.

Moving off in the car was very emotional and luckily I was facing forward so I could let some tears out. I am sure Alex was doing the same in the passenger seat. It was a monumental moment for everyone involved and it felt like it was an end to one part of his life and the beginning of his new one. Closing one chapter to open another. Jacob was silent for a good 15 minutes, and that selfishly suited us. It gave us some time to compose ourselves and steel our minds. When he did start to talk with us, it was as if he didn't really understand the situation. I would have loved to have known what the foster carers had said that morning, just to see what he had replied.

When we arrived at home, we purposely kept it very low energy and relaxed. Jacob was playing in the house and garden and seems to just be taking everything in his stride. He has been quite excited to sleep in his bed for the first time tonight; maybe it is because there are about 40 teddies stacked up to sleep in there too. If that is going to help him settle then he can sleep with as many as he wants. I just want him to be comfortable, feel safe and know that he is loved.

When we did get him into bed after the *exact* same routine he had in his foster carers, Alex read him a book to try and calm him down. We got lots of kisses and cuddles tonight and I absolutely loved every one. I could have kissed and cuddled him all night. When we did finally make it down stairs, he got out of bed 4 times looking for attention. We think this is to check that we are still there and keeping him safe. He was using any excuse to get out of bed. *'I need a wee'* (You've just had one). *'I want a cuddle'* (You just had 50) etc.

It was quite cute and endearing. We had to ensure that he knew that we were there for him whenever he needed us. Thinking about it, it may also be because he now knows he is allowed out of his bedroom in his new home as opposed to the rules he had in the foster home.

What we also discovered tonight was that Jacob decompresses and analyses his day through the medium of his teddies. He speaks from one teddy to another and discusses things in his day. It was very interesting to stand outside his door and listen.

I'm bloody shattered now. Drained, emotional but very happy. Our boy is home after all this time. I'm so happy. We are so happy. We are a FAMILY.

1st July - Hypersensitive

We didn't sleep very much last night. Both of us woke up at every move of his bed covers, every little bump and trump from Jacob. We were hypersensitive to everything. What we found however, through peeping around his door each time, was that he was sound asleep. Just as I thought I was about to fall asleep; he was making enough noise to suggest he was awake and ready to get up. We know that from his foster carers that they had to give him permission to come out of the room, so I had to get up to do that. We will work on letting him know he can come out whenever he wants to in the morning. This will be a slow process and adjustment, I bet.

Throughout the day we aimed to have another quiet one. This was so we could get to know him and vice versa. Additionally we wanted him to get comfortable within his new environment. Overall, it was a day with no issues or any event that made us think we needed to react to something. It is still a little unnerving to know we have responsibility for this little boy's life. It was a good day all-in-all and we think it is because we have kept it as quiet as we can based on the advice from the social workers to do so. We want to shout from the rooftops about our beautiful little boy, but it isn't the right thing for him. It's not fair to introduce others into his life just yet when he is still getting to grips with us.

2nd July - Playing and Exploring

Our sleeping was better last night, overall. We still had lots of reasons to get out of bed though to keep checking on him, but we certainly had more confidence tonight than we did last night. When I woke up this morning, he was at his door but didn't come out until encouraged. We had made a point on our calls prior to placement, that he can come and jump on our bed in the mornings. We tried to make coming into our room okay, and by telling him he can jump on the bed, we thought that it may work; something fun. Let me tell you, it worked and for about 45 minutes he jumped and jumped. He loved it and so did we. Just seeing him having fun was amazing and the huge smile was worth the DIY I am likely going to have to do to fix the bed.

We are playing in the garden again today, exploring more of it. We tried to have as much interaction as we can, especially physical as I've read somewhere that this will help with forming connections. To be fair though Jacob is such a tactile child and so we didn't need to try hard with him to get a cuddle and kiss.

A couple of things I have struggled with today are getting him to go to the bathroom without reminders and to have a drink without similar prompting. I am sure that will come in time, but he is just busy and exploring still.

At the end of the night, I did the bath routine. Whilst he was in the bathroom he mentioned his foster carers. We let him know how much they love and care for him and are so happy that he has now found his forever home. We are due to call them tomorrow, so that will help reinforce all of this to him too. It was inevitable that he was going to talk about them at some point and that's fine; we will never dismiss talking about them or even his birth family. They are part of his identity.

3rd July - Approved for Placement

Patrick called first thing to tell us the best news! We have formally been approved regarding placement so now it's official. We are absolutely delighted. I think I hugged Alex and Jacob for about 5 minutes. Jacob called it a *'forever family sandwich'*. He is just too cute!

We had another quiet day today and there was nothing much more to report on today frankly. I guess that's pretty good as things seem to be 'normal'. We are still keeping it all low-key so not to overwhelm him. We are taking it as slowly as possible.

I spoke to my mother as I know she is desperate to see Jacob. I am desperate for her to see him too and the same with Alex's family. We really want to introduce Jacob to the wider family, *his wider family,* but it wouldn't be right to add more introductions to his already buzzing brain.

Towards the back end of the day, we spoke to the foster carer and it was lovely to chat to them. They are very good at being positive and they still enforced the message to Jacob that he has now found his forever home with us and that we are all very lucky to be together. I am very pleased they are so good because Jacob trusts them, believes in them and most importantly will take onboard their message. I can see he is still processing it all though. I wouldn't expect anything less. It must be such a conflicting time for him.

4th July - Missing Foster Carer

Jacob has mentioned his foster carers this morning. He told Alex that he is missing them and he appeared visibly upset, but looked as though he was fighting back visibly showing it. It is as if he doesn't want to upset our little apple cart. Alex and I have spoken about this in private and we would rather he show his emotions so we can help him understand and manage them. We are conscious that he doesn't know how to show emotions based on previous feedback from his CPR (child permanence report) and social workers report. We will ask his social worker tomorrow when we have a chat with her what she thinks.

5th July - Social Worker Call

We had our call with Julie (Jacob's social worker) this morning seeing how we were getting on and advising us that our application for some further therapeutic support had been accepted and will be starting in due course. We aren't sure that he needs it, but we are wanting to be proactive with any additional support that can be offered to make this process the strongest for all parties.

We have been practising using letters and words this morning, spelling out Daddy Alex, Daddy Joe and Jacob Young. He is refusing to spell our family surname because he is 'just Jacob'. Although he isn't officially a Young, we are conscious of him going to school this September and not knowing his name if they use his birth name. We certainly aren't pushing him to use our name, but we are trying to slip it in subtly. We want to help him with his identity. On the whole and so far, I feel it all is going well and I know Alex seems pleased too. We have discussed it and the consensus is that we just need to wait a few weeks more to assess how we are all progressing. I think we shouldn't jump to conclusions on how it's going straight away as it is way too early.

Other than that, Julie gave us some advice regarding toileting and getting him to tell us he needs it as we had two accidents today citing the reasons for not going to the bathroom as he was *'too busy playing'*. This is something new, so we need to see if this is a one off or not.

Today we also did a big 'treasure hunt' that I set up in the local woodlands. George from next door was a pirate along with Jacob. I'd drawn a treasure map for them both to use and find the treasure (chocolate). Of course, they had no idea how to use it and both Alex, myself and George's parents had to lead it. What I did get from the treasure hunt was pure joy from both children when finding the treasure and a super amount of interaction between them both. They loved jumping in the puddles and being 'best friends' together. It was great for their relationship.

I've noticed today that I really enjoy children's programmes and books. They are so imaginative. The only one I am not sure of is that blasted Peppa Pig. She is so rude and I don't want Jacob with those manners, thank you!

6th July - More Social Worker Calls

Today we had a call from our social worker, Patrick. I'm not sure what the purpose was or why we had the call as we didn't really discuss much at all. Maybe it was just a check-in call and tick-box exercise. Usually the social worker would come to the house and spend some time observing what we do and how we are as a family. Of course that can't happen right now for COVID-19 restrictions. My mother is due to come to see the rest of the family in three days. She lives down on the south coast and we don't see her as much as we would like, so we can't not see her. Julie is not keen on seeing my mother, but agreed that we can because otherwise we may not see 'Grandmums' for a long time.

I'm very close to my mother, so I fought the case to the social workers for her to see Jacob. Thankfully, Alex agrees with me too even though they said 'no' to Alex's parents seeing Jacob. They only let my mum see him because of the distance.
After lunch we took Jacob out on his bike for a walk around the local area. That's all we can do really and I feel a little rubbish that we can't take him to play centres or similar things. I feel anxious that we aren't doing enough with him but the social workers think we are and have been very reassuring.

When Jacob had gone to bed, I arranged to see a friend after seeing my mum in a few days because I need some decompression time and someone else to unload on. Alex is happy for me to have some time out and I will do the same back. It will be the first time one of us has been left alone with Jacob for any significant time.

7th July - First Haircut

The COVID 19 lockdown has eased enough for us to be allowed to have hair cuts and Jacob's hair was getting very long and getting close to looking like a throwback to the 70's mullet. This will be his first haircut with us, so it's quite a big deal. We were told that foster carers have to gain permission to have a child's hair cut, so that's why it was so long. When we arrived we didn't know what behaviour we were going to get from him, but I gave him my phone and stood with him. He was a dream. Not only that, he looks super cute and even more gorgeous with his new haircut. Once again he took it all in his stride.

As a reward for him being superb in the hairdressers, we went to a local park. It's a big place with lots of walks in the forest and a cracking place for Jacob to explore and have fun. For us it was an eye opener having to keep thinking about things that we wouldn't normally need to. The park was beautiful too. Jacob absolutely loved it and just watching him run around the park in his wellington boots, jumping in every puddle and screaming in delight was an absolute reminder that we have made the best life changing decision. He is just a happy little boy. My heart really skipped a beat and I genuinely feel love for him. I've said it before, but that felt a little hollow when I'd said it previously and more for the benefit of Jacob, but now I feel like I mean it. I actually love this little boy to bits. He is amazing.

Oh, he had his first stand up wee today whilst we were out in the big park. It was really funny as he had never done it before and he had no idea what to do. I took it completely for granted and ended up with pee all over myself and him too. It made Alex laugh though. I know they say it's nice to have all the 1st's with your child, but....

When we got home it was a mission to get him changed. We had another first too when I got in the shower and he was adamant that he wanted to get in with me. I was a little unsure at first due to the comments previously at the foster carers, but then when speaking to Alex we have seen nothing that concerns us and he will see us with no clothes on at some point. So with that in mind, we got into the shower and all he was concerned about was drawing pictures in the condensation on the windows and making sure no water went into his eyes.

Bedtime was smooth though. He loves his books and will let you read to him for hours if you could. This will delight my mother as she is a bookworm (just like me too).

8th July - Testing Boundaries

I am pretty frustrated with Jacob this morning. He's changed his attitude and I can't work out whether he is tired or just testing our boundaries. Even though we have a morning routine of going to the bathroom and getting a drink, we couldn't even get past the wee point. He just stood in the bathroom naked and cried. I kept very calm and tried to understand what was happening, but I couldn't make sense of it. Eventually, before he was about to wet himself and had calmed down, he went. Then it was all pink and rosy.

A huge change again too. I don't understand? How can there be such a difference so quickly.

About an hour after the toilet incident, he started to talk about his foster carers and he is talking in the tense of it being 'his bedroom' and 'my house'. It is confusing for me, so I can't imagine how he is feeling, bless him. But at least we now know the reasoning behind him being a pain today. To help him understand the situation, I eventually had to draw a picture of our house and the foster carers house and explain that he will live here forever and not be going back to the foster carers. It has got me thinking that he's not accepted us as his forever family just yet and wants to be back (I think) at the foster carers. I've told Alex and it's clearly making him sad too. It makes me worry that we are missing something, but then taking stock, we are just under a week of him being here. I am being silly.

9th July - Grandmum's Visit

We are up at 07.15am waiting for Jacob to come through like yesterday, but he hasn't and I can't hear him so I thought we could chance another 15 minutes in bed. Sods law, as soon as I closed my eyes he was being pretty noisy and bounding in the bedroom and all over us. It is as if his body knows when it's time to get up each morning. I got up with him and left Alex in bed. Alex and I have now found a nice routine where I get up in the early morning because I'm more of a morning person and then Alex would let me have an hour to myself mid-morning.

He wet himself this morning when we were playing, yet it was only about 15 minutes after we had been to the toilet as part of the morning routine. It was as if he had held it. I'm so frustrated with this as I am sure that he knows when he needs it. I assume it's anxiety or controlling behaviours that is presenting. That is what all the blogs seem to say anyway.

My mother came today. She arrived at about 10.00am and was respectful to Jacob by only staying an hour or so. She didn't want to confuse or cause any anxiety within him, which is very thoughtful and considerate of her, to even acknowledge that this is a very different situation to when introducing a child that's born into the family. Both of our families have been really good about it all to be fair.

When my mother arrived she brought a small gift for Jacob and it was actually quite funny as he had barely said *hello* before he was asking if the bag was a present for him. It was cheeky of him, but so cute that it was endearing too. Mum laughed about it and said that's how I was when I was a child. She handed over the gift and I prayed he would have the good manners he has always shown. He did and I was beaming. It was such a proud father moment. We all went inside and had a coffee and tried to be 'normal'. Mum didn't want to give him too much attention but didn't want to not either. It was a fine balance, and she did a great job. After the coffee we went down to the local park and I got no attention from either my mother or Jacob. It made me smile really as they connected so well. I couldn't have wanted it to go any better than it did. We stayed there for a good hour enjoying the park before heading back to the house where I managed to get a couple of pictures of my mum and Jacob. I will treasure them forever.

I cried when my mother left. I usually do, to be fair. I have such a strong connection with my mother anyway, but this time it made me also think a little about what Jacob could be missing if circumstances were different.

After lunch, which again was great due to him being a good eater, I got ready to meet my friend, Duncan. Alex told Jacob I was going for a *'dirty beer'* with a friend and he just shouted *'urgghhhhhhhhhhh dirty beer'*. I couldn't help but laugh. He is so switched on and funny in the cutest way. But on a more serious note, Jacob asked if I was coming home in a tone that was worrisome. It said a lot about the way he was thinking today and probably a lot of the other times too. We both made a note to make sure we kept reiterating that we will always be there for him, forever.

When I met Duncan, I felt sorry for him because I completely unloaded on him with all of the child based stories. I did that parent thing where they share everything and you're not sure if the other person actually wants to know. Duncan was thankfully genuinely interested and wanted to know about Jacob and how we had all been settling. It was superb timing from him to ask for a drink because I was genuinely in need of someone else to chat. I will never underestimate how much a friend can really support you by just letting you unload on them.

When I got home, I told Alex I would take Jacob to bed and read his bedtime book. I mainly wanted him to know I was home for a bit of a psychological reason. It was important that he knew I was home and that I would always come home. I read a book called 'And Tango Makes Three'. I quite liked it as it depicts Tango (a penguin) becoming part of a family with two dads. Jacob has asked for this a few times now and I hope it's helping him understand a little bit about his situation.

Speaking of the two dads thing, I do worry about it for when he gets older. I know 'times are changing' but I am concerned how people will view him being adopted and having two dads. It is quite a lot of school yard ammunitions; or at least it would have been in my day. I guess there is no point worrying about that just yet, as it could be wasted energy.

10th July - Guilt

I woke up and felt quite guilty about going for drinks yesterday. I think I felt guilty leaving Alex to look after Jacob and also felt the same emotion because I left Jacob for a while when we are still in the connections phase. It's a feeling I need to adapt to as I will be going back to work soon enough and Jacob will be going to school. We need to be careful of his emotions but also not wrap him in cotton wool either. It could have an adverse effect should we do that.

Whilst having breakfast, Jacob spelt his 'big name' (our forever family name) by using the blackboard which we had written it out on. This is a big u-turn as he would previously refuse to say his name was anything other than *'just Jacob'*. It is a significant step forward and one that I really hope will help with him understanding and come to terms with his identity.

Later in the day and when the paracetamol had kicked in, we headed out for a walk and then to the park. He is getting more and more confident on the apparatus down there. It's really pleasing to see him making small progressions on the kit there. For example he needed us to help him down the fireman pole, but now he can do it alone. Small steps forward et al. We made some home-made pizza when we got back and it was a happy mess. It was great fun and Jacob laughed all the way through it. It's moments like these that make me really drive home the reason we did this and wanted a family.

We have also had no toilet troubles today either. He is definitely a *player.* There is surely more to the toileting troubles than we know about. When we have approached the subject with the social workers of other people in our circle. Nobody really has a firm idea why he is so inconsistent with the bathroom. Many just say *'that's what 3 year old kids do'*. I am not convinced and for some reason think there is an underlying reason for it. I will keep trying to work it out.

Teddies have been a source of jealousy. We have bought him 4 teddies but he keeps going back to his blue bear; the one he got at his foster carers. I worry he is attaching memories back to other people and not moving on and making them with us. Does he like them more than Alex and I? I'm probably being silly and he simply may just prefer that teddy, but it certainly make me think and wonder why that is the go-to teddy.

11th July - Pull Up and Bathroom Habits

We bought pull up pants yesterday and tried them on for the first time last night. Jacob was getting out of bed and going to the bathroom straight after his book, so it was wasting nappies if we didn't put them on right and it was also quite hard for him to do anything independently either. The change over seems to have worked to the extent that he wanted to keep going to the bathroom to show us how independent he is now. He must have had 4-5 wee's tonight. He has now got more freedom in the morning and as opposed to relying on us he seems happy that he can go unaided. He seems to enjoy that, so we are pleased. The concern with these are that they cost more money. Everything with a child seems to cost more money!

Later in the morning he returned to poo's being *'scary'*. What the hell has changed now? The frustrations are creeping into our voices as we chat to him. How can you go from loving having a poo and laughing about farting to being scared again? I've spoken to my best mate and he said his girls do the same. That makes me feel better, but still doesn't alleviate my frustrations. As an adult, I just don't understand the rationale behind it and I need to think like a child. Some would say that should be easy for me!

He had another accident whilst at the park too. Today seems to be a battle with the bathroom. I am pulling my hair out and I can't wait for him to go to bed so I don't have to think about it. Let the pull ups do the work for us.

Finally Jacob is in bed. I feel exhausted and a little guilty that I may have shown frustration in my voice and in some interactions with him today. There was no shouting, obviously, because I would never do that, but my voice was a little quicker and more high pitched. Life certainly isn't easy with a child.

12th July - Parental Disagreements

We went to a big country park and for a long walk today. We had been there less than 15 minutes and had fallen over 3 times covering himself in mud and water. I am a little worried about his spatial awareness and surroundings. He seems really clumsy; but it was fun!

From a parenting point of view, the time in the park was a tough one. Alex and I had a lot of differences of opinion on what freedoms when playing and exploring Jacob should have. For example when Jacob got within 3 meters of the shallow water (ankle deep), Alex would shout 'stop' and I was opposing and saying '*go ahead and explore*'. I just don't understand the over cautious, wrapping him in cotton wool approach. It must have been really confusing for Jacob to have the mixed messages.

Jacob also had an accident…again. He told us he was too busy to stop playing and have a wee. I got frustrated again and told Jacob we were going home, so he had a meltdown and cried lots. I think I was frustrated with how Alex and I were battling with each other and it spilled over to telling Jacob we were going home. We didn't go home, but it was pretty poor of me to use a 'threat' (of sorts) to get him to understand. I need to think about how I can articulate that better. In hindsight it was unfair and we need to be careful how our emotions translate across to Jacob. I felt really bad on the way home.

George was out in the garden when we got home and I really can't be bothered to take Jacob outside but I forced myself to let him go out and play. I am trying to think about Jacobs' needs over mine. It has to be that way even though I just want to curl up on my bed and sleep for a week.

Bedtime routine was lovely tonight. It seems to be up and down, up and down with how easy activities and routines are. As he was being tucked in he blurted out '*I love you very much*'. Well, I melted inside and my heart jumped. Little comments like this make you know it's all worth it. Jacob just wants to be loved and to give his own love out too. I just want to keep cuddling him.

I went to sleep with a smile.

13th July - Social Worker Advice

We had a call this morning with Jacobs social worker, Julie. It was quite a good call today as I went in with a bit more of an agenda on things we wanted to ask. We asked about the accidents and how we can manage it better. It seems to be the same as all the research we've done; acknowledge it, discuss calmly and don't make a big deal about it. We are doing that as best we can, but it's so bloody hard not to be frustrated as we know he can do it. We also discussed school. This is huge for us because tomorrow is Jacob's 'transition day' in school and in readiness for reception class. We feel it is very quick for him to go in September because he will only have been with us just over 2 months and we fear that he will be confused with regard to his permanence level. However, as time goes on we also believe it will be the best for him to make some friends, enjoy playing in a different environment and learn the things you do at school. It may actually help him understand the permanence he now has. Julie is pro-school and believes the same regarding permanence, so we are all on the same page. We just need to keep an eye on him whilst he is there and see how he reacts. The advice received has been to speak about school to Jacob and try and normalise going tomorrow and after that in September.

We even took him there and looked through the fence to do a 'dry run' in readiness for the transition day and to see how he reacted. He looked pretty excited about the playground, the toys he would be playing with and most importantly, that we would be waiting at the gates after school for him. The latter was the most important one for us, I think. We are very conscious about ensuring that he knows we will be there for him.

We also told Julie about how he is very good with his alphabet and spelling out words that he can see. We've been spelling out Daddy Alex, Daddy Joe and Jacob Young. He's still slowly coming to terms with having a second name (or 'big name' as he calls it). We believe he was told that he wasn't part of the birth family at one of the 'contacts' he had with his birth mother and her mother. We believe that is the route cause of him struggling with his identity. That makes me really sad. His birth family are still completely a part of his life and even though that is not actively, they are part of his identity and always will be.

Later in the day, I've a few tears on my own whilst in the bathroom. Jacob has mentioned his foster carers quite a few times already and I think it may have been triggered by seeing the social worker on the phone today. In his eyes, I want Alex and I to be his parents, yet he keeps talking about the foster carers. It's completely selfish of me and is causing lots of jealousy and a number of insecurities. He spent nearly a third of his life with them so of course he is going to talk and reminisce about them. I am also jealous of how much he loves 'Blue Bear'. I want him to love 'Sharkie' the transition teddy we gave him. My feeling is that 'Blue Bear' takes him to a place of other people, but on the flip side is that if it makes him feel safe and comfortable, then I need to get past my own selfishness.

Just before bedtime, Jacob had a bath and played 'school'. It is something we have encouraged and are hoping will help him tomorrow. He really enjoyed playing and loved playing the teacher role. We did lots of work on the way teachers take the register and will call out his name. We have asked them to use his new forever family name and not his birth / registered name because we don't want to confuse him or for him to have any regressions regarding his identity. When we were taking the register, at first he wasn't responding and saying he was 'just Jacob'. But we tried to make it fun and eventually he started to respond to his full name.

It was a very late night for him too even though he was in bed by 7.30pm. He was talking through his teddies and doing the register with them and telling them how excited he was about it tomorrow. We've found he does this when he is digesting his day. It's cute to hear, but I want him to go to sleep as I worry how he will be in the morning otherwise. A tired child is a grumpy and hard to manage child; we already know that.

14th July - School Taster Day

I didn't sleep much last night either. I have been anxious on his behalf and I don't think Alex slept much too. It may have been because I was moving around and fidgeting a lot. In addition to Jacob going to school, both Alex and I have set today as a 'sort out day' regarding clothes as he has a lot come with him.

We also got a little worked up as we realised we didn't really have much information on what he needs to take with him to school. It's been a bit of a guessing game. We just packed spare clothes as he's been having accidents, plus his medication for asthma.

Over breakfast we spent a lot of time discussing the day and what kind of fun things he may do at school. He was pretty proactive in talking to us about it, asking lots of questions. We answered them as best we could. He genuinely seemed OK and excited to go.

Just as we were leaving we remembered a nugget of information about having a connection toy to take to school so he can remember us and feel safe if he isn't feeling too good or *'funny in your (his) tummy'*. He chose to put in his pocket a little Fireman Sam figure and told us we needed to take Norman. We discussed in the car how he can just touch his pocket or play with Fireman Sam if he feels like he needs some love from us. We will also do the same with Norman throughout the day when we wanted to connect with him and fill him up with love. It went down really well with him.

It had been years since I have been in a school yard so going in I felt a little nervous but hopefully didn't express that to Jacob. I know Alex had the same feels because we discussed it in the car afterwards. Whilst waiting for teacher to open the doors we played some games and walked on lines in the playground. COVID19 has caused lots of waiting and specific rules. I used it as a tool to get him using his balance.

When we got to the front of the queue to get into the school classroom, we had a quick chat with his teacher and tried to introduce us to her and her to Jacob. It was the first time we had all met here, but we knew her name. Jacob refuses to say her name citing that he is scared. He then proceeded to be shy and hide behind my leg. I took two things away from this. I am really glad he feels safe and protected by me, yet we still need to work on talking about school with him so he knows it is a safe environment. Waving him off was a bizarre experience. We have only been with Jacob as a forever family for a month or so, yet the level of attachment and desire to protect him is so high, I just wanted to hold him and make sure he felt safe. However, I know how important it is for him to be in school, so I just hoped he would go on in and enjoy his day. He didn't even look back when we ushered him to go on in. He looked really happy, thank God. I felt so proud of him for being so brave.

Alex and I went for breakfast before we headed back home to sort out his clothes and throw some out. We both sat at the breakfast table and felt so drained of energy. All the excitement, nerves and worry had taken its toll and we could now relax for an hour or two. I went for a full-English breakfast and Alex for some posh over-priced eggs. That sorted me out!

When we arrived home we went through the process of throwing some of his clothes out that we don't like or that don't fit. It was a psychological step for us and one we have shared some concerns over. These clothes have come with him and some of them he will have attached memories or emotions to his foster carers, other people or events. We had to be positive in making the decision and just do it. We got rid of so many things and although it felt like a hard task, it was quite rewarding. It was a little like a positive identity shift; especially after the afternoon we had.

Having seen the lack of clothes, we went shopping with a budget of £100. We went silly and spent over £250. Every shop (and I mean every shop) we went into had clothes that we just had to buy. Skinny jeans, new underwear, t-shirts, jumpers and even things that we didn't need to buy because they are winter items… we just had to get them for him. We wanted him to be dressed in our things and our style for him. It would shift our subconscious mentality to him being part of our forever family even more so. I still can't believe how much we just spent but I can't wait to try it all on with him too!

Picking Jacob up today felt like a big task which we anticipated would be the case. We didn't know what to expect and had two ideas on how it was going to go. It could have gone very badly and he had a complete blocker attached to being at school or he will have loved it and be excited to go back. Thankfully he loved it and I am so pleased he did. The teacher said he was *'a dream today'*. He did have a small number one accident, but we anticipated that he may due to his anxieties about moving to his forever home, moving schools and possibly the detachment from us for the day.

When he opened the door and saw us, he ran arms wide open into our arms. Straight away he told us that he had kept Fireman Sam safe all day. Internally, I was emotionally exhausted. I am so glad that he was able to relax enough to enjoy his day and also have the maturity to think about what to do should he need to feel connected to us.

Whilst getting into the car, we had a new first. Alex tried to help him in as normal, yet he was adamant he wanted to get in alone. The car is a big car and so it is hard to get into alone. He went into melt down mode and just hysterically cried that he needed help. In hindsight he was definitely really tired, processing all that happened throughout the day and happy that we were there as promised. Maybe it was a release of relief and anxiety?

As a treat for him doing so well we took him to McDonald's. We had told him that we would take him after school and we did that to reassure him that we would be there after school. He loved his McDonalds Happy Meal and was soon digging into our food too.

I was expecting a lot of talking from teddy to teddy tonight, but he didn't do much of that. A minute or so after his book, he was asleep. He was knackered.

15th July - Mentioning Foster Carers

I'm sure I heard him in the early hours of the morning. He certainly shouted out this morning as he woke up. I think he may have been a little confused as he may have woken up suddenly. Either that or some of the trauma from his past is rearing its head. Possibly something that he is hiding when he is aware of what's going on.

Just after breakfast and even though we had been for a wee when he got up he wet himself again. He is clearly very anxious still and processing what happened yesterday. He's very hot physically and there isn't an obvious physical reason (like heat) for it. It must be internalised emotions raising his temperature. I really wish he could verbalise what he is thinking and not just talk about what is currently within his eye-line. It's quite frustrating and I must remember he is only 3 years old so will struggle to verbalise his thoughts. He then later cried when we went to get ready for the day and as I asked him to brush his teeth. He's mentioned the foster carers 4 times already this morning and its only 10.30am. His head is buried somewhere and I wish I could open it up and find out what he is thinking. I am really struggling but he must be struggling a hell of a lot more than I am. The amount of change and trauma that he has gone through is crazy. I just want to make it all better for him.

When Alex had sorted some of his things out that he wanted to get done, I went back to bed and read my book but fell asleep pretty quickly. I am completely exhausted and have had silly thoughts regarding the decision to do this. I am 100% sure it's normal to feel like this – some of our adoption friends have said the same – but I am also 100% sure we have made the right choice adding Jacob to complete our forever family. It's only a small portion of the time that he has some wobbles and it should be expected; of course it should be expected. I need to keep reminding myself that we are doing our best and that we can offer Jacob the things he needs to thrive as a child.

In the late afternoon we had another call with Julie. We talked about the introduction to school day, his recent behaviours and also we started the conversation surrounding the final contact with Jacob's birth mother. Regarding the behaviours and the actions, Julie reassured us that all of the emotions and actions we took are completely normal and well managed. To her that may have been quite a simple comment, but that really helped us validate our parenting skills and style, assuring us that we are doing well. The other conversation regarding the final contact with his birth mother is a little more complex. We clearly have to do this post placement (as he is here!) due to COVID19 and the social distancing restrictions. He wouldn't be able to meet her in the contact centre due to those reasons and that offers standalone risks, but may need to happen. Julie said they are going to start looking at completing a full risk assessment and identify when it may be possible to arrange the meet.

We have always maintained that Alex and I are completely and utterly in favour of him seeing his birth mother. It's morally right for her and Jacob. We don't see this as a favour either, but a given right for her. Someone the other day – who will remain nameless – said that we shouldn't let them meet for the last time until he is older. That angered me a little and I thought it was completely selfish of them to think that way. But then again, I would have likely thought that way prior to the training that we had.

Jacob has been okay this afternoon. He's just got on with things and just plodded through the day. Alex played with him lots after the call because I was still struggling. He's such a natural parent, but he doesn't see it in himself.

16th July - Playing Us

I'm feeling better today. Yesterday was a tough day for me and I mentally struggled.

It's been a good start to the day regarding Jacob, although it somehow seems like he is playing us a little bit. I'm conscious that he comes to me for a lot of things and not Alex. I feel bad that he does come to me and not Alex sometimes too. I am really trying to encourage Jacob to interact with Alex as much as possible.

He's clever and streetwise because he knows how to get things out of us when he wants something. We need to keep an eye on him. I think he knows that we need to parent him a different way, but I also wonder how he could know that?

We went for a walk in the park again this afternoon because he loves getting outdoors and exploring. He wore his new wellies and a jacket that was gifted to him by George and his parents. He looks absolutely gorgeous. I also think he relaxes when he is outdoors and really lets himself wonder. I wanted to play more and race with him when he asked but had to say *no* because of my spinal surgery. I felt like I wasn't being a great parent to him at that point. I must get it out of my head that being perfect is not the aim. We managed to take lots of lovely pictures too and I am so happy we did. These memories will last forever and we have added them into our family photo album. We can look back on these for years to come.

Overall, today has been pretty void of drama, other activity or crying (from any of us). I am taking that as a win but also not for granted. Quiet days are good. I feel we have really bonded and our connections are getting strong.

17th July - The 'Our Children Review'

Today we have our review with the social workers and an independent social worker who would chair it. It's called 'Our Children Review' and was pretty straight forward. The chair, Jessica, asked lots of questions about how Jacob is settling in, about his routines, about food and drinks and lots of other questions related to him and the last few weeks. The rest was our social worker, Jacobs social worker, the Chair and health visitor talking about us and Jacob between them. We played the passenger for a while, and it was very reassuring to hear what they had to say about us. It was very much positive. Again, this was great for our self confidence in being parents.

They also wanted to see how Jacob interacted with us on video (usually it would be done in person) and also, I guess, just to get a visual on how connected he seems with us. Jacob was jumping all over us and interactive with all of us. We got a tick in the box and it confirmed the placement is going well and accepted by all parties. We never had any doubt about that though. We are living the reality each day after all.

Other than the call we tried to have another quiet day. Jacob seemed like he didn't want to do much other than play with his toys and mostly on his own creating his own little world. We have been very impressed with his creativity and also his ability to complete things like jigsaws and building based toys. He absolutely nails the smaller jigsaws in minutes, so we need a more testing one. In fact I just ordered a jigsaw that replicates out first ever picture taken at the foster carers.

18th July - Mummy and Grandma

Alex is meeting his friend today in town. He's going for some boozy lunch and some more drinks in the early PM. I am really glad he is doing something outside of the family home today as I think it will be really good for his mindset and let him recharge his batteries a little. He needs some down time as he is an over thinker and unloading to someone else other than myself, will be good for him.

We drove Alex in this morning and on the way home and out of the blue, Jacob mentioned *mummy and Grandma* twice. That came as a shock and I was initially unsure how to respond, but it seems that each time Jacob sees or hears Julie's voice, he associates her with something or someone and causes memories to come back. We usually get a negative response. Once I composed myself I tried to ask what had made him think of them and speak about them. When he couldn't articulate it, inside I was going through all kinds of emotions. I really wanted to know what triggered him to mention them. Is he missing them and would he prefer to be with them? Does he really want to be with us? I'm drowning in my own negative thoughts, but I am sure they will pass soon.

I took Jacob for some food when we got close to home and I could see it in his eyes that he was thinking about something. He mentioned that his foster carer used to *'take me to see mummy'* so that confirmed it. I am sure, somehow, that he knows that he will see his mum soon for a visit. I had to take some calming deep breaths and compose myself. I know he is fully entitled to speak about his family and happy he is feeling comfortable enough to do so, however I just want him to be all ours. It's a bizarre feeling and one I thought I had fully accepted. Clearly I need to keep working on that side of it.

Alex got a taxi home, so I'm glad he stayed out for a little longer than he originally planned. It will have done him a world of good, even if he does get a little hangover in the morning. He managed to get home before Jacob went to bed, so it was lovely for them both to have some cuddles and kisses before bedtime. I believe it was also good for Jacob knowing Alex is home.

19th July - BBQ and Playtime

Today we are played in the garden and house with the BBQ getting fired up. We needed a slow day today due to Alex's hangover, the global pandemic of COVID-19 and knowing that Jacob had lots on his mind. We played lots of games that helped with his coordination too. I am convinced he needs some more guidance to improve on that. I will continue to keep playing games and working on it.

20th July - Doctors Appointment

Today is our visit to see the doctors about Jacob's eczema. It's a routine appointment and he seems fine about seeing a doctor. In fact, he seems excited to see them as they *'help my skin be better'*. I am amazed at how much he understands at 3 years old.

The hospital that we need to go to is local to the foster carers house due to it being arranged by them and we didn't want to change it as we didn't want to lose his slot. We are also hoping Jacob doesn't recognise the area as we drive through it and then experience some regression.

After an hour and a little in the car, we finally arrived at the hospital. What everyone failed to tell us was that it was shut due to the COVID-19 restrictions in place. The on site caretaker was very apologetic and told us the appointment could be completed, but we had to drive 45 minutes to get to that hospital. We certainly didn't want to miss it as we had driven so long and far anyway, so we went there instead. We did go via a shop to get some chocolate because Jacob was great after all.

When we arrived the nurse was superb and very attentive to Jacob. She said that she could remember him from when he first came into the care system and *'how bad he was that day'*. She told us that all of his skin was cracked, infected and *'just not looked after and neglected'*. Hearing the word neglected hit me for six. It really hurts having the knowledge that Jacob went through a bad and painful time and it was in fact the reality of his early childhood.

Overall, the trip was fine. We found out more about skin care routines and what we should do to keep Jacob's skin at its best. The nurse said we were doing a great job. Small snippets like that are absolute gold to us and again it reinforces that we are doing the right things as parents.

On the way home and because Jacob had been so patient (and because I love spoiling him), we stopped off at a Smyths Toy shop. I wanted to buy the shop but in fact Jacob just wanted one thing and wasn't greedy at all. It was atypical as the other kids in the shops were screaming for everything from their parents. I hope that is just his polite manner that caused him to not be greedy as opposed to something that we are unaware of. Maybe he was just tired and wanted to get home.

Captain Over-Thinker is back again!

21st July - Play Date with K & N

We had a play date today with our friends who have adopted also. What an amazing day! Jacob got to play with their children today and I think it did him a world of good to have some interactions with other kids. He had to show them all of *'my forever home'* which was also quite amusing to watch due to the way he did it. It was like an estate agents tour! It was also great for us as parents meeting up with other adoptive parents. K and N have been our rocks and a superb support for us when we need some guidance and reassurance. Today both Alex and I asked hundreds of questions and got their views on things. I also got some great advice that I want to try out too. K told me that children can take 30 seconds to acknowledge a question and then form an answer. Previously, when we have asked Jacob a question we would usually fill in the answer for him after a few seconds, should he be struggling. Now we are aware that we shouldn't it will be interesting to see if we get better answers or ones that make sense.

We can't thank K and N enough for what they have done. They probably don't realise how important they are to us and I am so glad we met them at the adoption training.

Tonight, when Jacob went to bed, he pretty much hit the pillow and was asleep. It's time for us to unwind and relax.

22nd July - Social Worker Call - Contact Centre

Julie called this afternoon with news that the contact centre has arranged for Jacob and his birth mother to have their final meeting. Alex and I anticipated a few weeks, so we can get him prepared and to understand more about the meeting. Well, it's on Friday – 2 days. Or a day and a half if we get really specific. To add a little more to the mix, we have a visit to the zoo booked in on Friday too, which Jacob is more than excited about.

I am frustrated at the time scales and angry that we can't prepare him properly for such an important life event, but I am also happy that we are getting it done and dusted. I know it's not the social workers fault and she was super apologetic about the short notice. I guess we just have to suck it up and get on with it.

We spoke to Julie about the best thing to do about the zoo. As its relatively close to the contact centre and because Jacob is very excited about going, then she said to go ahead and do it as it may also act as a good tool after seeing his birth mum that morning.

Our social worker, Patrick, called later in the day and had a conflicting idea on the zoo to Julie, but as she knows Jacob better we have decided to take her advice and not his.

In preparation for the meeting we have been asked to write a letter to his birth mum too with an update on Jacob. Just factual things and nothing overly detailed that can identify us and our location. Additionally, Jacob will do some drawings for his birth mum to keep; that was our idea and one we are really keen on him doing because we believe his mother has a right to receive something for good memories. I will do that in the morning when I have processed it all and before Nana and Grandad get here (Alex's parents).

23rd July - Settling In Letter

This morning has been tough as I've woken up with Jacob's snotty nose. He's passed that one on, thanks. Currently, I feel pretty out of sorts and so went straight for the paracetamol.
Whilst Jacob has been watching the TV, I have written the letter to send to his birth mother, after Alex has checked it. Jacob will take it with him tomorrow. I have tried to

write the nicest letter and a soft one too, but most importantly as sincerely as I can. I don't want it to be just facts as she will have feelings too.

Dear XXXX

We hope you are doing well. Both Alex and I (Joe) wanted to write and reach out to you as we wanted to introduce ourselves and offer you reassurances Jacob will be loved unconditionally and kept safe. We know you are aware of Jacob living in his forever family home; he is such a happy little boy.

Firstly and most importantly, we really wanted you to know and understand that you are his mother and always will be. Whenever Jacob wants to speak about you, we are happy to do so. We also speak highly to him about how much you love him and that will never change.

Our role is to ensure we give Jacob love, safety, encouragement, guidance and of course boundaries. All of these, we will do to the best of our abilities.

A little about Jacob and his progression. Jacob has settled super well. He has good routines around the house and also loves to play. He really enjoys playing and has a strong knack for building things. He can build better than us.

He sleeps well – often with a teddy you gave him and amongst other teddies like 'sharkie' (a shark) from about 8pm to 7.30am. He is such a ball of energy that he needs his sleep in the evening. We read lots of books and he knows most of them inside out already. He currently has a particular liking for dinosaurs, Fireman Sam and Paw Patrol. He is even in pull up pants. Something he has learned here. He is a very good learner.

His manners are superb... Jacob is also such a polite little boy. He is attentive to us, often asking if we are OK. He asks politely if he wants something and says his 'please' and 'thank you'. We are so proud of him. We bet you are too.

Since being here – about 3 weeks – Jacob has been doing so many things. So much of it is based around playing and helping him settle in his new home.

We often visit the park (now it's open again). We even created a treasure hunt in the woodland close by (he loves playing pirates), we have fed the ducks and he even has made a best friend with the little boy next door. We bet they will be a handful when they are teenagers.

Jacob has also attended his 'school transition' day too. He will be in a superb and very highly regarded school that will really help support his learning and personality. To be fair he could probably teach them some things too. He is clever. We are confident Jacob will flourish there as he is very bright. On the transition day, the teacher said he 'was an absolutely delightful little boy'. We are so pleased he seemed to enjoy it. Jacob is even growing a sunflower. We are to take pictures and send them to school.

In the future Julie (social worker) will be setting up a mailbox so we can give you updates on Jacob and vice versa. As we said at the start <u>YOU</u> are his mum and we feel it important for all parties to discuss Jacob and you. He will want to know about you too.

We will speak to you soon
All the best

Joe and Alex.

When I had finished the letter, Alex double checked it and confirmed he is happy with the tone and content. I left it on the side after reading again myself with the intention of putting it in an envelope when I found one after Alex's mum and dad had been. It was the first time they were coming so it was a bit of a busy day. We had put them back visiting 3 or 4 times on the advice of the social workers and couldn't change them at the last minute again, especially as Jacob was excited to meet them.

I was over the moon with the reaction of Jacob meeting Nana and Grandad – just as I was with my mother too. So far he has loved meeting all of the family and they have loved meeting him too. We couldn't have asked for better connections across the family.

It was quite a funny moment when they knocked on the door. Jacob was ready to greet them, which he did with big hugs, and then his eyes straight to the bag in Grandads hand. *'Oh what presents have you got? Are they for me?'* Although it was very cheeky, it was innocent and endearing. He clearly knows that people will bring him something at their first meeting. I just hope he doesn't expect presents from everyone though. Both sets of grandparents have given Jacob a lot of attention and he has loved getting it too. He really enjoys interactions with people. He will be a very social and loving little boy.

They stayed for tea and have inadvertently helped us out with regards meeting his birth mother tomorrow. We had no idea how to tell him, so when Jacob asked some questions, it transitioned nicely to how we can discuss it.

Jacob was talking about Nana, Grandmums and Grandad and it was clearly confusing to him as he couldn't understand why there are three. In his mind he should only have one set. We had to explain that Grandmums is my mum and Nana and Grandad are Alex's. When he had managed to process that, he said *'I have a mummy too and I love her'*. It took us all by surprise a little, but then again we are learning he will just say what he is thinking. We pivoted his comment into a conversation about his mum and how much she loves him, yet she couldn't keep him safe. He went on to tell us that he likes seeing his birth mum and so came our opportunity to *'ask Julie if we can see her tomorrow'*. That worked and he was happy enough and the conversation ended there.

When Alex's parents left, Alex told him that Julie had agreed that Jacob can see his mum tomorrow, but it would be the last time he would see her until he is as big as Daddy Joe (our way of helping him visualise an adult). I don't think he will understand what these time frames mean, but we tried to articulate in a child friendly way. We also told Jacob that we can make a nice picture and he can give it to his birth mother tomorrow. It is really tough and hard to explain how I am feeling about it. I have a mix of emotions towards his birth mum. Some are good, some are not. What I do have however, is a lot of empathy for the situation she was in previous and now finds her self in. I know the backstory of her life and I would suggest what situation she grew up in had a hand in how Jacob was parented. Frankly though, I still don't forgive her after what happened.

After drawing his picture, I forgot I had left the letter out. Jacob found it and asked if it was for his mummy which I told him that it was. I didn't anticipate him asking me to read it to him. I think it is very important that he knows about his birth mother and that we are open to talk about his situation should he want to. With that weighing on my mind, I read it to him and I broke down in floods of tears. Quite heavy, suck-in-for-breath type tears. I couldn't help but place myself in her situation and how she must have felt about the child she gave birth to living with someone else and not being able to see him. I tried to hide the reason from Jacob and told him I was upset citing that it is OK to be upset and cry. I did tell him though that they were happy tears as I am so happy that he is living with us – his forever family. There is certainly some truth in that, but it was mainly the aforementioned. I really feel for his birth mother.

I found it all very tough. One of the hardest times I have had recently. I wonder how he is feeling and significantly what he is thinking. I seem to be doing a lot of thinking about what he is thinking. I will never know unless he tells me though.

Jacob has been quiet for the remainder of the evening. He went to bed without any protest and fell asleep quickly. He said he was excited to see his birth mother and go to the zoo.

24th July - Final Contact Day

I am absolutely drained and shattered after today. It's been the biggest emotional roller-coaster that I've ever been on and I just want to get into bed. It has been a very tough day for all of us.

Jacob has been up since 4.00am and in floods of uncontrollable tears. I went to his bedroom to see if he was OK and he said his ear was hurting. He may have led on it for a while, but for the pain to last for hours was a red flag. It was at that point I knew that his mind was in a place that he couldn't and didn't know how to process. I tried him in our bed, his bed, our spare bed, but eventually we ended up downstairs on the sofa together. I felt completely helpless and as though I was failing in my job as a father to keep him happy and feeling safe. I also knew that he could be grieving because this will be his last visit to see his birth mother. Maybe we under estimated him and he actually did understand what was happening today? I just feel sh*t. I don't know what to do here and all I can do really is be there. A father should know how to protect his son. It has been a tough night.

When the clock hit 7.30am (our normal time to get up), it was as if a switch went off in Jacob's head. He went back to 'normal' and acted as if nothing had happened. It was bizarre. My mind was scrambled because I have no idea what the hell happened. It was as if he was a different child.

With breakfast complete, we set off to the zoo a little dazed. We were also thinking about scenarios and how the day could play out both before and after seeing his birth mum. I have played out every single scenario in my head and some come out very good and some are pretty grim. What if Jacob doesn't want to leave his birth mother and rejects us? What if someone says something at the meeting that ruins all that we have achieved so far? What if there is confrontation? What if someone takes our car registration and finds out where we live? What if… I could have gone on for hours.

We got to the zoo and met up with Uncle Ryan and his family. They have 3 children so we hoped to be able to distract Jacob with them all playing together and seeing the variety of animals. The first hour of the morning was very positive and high energy. He loved seeing the turtles and dinosaurs (his favourite). He was even making fun jokes about elephants having a 'bum the same size as yours Daddy Joe.' It was all jolly and happy families on the outside but both Alex and I were trying really hard not to show how we were feeling. We didn't want Jacob picking up on our feelings about the anxiety we had surrounding the meeting today.

Just before 11.00am, we made our way back to the exit and headed off to the contact meeting centre. It was only 10 minutes away, so it was a short drive. I am glad it was because we didn't have much time to think about getting there and the process that would follow. Additionally we didn't have to answer many questions from Jacob but to be fair he was relatively quiet. He knew where we were going and what was happening.

As we approached, I was on high alert scanning all cars and people to see if they posed any potential threat. Was anyone following or taking down our car registration plate? The military training kicked in there, but of course they were all silly thoughts. I would say that what was evident to both Alex and I was how much we cared about Jacob and his safety. It's a funny feeling to know and acknowledge how quickly you can form a bond and unconditional desire to love someone in such a short time. I didn't love Alex that quick, but don't tell him that!

Entering the car park of the building complex, we expected to see windows twitching however there was nothing. We had barely got out of the car and out came a lady from the rear entrance. She didn't really say much apart from to confirm who we were and then proceeded to take Jacob's hand. At this point I felt like slowing the process down, but in the same breath, I didn't want any hesitation. We told Jacob that we would be waiting here for him when he got out. We really wanted to reassure him that he was coming back to us and that we are his daddies and forever family.

Watching him walk away to see his birth mother was a sad, yet a very happy experience. It was conflicting. We are not selfish enough to deny the rights of Jacob and his birth mother their last meeting; at least for the foreseeable future (even though we don't have that power) as we deem this a very important milestone in both of their lives. He actually looked happy that he was going to see her and we are glad that he did. We don't want negative thoughts surrounding her as this may affect him as he grows up. Positive vibes all around!

With the door closed and Jacob in the building, Alex and I got into the car, both in a heightened frame of mind and very anxious still. We had an hour to kill and so headed off to find a coffee shop where we scarcely said a word to each other the entire time, preferring to internalise our own thoughts. Soon enough we were back in the car park at the contact centre waiting for Jacob to come out. The rear of our car was facing the exit door where he would come from, so we got out and opened the boot of the car and sat there waiting. We wanted to be in his field of vision straight away when he came out. When the door did open, well, it was possibly one of the most amazing moments of the short time we have spent together. He saw both of us, shook off the guiding hand of the social worker bringing him out and ran across the car park with open arms shouting 'Daddy Alex and Daddy Joe'. Inside, I was overwhelmed and I was overcome with relief. I was completely afraid of rejection and to my absolute joy it shredded any doubts I may have had. It was brilliant.

The social worker following Jacob joined us and gave us a bag of things from the day. In it there were pictures taken today with his birth mum and birth grandmother. We didn't know his birth grandmother was due to be there. It threw me off a little as it seems she is the one that has been very influential in the whole family's issue; not only that, it had been reported that she had previously told Jacob that he was no longer a 'Smith' (their family name).

Also in the bag were some clothes, crisps and some broken cars. It really saddened me to see the broken cars and once again I felt conflicting emotions. She clearly had every intention to give Jacob something nice, yet it backfired. I could see the disappointment in Jacob's face and could hear it in his voice when he told me it was broken and asking if I could fix it. On the other hand – and I had to suppress the emotion – I was pissed off that she could get such a thoughtless gift that would do nothing but disappoint him.

Overall, I think all three of us were super happy that we were back together; the Young family reunited. I also believe that it did a world of good for Jacob's connection with us too. Us being there when he came out will do wonders, I'm sure for his understanding of our forever family.

We headed back to the zoo and it was a relatively normal afternoon all things considered. He had a quick 5 minutes here and there where he was quiet, but that could be put down to him just being shattered.

Going home, we went for some food with Uncle Ryan and his family. We didn't stay long and within minutes of us being in the car, Jacob was sleeping. He looked so peaceful and happy cuddling his new 'Gerry the Giraffe' teddy bear. It had been a very long and draining 48 hours for him.

Alex and I were very pleased to get to bed. We were bloody shattered; emotionally and physically.

25th July - Quiet Day to Recuperate

We received a message from Jacob's social worker to ask about yesterday. I thought that was very thoughtful of her especially with it being a Saturday and technically not a working day for her. We just gave her a quick update because she wants to speak to the contact centre on Monday.

We kept today pretty sedentary and within the house and garden. We think Jacob benefited from a quiet day. We made sure we did lots of things that hopefully confirmed to him that this is his forever home. We talked about him growing to be bigger than me, watching his flowers grow over and how he will see them year after year. Small things, but tangible things he can look to the future with.

26th July - Cuddles and Kisses

Today was similar to yesterday, but we have seen some internalised thinking coming from him. He is almost certainly playing over the last few days in his head and trying to process it. It sounds bizarre, but you can actually see him thinking. Jacob has been giving lots of cuddles and kisses today. I am sure he is testing us a little and confirming to both himself and us that we are there for him. We just need to keep an eye on him to make sure he's OK and managing his emotions well enough.

27th July - Grieving, maybe?

We tried to have another slow day today. We collectively think it's really important for him to get his thoughts together. However, Jacob has had a couple of accidents today citing that he was too busy having fun to go to the toilet. We are certainly overthinking every scenario as to why he is doing this. He must have so much going on in his mind, bless him. I just wish I could go into his brain and switch off the negative emotions and reassure him that he is safe. Maybe he is still grieving but just doesn't really know it.

We had a proper briefing with his social worker today too. We explained in some detail what happened on Friday. There was very little additional information to offer other than what we had previously discussed with her, but we elaborated on certain topics and observations. Julie has been superb with her guidance and support but it seems like Patrick has now started to tail off his involvement now he has completed 'his bit' finding us our beautiful little boy. Maybe he has other things going on or that maybe there is genuinely little that he can add at this stage. All in all, we are OK with the limited involvement because we just want to get on and be a family as best we possibly can.

28th July - Extremes

There have been no accidents today and lots of playing. I don't understand how Jacob can go from one extreme to another. It's all very confusing for us as parents. Some days he can recognise when he needs the bathroom and on others we are unsure what goes on. Does he do it purposely so he can gain some form of control over us? Jacob is going to keep testing us I am sure. I don't think it is intentional, but I think it is because his subconscious mind wants to feel secure.

Mentally and physically I feel that my body is taking a beating. There seems to be no time to relax. That is definitely one of the hardest parts of being a parent so far. Alex and I have been great letting the other chill out but when we didn't have a child I could just relax when I wanted. Now there is something to do all of the time. Parent life!

29th July - Budgets and Money

Alex and I have gone through the budgets again and again because with Alex taking some leave and with me just coming off furlough, it's been tough in the finance department; even more so when you just want to buy everything you see for the little one. That has been a tough idea to contend with as we really need to keep as much of his first few months 'low key and normal'. The inert desire to spoil Jacob is high.

Although we want to keep it low key, we still really want to introduce him to everyone because they are all aware of our journey and want to be involved in welcoming him to our forever family and, I guess friends groups. We've been told a couple of times by the social workers that we should continue to do very little and meet up with very few people. It is a tough one given the past few days and as Jacob is presenting (externally at least) as doing really well and super happy. We are off to see Nana and Grandad tomorrow anyway and he's already seen my mum. We can't keep him (or them) away. Our friends have said that this was very tough for them too. It is certainly a tough call to go against the social workers' advice, but we have Jacob all day and everyday so we are going with what we feel is best for him. We don't want him getting bored and restless and we want him to meet his wider family. We think it will do him a world of good and hopefully, influence his feelings of permanence.

30th July - Time to Myself

Alex has taken Jacob to see Nana and Grandad today. Personally, I am absolutely shattered and so I'm quite happy to have some time to myself. I had two hours of sleep at around 1.00pm and until I had a child, I didn't realise how much this means and how good this feels. My best friend has been telling me for years how exhausted he is with 3 children.

Alex loves going to see his parents and they loved seeing Jacob last time, so it's a win-win for all parties here.

I also had the chance to pick up some presents for Jacob as it's his birthday soon. I was going in to buy some little bits just to bring up the amount of presents to unwrap. We have already got him a tablet (he loves playing ours and we limited the time on it, so don't judge!), a trampoline and Nana and Grandad have bought him a huge car garage too. He won't know the value of these so will just be happy to have some additional presents to open.

Anyway, I just bought a hell of a lot of little bits; way too much really. Rightly or wrongly, as his birth mother gave him lots of hand-me-downs and broken toys I want to give Jacob everything and I don't want him to feel disappointment by having current toys re-wrapped or cars that have 3 wheels. I hope we don't overdo it and add an unrealistic expectation for the future. Oh well, balls to it. It's his first birthday with us and he can have what he wants!

31st July - Learning Day

Today was a big learning day for us as it was our first time in the garden in the sunshine and this presented us with lot of things we hadn't considered before. That sounds weird to say but we needed to get our heads around lots of little things, which in turn can become quite large of a deal. For example, sun-cream, how much does he need to drink, when should he rest, what about how much time in the sun, what toys are suitable to keep him cool etc. We've had lots of disagreements on pretty much all the above and the evening was a little frosty when Jacob went to bed. However, we did talk things through and agreed to listen to each other's opinions. It is an eye opener thinking about someone else in this manner and not just yourself; we are now making decisions for Jacob because he can't as a child. He relies on us to do that, although he doesn't actually know it.

1st August - Frustration

Jacob just keeps having accidents and he knows he is doing it. It is purely a behavioural issue; it has to be because he never had these concerns at his foster carers towards the end and when he first moved to us. I must have read a million articles on children having accidents – although not number 2's. - and they pretty much all say to not make a big deal of it and have lots of reminders. How can you not make a big deal of something that we are pretty sure he knows he is doing? It is so tough.

We are off to a restaurant with our next door neighbours. George and Jacob love playing together. It will give us some time to let our hair down too and relax. I am really looking forward to taking him out for some food.

2nd August - Hangover

Well, yesterday! God, I never want a hangover ever again with a child. Today has been a mess. Routines and attention levels have been all over the place. We both feel pretty guilty towards Jacob because we haven't given him as much attention as we have in the past. I couldn't wait for him to go to bed tonight. I'm ashamed to think that way a little, but next door say that it is common for them to feel and think the same. Snippets like that help me feel better and I guess they are right as everyone needs downtime. We've certainly recognised that fact tonight. Those last few hours of the evening when the little on is in bed are a complete decompression and help reset the mind and body in readiness for it to all happen again the following day.

4th August - Health Advisor

We had a call with the medical expert / health visitor today. It was a video call to go through how Jacob is developing and to ensure we are doing the right things to keep on top of his physical and emotional health. It lasted over two hours and she had number of questions based on the aforementioned and we had the opportunity to ask questions regarding any other concerns that we had and that we needed some advice on.

We had filled out a big questionnaire a few days ago that helped the health advisor understand Jacobs current needs. We had to do lots of tasks and games like hopping, walking on lines, drawing shapes, knowing and repeating sequences etc. We actually had quite a lot of fun with them as we tried to turn it all into a game.

Overall, the call was positive and the health visitor said Jacob was meeting his milestones really well. What I was very pleased with was that she also said we are *'naturally doing a great job'* with Jacob. We seem to be *'natural parents'*. It is still pleasing to hear this feedback and also that our actions are correct and well thought out when we find something that we deem that we need to work on with him.

We brought up the toilet issue because this is the major thing that has been bothering us. He knows when he needs it, but just isn't telling us still. We had previously introduced a time to trigger the time to go and Alex and I have been advised to keep using it as hat association is working for him. We need to be careful that he doesn't become too reliant on it and if we can't naturally bring him back to organically telling us (or going himself) when he needs the bathroom, then we may need to seek some further advice.

We have said that we will always take any additional support, whether physical or psychological as we are completely pro-help if it benefits Jacob to process his life, trauma, loss and forever family (and the good things too!)

A minor contradiction to the my previous but this is day three without any accidents. Maybe it is the timer? Who knows?

5th August - Tragedy

F**king hell. Erm...

Alex's mother (and Jacob's Nana) has just passed away and very unexpectedly.

I have no clue what the hell to think or do. It is just not sinking in and I am in shock. Alex needs to prioritise getting to his side of the family and seeing his mum. He wants to be a great father and be with Jacob, but he needs to prioritise here. He has headed off to his parents house and I feel guilty that I can't be with him to support. He said he feels guilty for leaving us, but of course he shouldn't feel any guilt at all. I will look after Jacob.

I guess it shows the amazing feeling and connection of being a parent when Alex is thinking of other people's needs – his child - before his own.

I'm raising a glass for Nana now. Jesus. I am so shocked and very upset.

6th August - Alex Away

Alex stayed over at his parents just as we had agreed last night. He said that he didn't sleep much, so is pretty shattered. His first thoughts and questions were about Jacob, when they should have been about himself. Jacob is none the wiser to what has happened; he is just cracking on as normal. I hope Alex is OK and not putting himself under pressure.

Jacob and I went swimming today because I needed to occupy my mind as much as to keep Jacob active and engaged in something. I am numb and feel highly emotional. I had a good relationship with Nana and one filled with lots of son-in-law banter. It's a right of passage with the mother-in-law. I have so many fond memories of her and she was always very kind and wanted to 'mother' me. She'd give me eye massages because she said I would start to look old and tired soon with full time work and a child. Cheers!

When we were travelling to the swimming pool, I spoke to Alex and again he diverted the conversation back to Jacob and how we are going to tell him. He was being completely selfless and thinking about Jacob's needs and not his own. Another reason why I love him so much, but he does need to self-care more. I alway tell him that he needs to look after himself before others.

We had a lovely time whilst at the swimming pool, playing and jumping in. I can already see his confidence growing. While in the car on the way home, Jacob asked about the 'woman in the hospital'. It took me by surprise because how the hell did he know about Alex's mother, or was it a complete fluke? I can't remember him being within ear shot of any conversation about her. Both Alex and I hope that for Jacob's sake that he didn't have much of a connection with Nana and doesn't remember much about her. We really don't want any more loss or trauma for him as he has been through enough.

This afternoon I called Patrick, our social worker but got through to answerphone. He thankfully called back out of his working hours as he knew it would be something of importance for us to call him. He told us not to speak to Jacob about it and tell porkies as this would 'be the best for now'. We aren't sure the reasoning behind it just yet. Having chatted to Alex, we believe we should tell Jacob that Nana has gone to heaven.

We have decided we will tell Jacob tomorrow and tell Patrick our intentions. We can't lie to him and be at his birthday in a couple of days without Nana. This is heart-breaking; I can't comprehend or even begin to think how Alex is feeling. I would be in bits!

7th August - Telling Jacob

This morning was an emotional morning. Over breakfast we told Jacob about how Nana is now living in heaven. We had to try and explain through shaky voices and wobbly lips that Nana lives on a cloud and is looking down on us and looking after us. After a few seconds he turned to look outside, looked up at the sky and said *'I can't see Nana in the clouds'*. That got both myself and Alex right in the feels!

Sunday will be so hard when we have Jacob's birthday party. There will be a clear presence missing from the day.

We are playing in the garden today because we need something low key for us all as we are feeling the pain and exhaustion of the last few days. Jacob seems none the wiser really; he is just playing with Play-Doh and digging up all the garden stones border with the JCB truck – which is Georges. He keeps asking for us to buy him one and we keep telling him *money doesn't grow on trees*. Something my mother used to tell me too. I am sure she once told me to go and look for one in the field (we used to live on a farm). I wonder what sayings Jacob will pick up off us two in the future.

Patrick also called whilst I was out buying the balloons for Jacobs party and what a waste of time that was! There was no substance to it. It felt like a complete tick in the box exercise, and it is quite possible it is. He asked to look at Jacob's room and the house; all in the name of safeguarding, which we understand especially in Jacob's case. He was surprised at how clean it was, but then he knew how tidy Alex is.

9th August - 4th Birthday

Today has been an absolute blast. We stayed over at Alex's sisters and had a birthday party for Jacob there. COVID stopped us having one with his friends, so it was nice to have one with all of the family. The one clear missing person was Nana, but Jacob and the rest of the family managed to do really well and make sure the day was about him.

Out of his earshot we did acknowledge Nana and ate a piece of cake for her. She could have eaten the whole cake to herself.

We went overboard on presents too. I can't believe how much we spent, but as it was his first birthday we wanted him to really enjoy it. Why the hell not, huh?

My favourite part of the day was watching the delight of all of the family singing *'Happy Birthday'* to Jacob. It is clear and evident that Jacob is completely and utterly integrated into our wider family and looked as though he is fully accepting of it himself.

16th August - Walks

We have been on so many walks lately. The desire to do something with Jacob but to keep it relatively low key and so not to overwhelm him (and us!) has been pretty high on the agenda. The last week or so has been pretty quiet and uneventful overall. Maybe we are all still decompressing and processing the last few weeks as well. It has been emotionally tough and very hard on Alex, but you'd never know. I can't begin to think how he's feeling. He isn't really talking about it or showing any emotion around the subject should it arise and it worries me a little that he is compartmentalising and not dealing with his own grief for the sake of a brave face in front of Jacob. I would rather he just let it out when Jacob has gone to bed.

21st August - Diggerland Trip

We had the most amazing day today at Diggerland. So much for keeping it low-key! Jacob absolutely loves diggers so when we arrived he couldn't stop jumping up and down in the queue, completely full of excitement. People in the queue were smiling at us because they could see how much he wanted to be there; it was so cute! All day we went on the rides and diggers, over and over again. The joy and happiness that he projected was completely amazing to watch. He loved his day. I particularly enjoyed sitting on the diggers with him and controlling them. Just being with him and guiding him how to do things was exactly how I envisaged being a good father. Something I never had as a child. I also really enjoyed watching the dynamics of both Alex and Jacob. They both have a clear and amazing bond forming. I just see a happy family and that delights me. A normal, happy, loving family.

25th August - Nana's Dinner

Alex's mother was due to be cremated and it was decided by his family that we should all be together over some lunch at Nana's favourite restaurant. There were only 2 people able to be at the crematorium due to the COVID-19 policies, so that didn't work to be there. The day was a happy, yet sad day. Our whole family found it very tough, but also comforting to be together. I am so happy that Jacob got to meet her and vice versa. We got a couple of photos and that's something we will cherish forever. Lots of love to you up there, mother! We will miss you so much.

2nd September - 1st Day of School

Today is Jacob's first day of school. We took the obnoxious obligatory pictures at the front door in his school uniform but unlike others couldn't post them to social media and show off about how proud we are of him. I did find that a bit of shame to not be able to show how proud we on social media (thats life now, right!), but safeguarding him is the priority for us all. Both of us went with him to drop him off at the classroom door where he recognised his new teacher from the taster day. He liked her, so went in without so much of a worry. We got a massive kiss and cuddle and overemphasised that we would be there waiting for him after school. I was wondering if any of us would get happy-upset, but none of us did. Jacob was so brave and took to it really well. I am so proud of him. We both are. He is such a resilient little boy.

During the day we did very little. I actually had a snooze. Winner!

When we collected him at 3.30pm he was smiling and happy. He'd had a small accident throughout the day, but overall he loved it and that was confirmed by his teacher. Over dinner he told us that he got to play all day, and we could clearly see he was exhausted too. I bet he sleeps well tonight.

6th September - Duck to Water

Jacob has finished his first full week of school and he has really enjoyed it. I am so proud of him being so resilient and receptive to a new environment. He has even made friends and tells us about them over dinner. He is struggling to get much out and he is completely shattered, but he is loving it. He has taken to it like a duck to water and he is going to thrive in that environment, I can tell.

ADOPTION APPLICATION

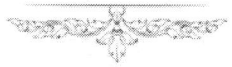

10th September - 10 Weeks

We have now had Jacob placed with us for 10 weeks and at the first opportunity this morning Alex had sent an email to the social workers to ask for the process and for any paperwork that we need to fill out to formally start to apply for the adoption order. Patrick got back to us relatively quickly with the paperwork required which in turn we are to then send back to him for checking. We will then send this onto the courts for processing. Not surprisingly there is a fee attached to the application, but we expected that. There is always a fee!

11th September - Information Required

Julie joined the email chain with further information that was needed regarding birth family and care order and placement order reference numbers. The application is very detailed and I am glad Alex is filling in these forms. The information is pretty factual and asks about us, Jacob and his birth family. All in all, it was simple enough (Alex said), but still a pain in the backside to pull it all together. Frankly, this is the application that will dictate our futures together, so however tedious it may be we would always complete it. Alex will send it off to Patrick and Julie for checking and amendments if required.

15th September - Social Worker Visit

We had Patrick visit today. We spent it out in the garden because that was where Jacob wanted to play. We discussed the adoption order application and what the next steps are and a likely timescale. It is all in the hands of the courts now, so we just need to sit tight and wait for a reply. We have been forewarned that it is likely to take some time as there have 'been delays'. Of course there have been! Other than discussing the adoption order application, Patrick just wanted to see how we had been getting on and if we had any questions. He told us that we were doing a great job and that he is very happy to see how connected we were with Jacob. That was lovely to hear. We think we are doing a good job! Jacob is engaged with us, shows love and affection and is polite and well behaved. He is also very loved as much as our hearts can. He is our little high-energy bundle of joy! We love him so much and we would be heartbroken should the order not be accepted. I shouldn't think like that. Positive thoughts only from now!

16th September - School and PEP (Pupil Education Plan)

Julie has been in direct contact with the school to ascertain who the designated LAC (looked after child) teacher is and to schedule Jacob's PEP. This one hour meeting will look at his current needs, development plan and how he is currently performing against the key metrics in school. We were advised that many children that have a similar background may have developmental concerns, so this PEP will certainly be a good marker to understand how we can help Jacob develop and grow. Julie also advised to be prepared to hear that he may be behind and not to be shocked by such information. It's common for LAC children to be a little behind the curve; that doesn't mean they will be, or that they won't catch up. I think she was helping us protect ourselves. No parent wants to hear that their child is struggling.

19th September - Request for Weekend Break

As we share parental responsibility with the LA (local authority) we still need to request to be able to take a trip outside of the home should we be staying over. As this one is on the south coast and for a few days, we have formally requested it today. We are hoping to see my mother just before Halloween and my birthday. I am sure there will be no concerns with us going away as it's in the UK after all. I believe it is much more difficult at this same stage of adoption, should you want to go abroad. COVID stops that anyway! Alex grew up travelling abroad at a young age and so wants Jacob to enjoy all of the experiences that he has personal and fond memories of. I would like that too, but I am also cool with the UK too.

20th September - Confirmation

After a couple of return questions from Julie, we eventually got the confirmation we wanted to be able to travel. We will be able to go to see my mother and spend some time in a little cottage on the south coast with her. It is superb and most notably it is our first holiday as a family. How exciting!

26th September - First Train Journey

Jacob has been desperate to go on a train for so long now, so today we decided to do it and take him on one. We planned to go to the city centre and have some food. He was so excited to get to the train station that he got ready in record time (which still felt like 4 hours long) but it was an improvement on previous times. Jacob loved the whole process of getting the ticket, going onto the platform, watching the train arrive and the boarding. He then loved the conductor asking for the tickets as he handed them over. I just didn't appreciate that what we as adults perceive as small and menial activities, he would really enjoy and gain some excitement out of it. I really enjoyed that he got some much excitement from it.

After waving the train off, we headed to a restaurant and for the next few hours he was a dream. It was nice to be able to have adult conversations and also to not have to constantly engage and battle with him to eat something. He just wanted to draw, eat and join in our conversations. I really enjoyed the day out and I am confident that he had a great time too. He certainly loved the train journey home too.

A bit of a side note which I found very interesting. I caught a few side glances from people in the restaurant as Jacob called us 'Daddy Alex' and 'Daddy Joe'. People were clearly trying to work it all out and what the dynamics are.

30th September - Email Exchanges

Over the past few days Alex has been dealing with a number of emails so he completed the documentation he can send off the adoption order application off. There is so much detail required and I am still glad he is dealing with it all. Things like ID, DBS checks, employment references etc. There was me thinking it was simple, when in reality there is a lot of detail needed.

Julie has also confirmed her next visit will be on the 13th October. She has unfortunately had some illness in the family, not related to COVID-19, and she has been so apologetic at not coming to see Jacob earlier. I have always been impressed with the level of investment she has had in him and the complete desire to make sure he has a loving and safe home. Similarly the level of support she has offered us has been fantastic.

6th October - Application Lodged

Alex has sent off our application. How very exciting! Let's hope this is a simple and easy process here on in.

10th October - Therapy and Mailbox

Julie is working hard today! We have been discussing the mailbox contact (letters to birth family and back) for the future and the agreement on what we would like to do. We are 100% in favour of annual letters without photos to Jacob's birth mother. We have always been clear on that front because we believe it will help both her and Jacob as he grows older and starts to understand and ask questions about his situation.

Additionally, we have accepted the therapy sessions that we have been offered. We are all in favour of additional support and guidance, so it makes sense for us to take it on. I am not sure what we will discuss and need support with at present because Jacob is presenting as settled and very well connected to us. We are going into these sessions at the mercy of the therapist and trust she will provide the direction needed to enhance our family relationships and Jacob's development.

13th October - Social Worker Call

Due to the current restrictions the social worker visit here has been cancelled. It is such a shame as we really enjoy our time with Julie. She has been fantastic from the moment we met her. We still did a video call with her and she was very happy with the standard of parenting we are giving and how happy Jacob presents himself. It is still very pleasing to receive such nice comments. She interacted with him on video and he got a little shy seeing her. Julie mentioned it is common when seeing social workers post placement that the adopted child can seem a little worried or anxious. Luckily we haven't had much of that as most of the interactions have been via video. We really don't want him connecting her with a move and certainly not one away from us. We have been working on 'permanence' with him so much, so don't want to take any steps backwards.

24th October - Half Term

It's half term and holiday time. Woo-hooo!

Jacob has been very fidgety this morning and he slept pretty badly. He has also been quite clingy and cuddly. I am concerned about him as he will be worried about his permanence and forever home status. The last time he was likely to have seen a full suitcase full of his clothes and toys was the time he moved from his foster carers to us. I wonder what he is thinking about so I can fix it. Alex and I thought we had done enough to ease his mind and offer the reassurance that all of us would be going on holiday and coming home together too. We have been talking about 'when we get back' and using similar terms to try and help him understand this is not a permanent move for him. I bet his mind is going crazy inside even if he's not really showing it externally. We will need to manage this carefully in the next few days. On the flip side, when we do get back and drive that what we said was true, it could work in our favour too.

Time to get in the car now… this could be a fun 4-5 hour drive! I am ready to play eye spy for hours!

We arrive at a good time and Jacob has been an absolute dream in the car. We did prepare well (tablet, toys and teddies). We even stopped off at a service station and bought some things. This was actually something that triggered an old memory, something I completely didn't expect and that took me by surprise. Alex waited in the car and I think I held my nerve and he wasn't aware when I got back in. The story… when I was a child, my brother and I were taken (some might say kidnapped) from my mother, by our so-called 'Dad' in what I remember as a very distressing scenario. I am quite certain I saw some domestic violence, but I was very young. My memory of it was that he took us and bundled us into the car. Halfway to where we were going we stopped at a service station with a Little Chef (it was the 80's) and I fully remember the layout of the restaurant too. At this point he bought us both a toy in an attempt to stop us from being upset. All I remember was throwing it out of the window. It was a small set of bubbles. The rest of that memory in the weeks after really makes me sad. Memories of 'PC

O'Neill' the policeman who used to bring his dog in the house and scare the life out of us. Our 'dad' would tell us things like we would 'go to jail' or 'set the dog on us' if we didn't go to sleep. What a horrible, horrible man!

It makes my childhood sound bad and it was far from it in comparison to most. Some of it was pretty crap, but my super-hero mother moved mountains to protect us and I wholeheartedly would lay down my life for her if needed. I don't know how to express my complete love for that woman. On the other hand I would hate to see him again in my lifetime. I would love to see my brother see him, however. Although I wouldn't want to see my brother go to jail as that is not his character in the slightest. He's a superb person but seeing our 'dad' would change that in 10 minutes due to the bond we share with our mother and the protective nature we have for her.

25th October - Grandmums

We had dinner (or tea as we call it up t'north) with my mother last night and we are seeing her again today. I am conscious of Alex and the recent event with his mum, but he doesn't seem to be fazed by it. He is bloody stronger than I have ever given him credit for.

Jacob is really looking forward to seeing Grandmums again today. We are off to the beach and he's been talking about it for ages because he wants to build a sandcastle. I think he might explode with excitement when we get there. He's so pumped to build a sandcastle.

We met Grandmums at her house. Again, I got upset with happy tears. I miss my mother so much and as she is so far away we don't get to see her so much. I feel like since I have become a father I cry more and I've never been a crier. My hormones must have shifted left. I'm unsure how to articulate why I got upset, but I think it is for a number of reasons. Alex's mum, my mum living 4 hours away, the protective mentality of my mother and so on; it just hit me that she is so far away. I know she wouldn't want me to think that way, yet I want to give her everything I can to give back to her for the most amazing upbringing. Alex was very understanding, loving and importantly, respectful.

Once I had composed myself we set off to the beach. It was lovely to see my family (Jacob, Alex and mum) really enjoying time together. Jacob ran straight for the sea and was paddling straight away. I struggled to keep up with him with my knackered back so my mother jogged on after him. Within 5 minutes both inevitably ended up on their backsides in the freezing cold sea. A small wave knocked Jacob off balance (it was less than small wellington-boots height) and my mother went to catch him. It ended up with them both falling over. I was laughing and trying to take a picture, knowing they were both OK and not hurt. It was also very interesting to see Alex run straight in there and 'save' Jacob and then my mother. Alex wouldn't have run in for me, so it just shows how his mindset has changed to be a protective parent.

Dried off, walk completed and a number of sandcastles later, we headed off for some Sunday lunch. I can't tell you how much I've loved this because Jacob went and sat straight next to my mother and for the next two hours, they just interacted and really enjoyed each other's company. I could see the love in both of them for one another.

I'm going to bed a very, very happy and proud father and son!

26th October - Pumpkin Picking

As Halloween is coming up we went pumpkin picking and my mother came with us. We had an amazing time and Jacob picked lots of pumpkins that we had to carve out. Luckily there were carving spaces at the place we visited so we all had a go at doing one each. I particularly enjoyed watching my mother and Jacob interacting again. It was as if they had known each other for years. My mother is besotted by him and it was actually hard to wrestle some attention of Jacob back from her. We took a lot of photos too and I know in years to come I will look back on them with very fond memories. It was a very pleasant few hours in each others company.

In the evening we went for dinner and Jacob wanted to sit next to Grandmum's without hesitation, again. They were having a great time together and he was giving her lots of love and kisses. The way she gave him love reminded me of how she used to show us love when we were children. Lovely memories!

27th October - Going Home

We travelled home today and I was pretty upset when we left. As my mother lives so far away we don't get to see her that much and with all the things that have happened recently with Alex's mother, I am all the more aware of how time spent with family is super important and we all know I am a mummy's boy anyway. I keep hounding her to come and move closer to home. We would love for Jacob to be able to grow up with his Grandmums around.

4th November - Kiss and Cuddle

Jacob did something I haven't seen before this morning. He refused to give Alex his morning kiss and cuddle. That is completely out of character. We are unsure why he has done this, although we think it is because he hasn't seen much of me in the last few days. I have been coming home late from work. It was suggested in some training we had that it maybe Jacob trying to show his attachment for me and subconsciously trying to win me over as he fears me 'leaving him'. We spoke to the social workers and they believe that could be part of it.

I need to make sure I come home earlier. Alex is OK with it because he has had a few days of lots of attention from Jacob recently. I am sure it will be a short temporary blip.

5th November - LAC Review

He's back to normal today. It must have been a bad day yesterday.

It was LAC (Looked After Child) review day today and was hosted by someone new, again. The lead of the call did very little really, bar going through the report that Julie had compiled. Patrick, our social worker, is a little redundant now for input but he is still there as a representation for us should we need him. We don't feel like we do need anything from him at the moment. It was a tick box exercise from his side. What we did take away however, was that we are doing a great job and that we need to continue doing what we are doing.

We have also had a meeting with the therapist today too. Julie has arranged this for us with the intention of having intervention based Theraplay sessions to help us as parents and Jacob with his mindset. The meeting was on Zoom because I was in work when it was scheduled for at lunchtime. We have said we would take any - and every bit - of support and help so we can ensure Jacob gets the best chance in life.

After spending an hour on the call, we've realised that we do need this, even though we thought everything is going amazingly well with the placement. On the face of it Jacob has been an absolute dream, yet we have come away seeing behind the facade he sometimes presents. These sessions will be looking at the actions and the reason to acknowledge support and possibly overcome some of the things we see. The best part for me was learning about permanence and *'talking to his fears'*. The session was only to set the expectations of the next 30 sessions we are due to receive but I went off on a tangent.

Within an hour of me getting home tonight Alex has already told me to chill out and calm down with the expressions of permanence for Jacob. I was going on about next week, Christmas, how long it would be before Jacob got as tall as me, etc. It was a lot and way too much in hindsight. I was trying to *'speak to his fears'*.

7th November - Uncle Ryan 2

'What is a d*ckhead?'

We went for a walk today and we had our first swear word; not from Jacob either! Jacob is very inquisitive and *'why?'* or *'what is/are'* are his favourite words at the best of times, however today was a beauty. Uncle Ryan 2 (another one) was holding Jacob's hand and also the lead of his dog as we walked up the hill. Dave (the dog) ran across the pathway and pulled the lead causing Ryan to be a little off balance; to which Ryan articulately and instinctively called Dave a *'dickhead'*.

Ryan:
'Oi dickhead'

Jacob - straight away…
'What is a dickhead?'

He is 4 years old and so sharp. (Jacob, not Ryan). At this point we didn't really know how to react, bar a sharp intake of breath and to suppress a huge laugh. Cue distracting tactics. Of course we don't want any swear words to be heard. In 4 months he hasn't heard any from us and then hilariously this happens. It was so funny - yet on a more serious note - we hope he has forgotten the word already. I won't bet on it as he has come out with some other things out of the blue when we didn't expect it.

Uncle Ryan - You're a d*ckhead!

THERAPY SESSIONS

10th November - First Therapy Session

The first session with the therapist was completed tonight. I'm not going to lie and say I was really looking forward to it. The session did exactly what I didn't need it to do, but also on the flip side of the coin, it gave me what I wanted too. That's quite contradictory but I have come to the realisation that I need to manage my expectations and emotions more than I thought I did. I really went in open minded, but I struggled.

Some of the 'interventions' got me overthinking and starting to look for things that I am unsure are actually there. The big question regarding some of the actions that Jacob does is *'Is he doing this because there is an underlying concern that we need to look out for and manage, or is he just being a 4 year old boy?'*

There were lots of buzz words being bandied around on the call and it came across as therapy textbook wording. I am not averse to different ways of thinking or *'looking through his lens'* but it seems very open ended and *'maybe this/that'*.

What we did get from it by the end of the call was the acceptance to work on different 'interventions'. We asked about why Jacob may have become so attached to his teddy in recent weeks. His current attachment is way more than it was previously. The therapist believes it's attributed to loss, attachment and comfort. She then talked us through some things to make sure we do; such things like accepting Bear (his name) if Jacob wants to take him somewhere or keep hold and cuddle him (he's a boy too). It was suggested that he uses this as a way of showing his emotions, but not consciously knowing what he is doing. We have also been told to try talking to Bear directly about things we want to know about Jacob. For example, to ask Bear how he is feeling, or what he would like for tea. She believes that Jacob will use Bear as a medium to his own emotions, effectively answering through Bear.

13th November - Personal Education Plan

Today was the first PEP (personal education plan) meeting with the school and Julie, our social worker. It was also attended by the local authority to confirm (or deny) the funding allocation as they are eligible for £2,000.

Jacob has settled in really well but I still have my concerns. I only see him before and after school, so I can only see the very small snap shots. I rarely hear him talking about his friends at school and he often struggles with any names of the children. I fear he may be left out a little, but I am assured they are my own fears and not ones others share.

It started with a bit of an introduction and then an overview of this session being a PEP and what this means. This being our first, I had to stop the Deputy Head teacher and ask him to explain the process and agenda. It was really quite simple. The school was to offer their ideas on Jacob's development and some ways to improve these. The plan would then be reviewed. Jacob's teacher then took over to give her update and opinion. She started off by telling us how much *'you can tell that Jacob is loved so much'*... well, that made me so proud and my heart melted. They say when someone has a child, their hormones change. I think mine have and they have made me become a little more emotional. I held it together but with a beaming smile.

Then the school went on to tell us how he is doing so well, with a couple of points to work on. He has some concerns regarding his social interaction, fine motor skills, speech and sharing. The last one took me by surprise a little, as he has been so good with George next door. Maybe I see the good bits only and the best in him as opposed to a non-emotional and impartial view. The school has set him some goals but also used the money they have been granted to bring in a play therapist and buy some tools to help with his fine motor skills.

I was also worried as his teacher suggested she had been to see the 'special needs' teacher. In my head that meant that he could have special needs. I had to take a breath. The special needs teacher is used for all sorts of information.

The first thing I did after the meeting was to Google *fine motor skills* and things to help Jacob improve on them.

14th November - Time Alone, Well Needed

Alex took Jacob to see Grandad this morning after his swimming lessons. I absolutely love watching Jacob swimming and seeing him develop and improve week on week. We had a few issues at first with him having some worries around us handing him over to the instructor, but once he knew we were watching and waiting for him then he overcame his fear and enjoyed it. We also get in the pool together after his lesson and he loves messing and playing around, bless him.

They were out at Grandads and I feel as though I should have felt a little guilty for not spending time with him, but I really enjoyed being on my own and not having a constant noise and need in my ear. I was happy to have the time alone and know I have no reason to feel guilty. When they got home though, I was completely ready for the cuddles and kisses. I did miss him… and Alex.

17th November - Anxiety

I got a call out of the blue, whilst at work, from Alex at about 4.30pm. Jacob asked for the first time today as to whether any *'other little boys have lived here before'*. Well, that took us by surprise and assume there was some form of anxiety in his mind. I think he may be viewing us similarly to the foster carers where other children had been in and out of the home whilst he had been there. Maybe we need to do more work on him understanding his permanence still.

It was quite hurtful for me to hear him thinking in this way. It hurts because I don't want him to feel the insecurity that he may be feeling. He also told Alex that he misses him when he is in school; although school has never mentioned it is affecting him, or more likely, that Jacob is displaying the signs that he is missing us and feeling insecure. I find it hard and upsetting that I can't make him feel secure **now** and have to take it really slowly. I completely recognise that he has had a poor start to his life and his brain and emotions are going to be everywhere. Quite often I would bet that he won't have a clue as to why either. I know it must be so tough for him to make sense of it too. I gave him lots of love and cuddles when I got home.

19th November - Second Therapy Session

We had our session with the therapist this evening. She was quite complimentary in the way we are parenting, but the cynic in me felt that she was building bridges from last week when I was a little frustrated with the start.

The main topic this week was *really* helpful. We spoke a lot about 'ruptures' and 're-builds' and I took a lot away from them but I still feel like she is looking for things that just aren't there. I want to give her some time and have faith in her, but I am struggling overall.

24th November - Third Therapy Session

We had another session tonight with the therapist. It didn't go very well. Although I know Jacob has had a different start to life and there will be missing cognitive connections affecting different parts of his brain and development, I felt like the therapist was throwing out far too many boxes to put Jacob in.

It was so frustrating. At one point the therapist suggested some actions to note that if Jacob did / didn't do, then there could be some cause of concern. Alex sat and nodded at pretty much all (things like 'is he clumsy, does he grab at things and miss them?') and I sat there and thought *'pretty much every 4 year old does that.'*

I felt it was like when you have a cold and you go onto the internet and all of a sudden you have lung cancer. I just want the therapist to come and spend time with Jacob and actually see it for herself as opposed to *'might'* and *'could'* have a concern. Stop putting him in a box, please. Just come and meet him!

I really can't carry on with these. I am so protective of Jacob already and I can't bear to listen to any more rubbish or generalised theories based upon very little, to no, evidence.

25th November - Reflection

In hindsight, I can understand what the therapist was trying to do, but I can't get off my emotional high horse. I am obviously protecting my little boy and not wanting for him to be pigeonholed; yet I am still very aware and accepting that he has had a different and challenging start to life. This is about playing the percentages game and there is a high percentage chance that not all the cognitive and physical connections have been made from being a baby and the neglect that he received.

This afternoon we also got an email from the therapist with her addressing both social workers and us. I felt a little like the therapist was a little condescending; although she was probably not. *'...I appreciate that therapeutic support can be a difficult journey for parents...'* Piss off. That's it now with her! I don't fancy it.

30th November - Santa's Letter & Decorations

Santa delivered Jacob his letter today. We have been very careful on how we wrote this and tried to be subtle with some tools to support his thoughts on permanence. For example, we spoke about next year and how Santa is keen to see how he *'grows up with his forever family'*. When he opened it there was some excitement that Santa had written back, however I am unsure whether it brought up some old memories as he was pretty subdued and looked a little glazed over. We certainly need to be conscious and aware that this time may bring up memories of his birth family and maybe also last year with his foster carers.

We also put up the tree and decorations which we had a blast doing. The Christmas songs were on, the mood was fantastic and the energy high to get working on the tree. Not long after we had got started, Jacob got bored pretty quickly, however soon became excited and re-engaged again when it was time to switch on the lights and put the star on the top of the tree. He was adamant he was going to be the one that did that. His sheer delight at doing it was enough to justify the 30 minutes it took to put the tree up. We even got a rendition of *'We wish you a Merry Christmas'* from Jacob too. He sings like Daddy Alex… badly!

I have had such a lovely day today seeing how much Jacob loved it and how much joy we had as a family.

1st December - Mountain Out of Molehill

We had a call with Patrick about the therapy sessions and it seems that there has been a mountain made from a molehill. I am just struggling with the process and not understanding a 'potential' diagnosis or suggestion of something I do not see through evidence based knowledge. Everything seems to have a 'potential' negative connotation to it. I don't doubt that Jacob has some demons in his mind that he can't control for the reasons of his younger life and the trauma he has gone through, but because has knocked a glass over - like every bloody 4-year-old - he seems to have X problem. I am pretty pi**ed off and it may stem from being overprotective and blind to some things, but I don't doubt that some of it is crap.

It's all very frustrating. We need to cancel them. I can't do any more sessions.

2nd December - Therapist Call

Patrick asked for us to have a call with himself and the therapist. I don't want it to happen right now as I am emotionally drained and frustrated by it all. I called him and told him that was the case and that I want to wait until next year to do it and restart the sessions.

I feel like the bad guy here and I can kind of see why; however, I can't see the value in something that (selfishly) makes me feel rubbish and that I don't understand. Because there is no concrete evidence as to 'why' regarding the theories, I just struggle to buy into it and I think it will affect the way I would parent Jacob. I want the therapist to be present in a live scenario watching Jacob, Alex and I via video, in person or a recorded session and then offer some form of diagnosis or theory. Right now it's based on complete theoretical scenarios, not evidence. I am not buying it, still.

10th December - Parents Evening

Parents' evening and I wasn't sure what to expect or how it would go. I was worried but also quite calm going into this because we had not long had his LAC (Looked After

Child) review and the school gave us a superb update and plan regarding his current progress and opportunities to grow then. What we didn't expect was the manner in which his teacher spoke about him. Jacob was said to have come on with such things as his gross motor skills and sharing. I was so proud of him, again. I am 100% attached and love this little boy and I couldn't imagine our life without him. My heart gushes each time I see him; although when it's 7am and I am knackered, I could do with 5 more minutes (please).

14th December - Social Worker Visit

We had Patrick around at the house tonight. I know he is our social worker, but I am not at the stage where respectfully, that if he didn't come around again I would miss him. I am just not sure what we are getting from the 'visits' now. I acknowledge these visits are not primarily about us and are for seeing Jacob and for his safeguarding. Alex feels the same too, frankly. We only have a few more months left of his visits until the full adoption is completed we hope and speaking of that, we have been advised we need to go and do the medicals again because it was over 2 years ago since we did those. I may need to head out on a few runs and have some salads before the big weigh in. I have put on a few pounds since then and last time they told me my BMI was a little high. I need to stop snacking on Jacob's leftovers, but I keep reading the 'dad-bod' is in.

20th December - Gullivers World

We went to Gullivers World theme park today. I was consciously aware of other parents and how they 'parent' today whereas previously I would never really have been bothered. I can safely say, from the very quick outside view, both Alex and I are doing a good job. I know observing parents and children at a theme park in a queue for a ride isn't the best measuring stick, however it has highlighted how patient, tolerant and loving we are to Jacob.

One child actually kicked his mother and it made me really sad to see it. She was very embarrassed and upset by it yet tried to keep a brave face. I do wonder how it may be at home for them. I hope her boy isn't that much of a pain on a day-to-day basis and I am not judging as I certainly don't know the circumstances. One major learning I have had from being a parent of an adopted child is that I don't now judge people and how they are parenting or how their child is behaving. There are so many varying factors to it and without the full knowledge of the situation we shouldn't judge them. My opinions have changed.

Jacob was a very good lad today and he was willing to try lots of the rides and explore things he has not done before. I have learned to have a lot of patience as a parent too. On the whole he was very well behaved and he had his 'listening ears' on most of the day. It was another cracking family day and one we will have fond memories of for sometime.

21st December - Cousin's Birthday

We went to see some family today as it was one of our nephews' birthdays. Before we set off, I had the idea to go to Build-a-Bear as his current bear that he is completely obsessed with was from his foster carers. He seems to be stuck to the bear a lot and quite frankly I am jealous of it and the memories that he has with it. I know that is selfish and silly, however I want him to feel part of our family and let go of some of the past. I don't want him to forget his past, but to be more mindful and in the moment regarding his current situation. The idea I had (selfishly) was to create our own bear and memory. I want him to have both bears and be happy with the one we got him too. Maybe I subconsciously want him to acknowledge that he has a forever family with us, putting us on a level playing field with his foster carers. I am pretty sure I am overthinking it again.

Speaking of which he has been mentioning his foster carers an awful lot recently. We are putting that down to the fact that it is coming to Christmas and it is likely his only memories - or good memories - of this time would have been last year when he was with them. I bet there are so many triggers (not including the Build-a-Bear one that we created) that are making him think of his past.

In the car home he started talking about his foster carers. At 'X' we did this and at 'Y' she did that. It really hurts inside as it feels like you are being compared all the time to them and quite often it feels like I am not as good as them. We do reassure Jacob that it is OK to speak about them however, because we would not want to stop him, yet more importantly we acknowledge that they were a huge part of his life and his only safe space at the point where he needed it the most. They gave him the things he never had but needed.

Alex thinks it's the triggers and time of year that are causing it. He is likely correct but it still hurts to feel second best. I had some tears to myself earlier. I know we are doing a good job. I (we) love him so much that it hurts to think he may not reciprocate in some form.

24th December - Magical 1st Christmas Eve

Tonight was such a magical day and we had a wonderful evening too. We spent a lot of the day watching Christmas films, eating chocolate and just generally being excited about Christmas Day.The family time we spent today has been invaluable and I have loved each moment of the day making memories.

Surprisingly Jacob went straight to bed at 7pm and straight to sleep. I think this was two-fold through fatigue and the desire to wake up on Christmas Day as soon as possible. Before he did go to bed we spread the reindeer food in the garden and put out the milk, mince pie and carrots for your visitors tonight.

Now all the presents are under the tree, we can get straight to bed. I am sure Jacob will be up earlier than we would prefer! I know I was when I was young.

25th December - Christmas Day

I was quite emotional watching Jacob opening his presents this morning. He was so grateful and appreciative of all of the things he received. I am pretty sure that it is his natural nature and personality shining through, but I also do suspect based on the evidence of information we are aware of, that he was genuinely happy to receive the gifts he did.

The day must have been very overwhelming for him as we had all of the family around at our house too. It was busy, noisy and he had so many things to play with his brain must have been working overtime. He also ended up staying up late, so he was shattered by the end of the evening.

We had an amazing day as a family. One I will cherish forever and one that I hope he will remember too.

P.s. - next year, not as many gifts.

31st December - New Years Eve

We had a couple of days just after Christmas where some of the family stayed over post Christmas, so it was all go. In between then and now, we have done very little to try and bring the excitement levels down. We felt it to be very important for Jacob to decompress and have zero agenda. Tonight however, we will have the neighbours over and celebrate the coming of the new year.

1st January - New Years Day

Jacob absolutely loved yesterday. He got to spend lots of time with our neighbour's little boy, George. They just played the night away whilst the adults put the world to rights. It was a superb night and a great ending to the festive period. I'm back to work in a few days so happy to have some family and down time.

5th January - Back at Work

I am back at work and I can honestly say I am glad that I am. It has been so full on for the past few weeks, that I am very pleased to be back in some form of structure. I never thought I would say that!

20th January - Social Worker Call

We had our chat with Patrick tonight, and he came up with some really good points. This was the most useful chat we have had with him in a while. The conversation was started with no agenda but progressed into talking through some of the behaviours Jacob has presented recently. Some are good and some are not-so-good. One was around his teddy that he loves so much. It's the one that came with him from his foster carers. This progressed onto Patrick asking if we'd had any contact with them at all. We haven't, although we had spoken about it over Christmas to send her a card or send a text; although we didn't want to intrude on their family time over the festive period. In addition, we didn't want to re-introduce Jacob to them at that time either as we could already see he was battling with some emotions and thoughts. Anyway, it has got us thinking about whether we should speak to them and see if they want to have a chat with Jacob over video. Patrick is pro this idea and he believes that although it may cause some uncomfortable emotions it will be great in the future as he will grow up with his identity intact and not have any missing pieces. We agree, although we hadn't fully thought about it in the past.

We also discussed the same about his birth parents as we are due letterbox contact soon. Again, the same scenario applies here and we will speak tonight (Alex and I) about how we will re-introduce the conversation about his mother; or high level, about mothers in general. This one is a little more controversial than the foster carers discussion, but maybe it has to happen at some stage.

28th January - Message to Foster Carer

We decided to message Jacob's old foster carer to see if she would want to chat to him. She replied pretty quickly and was very responsive to arrange a video call and chat with him. She had said she had missed him lots and that she was happy we had sent lots of photos over which she commented about how much he has grown and changed.

It was not a tough decision to make in regard to wanting the call to happen, but more of a worry that it could bring up lots of emotions or memories for him. We constantly worry and are conscious about his past and we don't want to bring back any memories that may cause hurt; even though in this case those memories would be lovely ones of love and safety. We don't want the call to set him back emotionally.

I guess we will only find out when it happens. In the grand scheme of things this should be a positive experience.

30th January - Foster Carer Call

We had the call tonight with his foster carers and what a lovely call it was. It was superb for us adults to chat again, however it was a bit of a weird call in regard to Jacob's interactions. He wasn't completely attentive and showed some small dismissive behaviours when chatting to the foster carer. We aren't sure if he was protecting himself or had just forgotten about her a little bit. His foster carer thought it could be that he was thinking about his birth mother and confusing them both as young minds often confuse timings, events and even people. We are not sure.

One thing that we hadn't seen before was when Jacob was taking out some of his toys to show them and he pulled out Spiderman. This was a present from his birth mother and it looks as though he had some memories in his mind at that point. Alex swore that he saw Jacob a little upset; it wasn't obvious and if he was, he quickly re-compartmentalised it. I didn't see it, so I am not sure.

After the call he seems to have been fine and taken it all in his stride. I hope he is OK in the morning and coming days. We will have to keep an eye on him to see if anything changes.

31st January - Day After

He seems to have taken the call all in his stride and we haven't seen any immediate reaction in his emotions or behaviours. All seems well and we hope that continues.

3rd February - Wet Nights

Jacob has been wetting his pull ups at night again. He had been going through a stage of not doing this overnight, yet it seems like it's back. I hope it's a coincidence and not anything to do with the call, however I suspect it has brought back some subconscious memories and feelings. Or maybe he is just being lazy and not getting out of bed in the morning. We will keep an eye on it and see if we can understand.

9th February - Friends Suicide

Today has been a very tough day for me! I received a phone call from one of my friends to tell me that another friend from our social group has made the ultimate decision to end his life by suicide. I have been in floods of tears all day wondering if there was anything I could have done for him to have not done this and for him to have changed his mind. I think the shock of it being him was the hardest part as if someone had presented me with a list of all my friends, he would have been the last on the list of people who I would have said would have thought this was his way out. I am devastated for him, his family and his friends. He was a huge influence on me when I moved here back in 2008. We actually met in 2009 when I bought my motorbike. I was going through my own mini-crisis not knowing my own identity and reason for being where I was. For the previous 8 years, I'd had a purpose and reason and (in hindsight) a very good job that I loved. All was good until I thought the grass was greener. My mate had been there for me, probably without even knowing it. A motorbike ride and a cup of coffee goes a bloody long way.

He is (was) an incredible bloke with bags of empathy and love for all people around him. He didn't deserve what happened. Weirdly, I hope he is now happy. I have a lot of love for that guy.

Back at home I think Jacob has surely seen me affected by this because I have been a little subdued and often in thought. It's so hard, emotionally. I have been a bit snappy I think with both Alex and Jacob too. I shouldn't take it out on them. I certainly don't mean to.

I didn't know whether to write about this tragic event in this diary, however I really wanted to reference him for a number of reasons. The main one was a complete and utter 'nod' to how much of a bloody great guy he was and how much I know I will miss him. Each time I read this, I will remember him as a superb bloke and one that influenced me in many positive ways. He also met Jacob on a few occasions when Alex dropped us off at the pub. He was a great outlet for me in the run up and early few months of Jacob being home. A top bloke!

For you, mate. Lots of love. X

13th February - Measuring Love

'I love you to the moon and back'... or France, or London, or Uganda. It has been very funny. Jacob has been learning new countries and has been measuring how much he loves us by using the distance to them.

We have also been using the same with him. We are aware that we need to reassure him that he is loved by us and so we use the same thing he does to tell him back. He loves the game and tries to go further and further. He has no idea where these places are or how far, but it is a fun way to engage.

14th February - Not Listening

He is just not bloody listening and we are both getting to the point of nearly shouting at him. We know we should not - and we haven't - but it's got to a point as to where we need to do something to stop this cycle. It's really hurting Alex's mentality as Jacob seems to not be listening to him more so than myself. I can see that it is really starting to affect his mood. I think some of this is due to my mood this week too. I have been pretty withdrawn and lacked any patience.

22nd February - A Huge Shock

Today Alex called me at about 3pm as I was in work and before he picked Jacob up from school. We have now been advised via Julie that there is an auntie - maybe two - from Jacob's birth fathers' side that have only recently found out about him and expressed a desire to know more about his situation and whether he is in a forever family home. Julie did say that they expressed that they would have put in an application to adopt him if he wasn't so far in the process with us. Clearly his birth father hasn't told his family about Jacob, which angers me and saddens me too.

I called Julie directly to ask a little more detail as Alex was in a little bit of a daze and shaken up, so I just wanted to get my head around it myself; straight from the horse's mouth as they say. I wanted to know the intention of these aunts as this could be a complete game changer in regard to the legal part of the adoption that we are waiting on. Julie was very honest with her answers and has said that if they do lodge an application to adopt Jacob, then it could be seen as beneficial to him in the long run to be part of his birth family. Jacob is part of a loving and very stable family now, so I personally think it would be catastrophic to his brain causing significant and further trauma. Part of that being due to the messages of us being a forever family and all the work we have done to help him understand he now has permanence in his life.

Julie doesn't think that they will lodge a formal application at this stage. We bloody hope not. I will be devastated should things go belly up from here.

23rd February - PEP Meeting

We had Jacob's PEP (personal education plan) this morning. He has come so far and has progressed in so many ways since the previous one. His social skills and fine motor skills are coming on so well. His sounding out of phonetic letters is coming on and he can read some basic words. She said he is *'significantly closing the gap and you can see that the consistency of school has helped him no-end'*. I am very pleased with him and so happy that he has progressed. Good lad!

They said the main thing that they would now like to work on is his concentration levels towards tasks and sitting still when on the mats. We know he likes a wiggle!

25th February - Unannounced Social Worker Visit

It is as if we haven't heard much from the social workers for a while and then all of a sudden, we are never off the phone. We are happy to have meaningful contact. I had just got home from work tonight and Patrick, our social worker, called out of the blue. I did wonder straight away if it was any news (bad news) regarding the aunts, but it was just the annual unannounced visit. Jacob had just got in the bath and Alex was off to see his father so that was a bit of a whirlwind start and it was quite hard work to keep tabs on the call and a naked Jacob splashing around. Normally he would want to see Jacob, but for obvious reasons we didn't. The call didn't really have much substance to it. More of a check in and house check. Of course, Alex being the cleaning freak that he is, the house was immaculate. Obviously to show Patrick the house, I had to leave Jacob for 20 seconds to run downstairs and in hindsight, Patrick asked if I was sure 2 or 3 times if I was OK to leave him on his own there. Over the time we have had Jacob and bathed him he has been absolutely fine and also played safe, so we feel fine not to have eyes-on every second. Now I am wondering if we are doing something wrong. A classic overthinking issue.

Overall he seemed happy enough with how we are progressing.

27th February - Our First Pet

I am not sure if this was for me or for Jacob, but I went and bought some tropical fish today. I have wanted some for a while and I thought I would make an executive decision today; Alex wasn't all that pleased and made sure I knew the responsibility of the fish, cleaning and any events (i.e deaths) were my responsibility. I got 8 fish and 2 shrimp and I think they look superb. Jacob was very invested in the process of getting them settled into the tank. He is such an inquisitive little boy and constantly wants to learn. Alex wasn't bothered.

28th February - Fish Heaven

Well, that didn't go to plan because it's the morning after and we have only 2 fish left. I really thought I had done everything to make sure the tank and 'ecosystem' (that's what the guy at the pet shop had called it) was in good order and correct. Clearly I got that wrong. Alex laughed a lot. I think it was more regarding the process of what and how I was going to tell Jacob. How was I going to explain this one?

I was at the tank when Jacob came to look at the fish. I had quickly managed to extract the dead fish and send them to heaven before he noticed. Alex was behind Jacob and of course face to face with me; laughing. A lot!

I told Jacob that I had to return them to the pet shop because there wasn't enough space in the tank. *'But Daddy Joe, there is lots of space, look'*. He was right and he caught me out, but I had to stick to my guns. Alex was in hysterics laughing at me behind Jacob's back.
I think I've managed to get away with it; but probably not.

2nd March - Overthinking & Hugs

Jacob went into school this morning with the intention of doing some additional work for his fine motor skills with the PE Teacher. Alex finally managed to have a quick face to face and she was lovely.

'Whatever you are doing at home, keep doing it. Jacob is the most lovely little boy.'

I am not sure she is aware that such a simple comment can give such a HUGE boost to a parent; it certainly has for us. I've mentioned before that overthinking is common for us regarding our ability to parent well and the constant question of *'Are we doing that correctly?'* We know there is not always a black and white answer and it's likely that because we are both exposed to parenting via adoption, we have been semi-indoctrinated to think about the actions we take. When speaking to my mother and other parts of the family they say they hadn't ever thought about the psychology of an action they took as parents or lack of. They just *'get on with it and use our best judgement'*. I guess we just need to do that and trust our instincts but still be mindful of the traumatic experiences Jacob has gone through. So, yeah, I have contradicted myself.

6th March - 'Hurry Up'

I am sitting downstairs and all I can hear is Alex telling Jacob to *'hurry up', 'be quick', 'please just…'* It has just made me realise how much we have to ask him to do something. I know we are not the only ones, but it does get frustrating. I wonder if I was like that as a little boy? I must remember to ask my mum when I next speak to her. I bet I was a complete pain in the backside too.

7th March - Common

Today we had an outdoor photoshoot from a guy on the estate we live on. It is a really nice community that we live in and around. He has been doing lots of photos for other families on the estate too and of course he has had plenty of opportunity to meet the families and talk to them. Whilst we were taking the photos with Jacob we found out that there is another family on the estate that have also adopted a little boy. We have asked if the photographer will approach them for an introduction. It would be nice to have another family close by to share experiences with. It also presents us with an opportunity to ask lots of questions about such things as big school and life events. I hope that we can share some support in return; all being well.

11th March - My First School Pick Up

Today I got to pick up Jacob from school. It was my first time. Not through lack of desire, but more because of timings and work. I have previously felt pretty left out not being able to pick him up but it has been circumstantial and unavoidable. I felt like a novice as I was there early and as I was walking to the gates, all of the other parents were in their cars texting or chatting. I was clearly too keen or naive regarding the timing and process. I texted Alex and he laughed at me.

When the door finally opened to let the children out, the teachers were not sure who I was; they were used to Alex or Grandad picking up Jacob. I had to tell them I was here for Jacob. They shouted for him to come to the doors, probably with the intention of him recognising someone, but when he saw me he absolutely forgot about everything and sprinted to me for a cuddle shouting 'Daddy Joe'. It made me feel so loved by this little boy. There was a nice little touch from his teacher too as she wanted to tell me how well he was doing regarding his grip on his pencils. It is one of his development points.

It has been a very pleasant experience for me. One I think that I took for granted, and one that I really want to do more where possible. I guess the takeaway is that I shouldn't put pressure on myself to do it either due to my work pattern. We have a system that means he is picked up each day and feels safe.

14th March - Mother's Day

I called my mother this morning with Jacob. He was very much interested for the first 30 seconds and then it was back to his cars and building blocks. Alex was still in bed; but I intentionally made the call before he got up. I am acutely aware of this being the first mother's day without his mum and I am unsure how he would be affected by it. I know full-well that he will be sad, yet he will put on a brave face for both Jacob and I. I don't doubt that he will be speaking with his dad and sister later as a nod towards his mum. I hope he is OK; of course I do.

Jacob is also without his birth mother and of course, we are of course two dads, so there is no acknowledgement for him, where others (like me) talk to our mothers about it and celebrate. I do wonder what he is thinking when someone brings up the term 'mum'. He certainly knows he has a mum but I am not sure how he feels about the whole situation; he is only 4. I've also wondered about the arrangement that would have been in place last year when he was in foster placement. He was still having monthly visits to see his birth mum. I would assume that he would have spent some time with her around the day. He hasn't brought anything up, but I think we were both ready to speak through the whole 'mothers day' situation with him.

He hasn't shown any signs of knowing what is going on, but he may in the future if they speak about days like this at school, or of course, he sees it at home with my mother and I. I do have concerns and apprehensions regarding the questions we may receive as he grows older and starts to actually understand his situation.

LEGAL PROCESS

15th March - Court Date

Any chance, or what? I mean come on! We are still waiting on the bloody courts to give us some news and a date for the adoption hearing. It is very frustrating as it's been with them for months now. Both sets of social workers have completed their paperwork and the court has ours so there should be no issue and certainly not this long of a delay. We really want to get things fully formalised as there is the whole situation hanging over our heads that he is still only classed being on a placement order and not fully adopted.

If I am very honest; subconsciously it is currently hard to completely and fully accept that Jacob is part of the family as he technically isn't. To be clear, I am 100% invested in him being 'one of us' and that will NEVER change, but at present there is still that small chance that he could be taken back to his birth family somewhere, so maybe there is a part of my brain protecting my emotions. I love this little boy to the moon and back (and some) and I couldn't imagine my life without him. I am worried about the aunts rearing their heads.

'I love you to everywhere and back' That is his current favourite saying. Me too sunshine!

19th March - 'I've never been a baby'

Last night when putting Jacob to bed he got inside his duvet cover. Smiling, I told him that it was something that I used to do as a little boy too. He then said that *'I haven't ever been a baby'* and also asked if I was a baby at his foster carers too. I explained that he had been a baby and that he had a mummy too.

I also described to him that Grandmums was my mummy and that Grandad was Daddy Alex's daddy. He looked a little confused. He has clearly been thinking about things a lot as he had also told us that he didn't have a middle name. A sign that he is thinking usually is either him completely zoning out or not sleeping for a while. He was 2 hours past his normal time until he fell asleep tonight.

Maybe the above explains why he sometimes acts like he is a baby? Is he re-enacting being a child to compensate for that phase? I read something about that somewhere; children often regress to a phase that they may have missed so they can feel like it has been completed.

23th March - Social Worker Visit

'I know I don't need to be here, but I have to be to tick the boxes. You are both doing a great job and we are now just waiting for the court dates'

The visit was a waste of time really, according to Alex. I wasn't there as I was still working. It was lots of generic small talk that was, as Patrick said, just a tick box exercise. We won't need any visits if and when we get our court date and the adoption order issued. Hopefully it won't be long now until we get the dates and completion.

25th March - A Date

I went to bed last night at the same time as Jacob. It was only 7.15pm but I was absolutely shattered and just wanted to catch up on some sleep. I think the last 9 months have taken its toll.

This morning I was about to start the usual routine of taking Jacob to the bathroom at 7.00am and Alex sat up in bed, called me over whilst Jacob was using the toilet and excitedly told me about the previous evening. It transpired that at about 8.15, Julie (Jacob's social worker) called whilst I was asleep and advised us that she had been issued with a court date. When Alex told me I was in a bit of shock and having just woken up, it took a second to sink in. I am delighted; we are delighted. Julie said she wouldn't normally call at that time but as it was such good news, she couldn't hold it until the morning. Bloody fantastic!

Julie has also tried to ease our mind in regard to any contest from the birth family. She doesn't believe Jacob's birth mum will contest but will attend. Birth dad; it's likely he still has no interest. A shame really as we would love to have been able to share that they both showed an active interest in his future. Birth mum is showing that, and it must be mega tough for her; we have a lot of empathy for her. Nothing from the aunts and we were advised they wouldn't be doing anything in the knowledge Jacob is in a very happy and loving place.

When it sunk in a little, I was thinking how do we tell Jacob? Do we tell Jacob? He is already using our surname as 'normal' and if we told him he had been adopted on the date then will this confuse him? Personally, and on the assumption the order is granted, we would love to mark the day. We will ask Julie how it is usually done with younger children.

On another note, Julie advised that the birth mum has not received our letter from the mediation letterbox team. It's very frustrating as we are very keen for her to know about Jacob's life and we would love to receive letters back so we can share her stories with Jacob - when it's appropriate. That won't be in the next few years, however, but when he has the capacity and understanding to take on the information, then that is when we will share them. It's all part of his identity so it's important he knows; if he wants to.

Overall it has been a very happy day for us as a family.

27th March - Meltdown and Jealousy

We went for a long walk today and Jacob just wouldn't bloody listen to anything that both Alex or I asked him to do. We are very happy for him to have fun and explore, but he just wouldn't do anything we asked. It was bloody frustrating!

He also had a massive meltdown but just wouldn't or couldn't express the reason as to why he was upset. It was the biggest meltdown he has had so far since being here. I have learned how to deal with them now and it is to simply sit with him and let him know he is OK and safe. It was a bit tougher this time. He also did it whilst we were at the park, and I have now experienced the first time of being self-conscious of people judging me as a parent and how I am handling the situation. Other parents staring at Jacob crying quite hysterically and then looking at me to check how I am dealing with it was making me feel very inadequate and self-conscious. I just wanted to tell them to piss-off and get on with what they are doing.

When we got back to the car, he spoke about his foster carer too. Maybe he had that on his mind? Could that have been the cause or am I just overthinking it...again!

Speaking of the foster carer, I am still very jealous when he brings them up. I don't have any feelings of malice towards them and thank them dearly for what they have done for Jacob (and other children in need), but it doesn't stop me being jealous.

4th April - Easter Sunday

What an amazing morning we have just had. As soon as Jacob woke up he was out of bed and just wanted to search for Easter Eggs. We under estimated his egg finding capability and he found them within minutes. He was so excited (egg-cited - sorry!) to find the eggs and it was just a joy to see him so happy. Somehow we managed to calm him down enough to have some breakfast; this gave me enough time to get out into the garden and plant the remaining eggs for the hunt that we had sorted with the neighbours.

George (next door's little boy) and Jacob loved it when we finally opened the patio doors. Again it was an absolute joy to watch the boys have so much fun together and also to share the experience too.

Jacob opened his card and book from my mum (Grandmums) and I had to take a bit of breath as it was getting me choked up. Little things like this really drive home how much our family love Jacob. We have the other side of the family coming later. Grandad, as per his and Nana's tradition is getting Jacob his first big boys bike. It will be a really strong memory for him as he grows older. I am sure it will be tough for Grandad today as they would have preferred for Nana to be part of gifting the bike.

5th April - Easter Weekend

We had our first family Easter weekend and the family have just left. It was with Alex's side of the family and as usual when they leave, I am pretty tired and hungover.
I had 10 minutes to myself when they left and felt a little upset for some reason. It wasn't unhappiness, it was more the overwhelming pride I feel as a father to Jacob and how well this superb little boy is dealing with life. He seems to be taking everything in his stride and getting on with things. I really do wonder if he subconsciously bottles things up and hides it by just cracking on, or whether he genuinely is just OK with things.

He looks and presents as such a happy little boy. I really hope he is.

7th April - 1st Party Invite

Alex just got the first invite for Jacob to go to a children's party via the school and class 'mums WhatsApp group'. I feel a bit left out not being invited to the group, but Alex thinks I will end up getting frustrated with the rubbish in there and then eventually resort to taking the piss; my default. The party has mentally put us on the back foot a little. I am pretty much cool with it, however Alex has a thousand questions and I think he is feeling a little stressed out by it all. *'Do we buy a present, what does he wear, do we leave him there or stay with him, how do I interact with the other parents, do we arrive early, etc etc'.* It is the first party so it is normal to feel the way we do about the etiquette. We have decided to both go together for a bit of moral support and since it is the first. We will be fine, I am sure.

10th April - No Pull Ups

Alex and I have decided that Jacob has had enough nights in a row with dry pull ups and we have agreed to try with no pull ups overnight. We have asked Jacob too, and he would like to try. Let's see how this goes.

11th April - 1st Party

We had a wet bed. It's only day one! Oh, well. We tried not to make a big deal about it but told him that he must not lay in bed when he has had an accident as we don't want him to feel uncomfortable and dirty.

Regarding the party and in hindsight, there was nothing to worry about. Jacob had a ball when he played with the other kids. Upon arrival to the party the parents of the little boy - whose names I can't remember - welcomed us in and were very accommodating, but not overwhelming. They offered us a drink and pointed us to the big bouncy castle in the garden. We were the first there. We gave the present to the birthday boy, but he said straight away after unwrapping it that he had already got that gift. Kids are very honest. Jacob was very quick to tell us he didn't and that he would like to keep it. It was on £10 or something, so we were fine with that. Jacob and his mate were best mates for 15 minutes or so until the next boy got there and then Jacob looked like he lost interest and became a little bit of an outsider, choosing to get a drink and food by himself, but still close to us. We just continued to talk a load of random chaff with the other parents; *where do you live, how many kids do you have, who do you support etc etc'*. It was all just generic small talk but enough to still feel comfortable.

As more and more children started to arrive, Jacob seemed to come out of shell and play amongst the others, but not really with anyone. It made me feel sad for him, but he insisted he was fine; of course he did, he always says that he is fine.

18th April - Feelings

Funnily enough my last entry to the diary is about Jacob always telling us he is fine. Well today, I am 99% sure something is troubling him inside and also he has a high temperature. Last night we put him in our bed to fall asleep (he really likes it) before we move him to his bed. During a dream he shouted something that sounded like *'No I don't like that'*. I am certainly reading into it - because that bloody therapist said we should consider everything - but I really hope he has not had any flashbacks to poor memories. I just hope he is having a generic nightmare.

It really hurts when you can't get any information out of him, but then I have to remind myself he is only 4 years old and still learning. I have questioned myself and the trust he has in me if he doesn't want to answer. If I was to ask him about what he is thinking when he is looking blankly and with the 'thousand yard stare', he would snap out of it and then just say something along the lines of *'I am thinking of you'* or *'I love you'*. Complete diversion tactics.

It is very frustrating as I really want to know so I can make him feel better, safe and most of all, loved.

19th April - No Pull Ups

Another try at the no pull ups in bed at night and another accident. It's 50/50 at the moment and although the washing is stacking up (thanks Alex) we are going to stick with it. Jacob tried to creeping to the bathroom and back to his room this morning, and then lied about when he had his accident, so I think he is worried about telling us. This is actually quite unusual for him as we have really tried hard to create and establish a culture of open and truthful conversations in the house. As an example, when I told him not to tell Daddy Alex that I had a sticky toffee pudding at the pub the other day, he corrected me and told me that we don't keep secrets. It was the first thing he told Alex when we got home and I was happy and laughed about it.

20th April - Sharted in the Bath

One thing I have learned about children is that there are some hilarious moments and they are always eager to make you laugh and smile. We were at the dinner table and the old myth has been passed down about what beans make you do (fart). We were laughing that he may be in a bubble bath if he eats all of his beans as he was due in straight after tea. That was the tool to make it fun to eat his beans. What we didn't anticipate was that when he just got in the bath, he tried to trump and sharted in the bath. It's obviously not right to laugh but it's hilarious.

Alex got him out and then Jacob proceeded to have the largest poo I have ever seen. They didn't tell you in training about the size of some of the things that kids produce. Where do they keep it?

Maybe it's because I am a guy that I am laughing so much.

25th April - K & N Visit

It was a beautiful sunny day today and we had our lovely and amazing friends around in the garden with their two adopted children. They are superb and have really helped us by just being a good ear and soundboard. K & N are amazing people who I respect a lot as parents and just watching them parent their children has helped me take some ideas and offers us a different perspective. They are both amazing people and I am glad we hit it off at the training sessions way back when.

Out of ear shot we discuss the pending court dates and the situation we are in at present with regard to the birth family. They were very reassuring to us and it was a great help to have friends who understand our situation that we can talk to.

I am immensely grateful that we had created our friends group at the start of the process.

27th April - Court Day

I didn't sleep much last night and I am not sure if that was caused by today's big life event, or not. It may also be the fact that we send across the letterbox contact letters to Jacob's birth-aunts and grandparents. The letter was pretty much the same as what we sent to his birth mum as that letter was written very much as an update. It still pisses me off that his birth father has zero interest as I know from experience that it is likely to have some form of emotional effect on him when he is old enough to understand his feelings and situation a little more. More importantly in the immediate timescale, today is the day that Jacobs' adoption journey goes to court to decide whether he will legally and fully become part of our family and share our last name. I am outwardly calm about it as we have had all of the assurances that this will go in our favour, but there is some concern that something could crop up and cause a delay. All of our friends in the process have had that scenario, so I think it's prudent to be cautious of celebrating too early.

It's now the afternoon and the hearing has been completed. Julie, the social worker, called and as soon as we answered we could hear the trepidation in her voice. With lots of caution we asked what the outcome was and the meeting had to be adjourned. There was a suggested and suspected breach of confidentiality with, allegedly, someone feeding Jacob's birth Mum information which ultimately led to her offering up a contest to Jacob being adopted. This was to the complete surprise of all parties. She had been given ample opportunities to do this well before the court date and never suggested she would.

I am not sure why, but I had the urge to look at Jacob's CPR (child's permanence report) and it made me get emotional with anger and sadness. Bringing back all of the detail and the pictures of him from before his time with us brought a big wave of emotion. I can fully understand the rights and the desire from a birth parent to want to contest their birth child being placed for adoption, but surely should at some point accept what is best for him. It makes me really sad because they could have avoided the whole situation if they could have done it right from the start, yet I still don't blame them as his birth mother just didn't have the capability. I find myself still having some form of sympathy for her, even with what happened to Jacob in his early months and years.

2nd May - Projectile Vomit

We have just dropped Daddy Alex off in town to spend some time with his friend. I really hope he goes out and just lets his hair down and has a few drinks with her. I think it will be a really good release of pent up energy and constant thinking about Jacob.

Speaking of Jacob; when we got home we had our first ever projectile vomit. It came out of nowhere and he never mentioned anything about having a bad stomach. He did bring up memories of his foster carer and the last time he remembered being sick. It is such a difficult thing to process for me as I really want him to psychologically be present in our forever family and feel that is the case. I fear he still believes he may move on at some stage and doesn't fully believe us when we say that this is forever.

He went to bed with a smile on his face though as he got an extra 30 minutes out of me because he wanted to watch some 1980's Transformers cartoon. It took me back to my childhood, so how could I say no.

I hope he sleeps well tonight and is feeling better in the morning.

4th May - Grandmums Moved

Amazing news! My mother has moved close to us and the rest of the family. I am delighted that Jacob will be able to spend some time with his grandmum. I am also delighted that I will be able to spend some time with her myself.

5th May - Birth Father Drama

We had a call from Julie today. She was angry, upset, apologetic and quite frankly pissed off with the birth father. For over 4 years - since Jacob's birth - he has shown absolutely zero interest in him and his life to the point of not even providing any medical history or even a photo, yet all of a sudden he now wants to contest the adoption order. Julie thinks that this has come about due to the formal letter advising him of the contest from birth mother. It is all very bizarre as he has absolutely no leg to stand on in court due to his history; which Julie quite candidly and very frankly told him.

On a personal note I am very, very frustrated and angry at Jacob's birth father. We have not long written the 'letterbox contact' letter to the paternal grandparents, and it seems that they are also very much influencing this decision as they got a large mention on Julie's call with the birth father. I really hope the letter that we wrote hasn't triggered the desire to want some contact. I want to say I feel sorry for his birth father and have some empathy towards him, but I really can't and certainly wouldn't mean it if I did.

6th May - Happy Tears

'I've got happy tears'

I went and had a quick beer on a school night and when I got home, I went to say goodnight to Jacob who had just got in bed. I was just chatting and asked him to cuddle one of our family bears in bed. He reminded me that the one I asked him to cuddle was the bear we gave him as a transitional teddy when we first met him at introductions. At this point he had tears in his eyes and I asked if he was OK. He told me he had *'happy tears because you're my forever family'*. That got me in the feels right there. Many times I have been close to happy tears thinking about that little boy and how complete he has made our family. He's such a beautiful boy inside and out.

8th May - Kids Party

We went to another kid's birthday party and this time it was a friend of ours and not a school friend. The good news is the children get on really well and are a similar age. When we arrived Jacob went straight off to play with his friend, checking out all of the toys, whereas we grabbed a drink and mingled. We didn't know many people so we got introduced as Alex, Joe and their little boy Jacob. It's quite interesting to see people register that we are two guys and have a child and then finally making an assumption that we have likely adopted him. The secondary part to that same process is seeing the person mulling over and finding the courage to ask about Jacob and adoption in general. The default and standard way I've found people break the ice is to tell us how amazing we are for adopting a child or that they have heard the process is so long and in a huge amount of depth. When replying, I tend to agree with the latter regarding time frames, but I politely challenge the first by telling them that he has done just as much for us making us parents.

I must say I do actually enjoy people asking questions about Jacob and the process so long as it doesn't get personal regarding his own backstory. We have our default answers to those questions.

'He was placed in care to keep him safe' We have found being honest, but very vague works and is important. It is his story and not ours to tell, really.

Other than that we just got asked a load of questions regarding the process and how we found it. We want to normalise it as much as possible, so welcome inquisitive people and their questions.

13th May - Court Case 2

This afternoon we got a call from Julie which was way past the time we had expected it. Due to it being so late, we expected bad news and not only was it bad, it was so very frustrating. In fact I think frustrating is the wrong description for it. I am bloody angry. I am furious with Jacob's birth father, yet not so much with his birth mother. Both have contested the adoption order. At least she has shown some form of desire to want to do well by him and has demonstrated an active love for him (to a degree), whereas his father is just being a d*ck. A big whopper!

Jacob's birth mother will also be offered someone to support her. They will also appoint a guardian to give an independent view as the 'eyes and ears of the court'. They are not often appointed in court at this stage, but she was appointed so she can give first-hand information directly to the court from both sides of the adoption.

This has also really started to affect Alex too. It is all very upsetting for a number of reasons, but mostly because we really want closure for Jacob. Even seeing the social workers online and on calls, he is likely to have associations that are negative and attributed to his past. We just want to get on with our lives now.

20th May - LAC (Looked After Children) Review

'Well, I wasn't expecting us to have to do this' was the opening line from the independent reviewer. This review was another progress review to check in on Jacob's progress and was attended by both Alex and I, Julie, Patrick, the reviewer (Jessica) and Mr Davies from school.

Once the meeting was opening, it was handed over to Julie for her input and an update. It was clear in her voice that she is emotionally invested in Jacob's case (which we are super grateful for) and that she is desperately in favour of Jacob's adoption order to be passed at the earliest so we all, as a family, can just get on with our lives. The noises and grunts of agreement from the others on the call made is abundantly clear that they are all also in favour of this whole situation to be resolved in quick time. It is very reassuring to know that the professionals are on our side.

Julie also made reference to Jacob's birth father citing some tosh about Article 8 of the Human Rights Act. I think the line that I can see from the website guidance that jumps out as the obvious citation is *'You have the right to enjoy family relationships without interference from the government. This involves the right to live with your family and, where this is not possible, the right to regular contact. 'Family Life' can include the relationship between an unmarried couple, an adopted child and the adoptive parent, and a foster parent and fostered child'*

To put this into more context, Jacob is nearly 5 years old and his birth 'father' has never had any form of interest in him nor ever shown any desire to get to know him. Furthermore, he explicitly said he did not want to oppose Jacob being put into care.

They now have 21 days to put in their leave to appeal.

28th May - Family Lesson at School

We have just received a message from school via the App. It's typical that it is a Friday before a half term, and they have asked us for a picture of Jacob when he was a baby as they are doing a session discussing how they have changed and grown since then. To say we went straight into protection and worry mode, is an understatement. *'What if they talk about things that bring up bad memories, what if he feels left out, what if….'*

The obvious choice was for us to call school and discuss it with them, but as we were on the phone to Julie (Jacob's social worker), the school called. It was refreshing to know that they thought of us and were conscious of how we may take the message from the app. It's another reason why we both are very happy with this school; we haven't had any other bad experience bar the name issue on day one.

Having spoken to Jacob's teacher we have since received an email about the lesson plan, and although it still presents some worries, we have to be very honest about his situation and not shy away from the fact that he is adopted and that he didn't have a great start to life. I guess it's all part of the acceptance piece and if he can do that now, and we are open about it, then I am very confident that will really help him when growing up.

14th June - Plot Twist?

We had a phone call from Julie this morning regarding where we are up to with the court cases and the leave to oppose from both birth parents. Alex took the call as I was at work so I got the second hand and frustrated version. It sounded as though Julie was frustrated too, as she is completely on Jacob's side (and ours) and has his best interest at heart.

Julie has advised that Jacob's mother, despite the support and offer of guidance, has not put in any statement or request for help. His birth father has at least personally conceded that his situation will not allow him much of a chance, legally, to look after Jacob safely but has now formally stated that *'if I can't, then I want to put forward my sister (Jacob's aunt) to be his guardian'*. Julie has actually spoken to the paternal aunt to check whether she would want this and accepts this notion, yet my view based on the information we have is that she is doing this as a front to maintain her relationship with her brother rather than seriously considering wanting to adopt (I think) Jacob. She has said she will go with whatever the court and judge decide is best.

It is a huge plot twist and one that nobody has seen coming and a bizarre situation. We are very lucky that Jacob has no idea what is happening behind the scenes. We are doing our sincere best to ensure his quality of life is not affected by the legal process. In his world we are his Daddies and his forever family.

Frustrated, annoyed, angry, sad, empathetic and yet I am still so happy that we have had our lives graced and enhanced by our amazing and resilient little boy, Jacob.

We had also received a call at lunchtime that we were anticipating from the court guardian as she is acting as the impartial and independent case reviewer regarding Jacob's birth parents' leave to oppose. I can't keep up with all of the legal in/outs. It is very much in depth and full of jargon and steps that it's tough to understand where we are up to. Anyway, she will come tomorrow at 9am - so more time off work needed - to speak to us about how Jacob has settled in and how we see him as part of our forever family. Julie advised us to be mindful of what we say and how we express some of our more emotive feelings; especially if the birth father comes into conversation. I am sure we will see tomorrow.

15th June - Guardian Visit

I had a rubbish call from 0830-0900am from work. There is a guy there that just knows how to rattle me and always seems to have the opposite view to me regarding any subject and it p*sses me off. It was just before the guardian arrived at 9.00am and I was already sleep deprived through being nervous. This woman can change our family life as she has so much influence on the courts and their decisions.

She was also late to arrive which just gave me a few more minutes to overload my brain with various worries and minor anxiety. I guess it didn't help that Julie had forewarned us to be careful on what information and emotions towards the birth family we shared. She did end the call with a very reassuring comment expressing how she thought we were quite possibly the most receptive and attentive adoptive parents she had worked with over her time as a social worker. I am not sure if that was her way of shit-sandwiching the warning, but it helped.

When we did finally get sat down, the conversation was light-hearted and pretty much based around the process and why she was here. I can't remember any direct questions from her and by the end and after some reflection the session seemed like a bit of a tick box exercise. The guardian did also share that she thought the process was a bit of a strange one due to the nature of birth mother not submitting the right of leave and evidence and because birth father had now conceded and passed on the desire for his sister - Jacob's birth aunt - to be considered. She did also say that if he suggested this at the court case, then it would be highly likely that the judge would have granted the adoption order there and then and not 'messed around with all of this'. Reading between the lines, this is very reassuring and I sincerely hope I am reading it well.

In hindsight, it was wasted energy worrying. I don't often worry about things, but if things took a sharp turn left and out of our favour, my mental health would take a complete beating. Jacob means so much to Alex, me and all of his forever family. It would break our world, but I am thinking positively I am sure we won't need to go down that route.

16th June - Jacob's Joy

This morning summed up why I love being a father and it was such a simple thing. As always, Jacob came into our bedroom and he was confused as to why I was in bed because he thought I was working away from home (even though I put him to bed). The absolute joy, the love in his eyes and the huge cuddle was just enough to melt my heart. I think I hugged him for about 15 minutes. I can't describe the feeling of how much I love this little boy, but by God, if I had to give him my heart to live, I would have no hesitations on putting him first.

He is just so loving and an amazing little boy overall. I do still wish I could read his mind though! I think all of the above is down to some insecurities he still has.

19th June - Visiting Grandmums

We went to visit grandmums (my mum) this morning and it made me so happy to see my mother, but most of all the way Jacob interacts with her. She adores him and you can see he adores her too. Grandmums read a couple of books to Jacob and he was completely engaged with them and how she told the stories. He sat on her knee for about twenty minutes absorbing and listening whilst I just sat silently watching and sipping on my coffee. It was almost perfect to see.

We also went for a little walk where grandmums' natural parental instincts came out. She is always thinking about Jacob and what he's doing. Speaking of parental instincts, as we passed through a cemetery walking back to her house, Jacob asked about why he can't walk on the grass and next to the 'big stones'. It's a tough one to explain what a cemetery is, but I didn't want to shy away from it. I think my mother thought I shared a little too much, but I want him to learn.

The afternoon was filled with dinner at a restaurant for Grandads (Alex's dad) birthday. For the first time Jacob did something we have never seen before; he drew on his brand new white trainers whilst sat at the table. I gave him a quiet telling off, explained why I wasn't happy and asked if he understood why he was in trouble. Then I told him that we had to move on and that we would move past the telling off. I was very happy with the way I handled it.

Other than that, he had a lovely day.

20th June - First Fathers Day

I had zero sleep last night; well it feels like it. Jacob and I shared a bed last night and it was one of the worst nights of sleep I've certainly ever had. He is a mover, cuddler and dreamer.
At first it was all nice to get the cuddles, but then to be woken up 15 minutes later with his bum pretty much in your face wasn't the most pleasant thing in the world. Not only that, he is a dreamer and kicks out a lot and talks. I've never been close enough to hear his words, but last night he was sleep-talking about a big house and then 20 minutes later, he woke up crying and clearly in distress. It's hard not to make theories up on what he was dreaming about; but maybe he was thinking about moving to another house. My mind is racing about what he could be dreaming about. His standard answer when he is asked is about a crocodile. I think I have said a hundred times in this diary, I wish I knew what he was actually thinking.

I also received some lovely presents. I forgot to get Alex an actual card, but not a present; he got one of those. It was online, so not a present Jacob could give to Alex directly. I have always been rubbish with things like that and I must get better and be more thoughtful to both of the boys. After all these are memories that we will have as a family. I feel pretty guilty that I was poor with my effort levels.

Later this afternoon when we had got home from Alex's sisters, I got the nod that I could get in bed and catch up on some sleep. I was bloody shattered and have not long woken up from a 3 hour nap. I could have gone a lot longer. When I did wake up Jacob jumped on the bed and we played a small game where I kept hold of him and told him that *'I'm going to keep hold of you forever'*. Without missing a beat and with such an organic natural reply he said *'You have got me forever anyway, Daddy Joe'*. It was said in the tone that suggested I should have known, like *duh*. If I am reading into that, it seems like he is really and fully invested into the work we have done on permanence and him being 100% part of our forever family.

Father's day has been amazing, but what he said to me was worth more than any present.

22nd June - Hitting Out

We had Uncle Ryan around tonight and Jacob had a meltdown just before bed and in front of Ryan too. Although Ryan let me deal with it there were a few comments after that made me feel a little judged. None were meant with any malice or undermining tones, but the comments made me feel a little like I didn't present as if I knew what I was doing. Jacob also pushed out and something that felt a little like a lash out when he was angry. This is a first and he was quick to apologise when he was told what just happened. That made me feel really sad that he has resorted to this to express his frustration.

23rd June - Again

Straight away Jacob went to Uncle Ryan's room this morning. That's fine and usually part of his routine when Ryan stays over, but when Jacob was asked to go down and get his breakfast he had another breakdown shouting and stomping around the rooms. *'Noooooooo, I want….'*. This alone has not been seen at this level since Jacob came home. Recently when both Alex and I said no to what he demands, he seems to think he can cry and get what he wants all the time. We need to break the cycle. When I went to calm him and chat to him at his level, he once again hit or pushed out. I just don't know where this has come from and it's quite distressing for us as much as it is likely for him.

Alex has had to go and sort Jacob out as it's actually quite upsetting to me that he has done it completely out of the blue. My feelings initially are to go to strict parent mode and to take away his privileges like his screen time, but I don't think that's the correct approach. He needs nurturing, shown love and most importantly, he needs to feel safe. He is still clearly working out how to express his emotions.

I really hope this isn't a trend. Regardless, I will still love him unconditionally, of course.

24th June - Pending Court Case

Alex received a call from Julie to update us regarding the pending court case on the 9th July. It seems that we have another *'this is a new one to us'* scenario and it is starting to feel like we have so many things stacking up to overcome. We are lucky that Julie is superb and has been so proactive with her investment in Jacob's best interests. I called her even after the call I'd had with Alex as I wanted to hear about it all myself from the horse's mouth, as they say.

Because Jacob's birth father has now put in the desire for his sister to be considered, the legal team at the local authority - chased by Julie - have advised that the relevant parties need to find out and assess as much as possible the intentions of the aunt so the judge can rule for a full assessment of her or for him to grant the adoption order in our favour. Julie sounds worried and also concerned for us. Her usual demeanour regarding things that we have come up against is usually and frankly very reassuring, however at this stage she said *'I can't downplay this one as I just don't know'*. That coming from her really worries me.

25th June - We Might Lose Him!

'We might lose him!'

Alex said this morning after dropping Jacob off. I am fully aware of the possible situation and the same worries because I have been thinking about it all night and this morning. I am very mindful that the outcome here could be catastrophic to us but I am trying to put it to the back of my mind. I really can't comprehend how someone might think this could be a good move for Jacob (if they do), to potentially move him to a woman who has shown very little interest anyway (aunt), one who's expressed she's only doing it for her brother and a person who's clearly got a close relationship with her brother; Jacob's birth father. That alone could put him in danger. It just doesn't make sense to us.

This afternoon I was chatting to our good friends next door and I was explaining the top level detail and the possible outcomes and I just started crying because the outcome could be bad. I was lucky that I was quite a distance from next door and he couldn't see.

We will fight to the death for Jacob as being here is what's best for him. We have done so much regarding permanence and his forever family, that it would be catastrophic for his short and long-term wellbeing.

This evening we invited our friend around for dinner. He is just starting his journey of adoption so we have lots to talk about. Both he and his partner are using the same agency as us too, so we could talk about the things we learned and the hurdles we have come up against.

Halfway through the evening Jacob came out with a couple of crackers. His character is really shining through. *'I just want to show off'* he said to my friend when getting some toys out and *'I am gorgeous aren't I?"* or something along those lines. It is so nice to see this little character growing and I can't wait to see it continue.

28th June - Patrick's Visit

We just had Patrick around for his tick in the box. He has completely checked out and hardly seemed interested in us telling him that there are some complications in the court case.
It's hard work for us to spend 30 minutes trying to talk to him about something. I think we ended up speaking about Jacob trumping for 5 minutes; that's how hard it is.

On a more positive note, Alex has just shown me the photos of some of his work colleagues who have just gone through the process and they have now been formally signed off with the adoption order of their child. It's fantastic news. I just wish it would hurry up for us.

29th June - Patrick's Follow Up & PEP

This morning we received an email back from Patrick regarding the conversation he had with Julie. The content didn't really offer much and didn't really offer any reassurances about the outcome. I guess she can't as she doesn't know; just like the rest of us.

The part that suggests *'different outcomes when other placements are considered'* gave me goosebumps and made me uneasy and uncomfortable. I know I am reading it with a negative connotation to it. I know full-well that the courts have to consider the aunt put forward legally, but my mind naturally keeps wandering to the worst-case scenario. It is so upsetting to think that Jacob could be moved again. Of course my biassed mind keeps telling me that Jacob staying with us - his forever family - is the best thing for him and his mental health. We have done so much work on permanence that if the move was to happen, he would never trust anyone again. Surely going to a place and person he knows NOTHING about would also be 10 steps backwards. Ahhhhh, I am so angry, upset, frustrated, worried….

Patrick also has tried his best to ease our worry. He suggests that the assessment of the aunt is *'in my opinion unlikely'*. Let's hope that he is correct. We really don't want to keep going through the mill on this one. It's really starting to burden us all to a point we are exhausted and feel the pressure. I believe it's affecting my parenting. Please just hurry up, for everyone's sake.

The email from Patrick read…

> *Dear Alex and Joe,*
>
> *I have spoken with Julie this morning to understand the situation in more detail.*
>
> *Julie does have some unease and frustration, but her concerns are more around not being able to offer you definite date regarding the responses of the court. From our conversation it is clear that this is a new situation for the local authority (LA) but they have clearly gone a long way to answering questions the court may have prior to*

them being asked. Reports have been submitted making clear points re the best interest of J and the different outcomes when other placements are considered.

No one can be sure if the adoption order will be granted on the next hearing, but what is very clear is that the LA including legal have worked hard to second guess the response from the court and address everything in as timely manner as possible. It is my understanding that at present birth mother has not submitted her statement to the court in support of her wish to apply to oppose the order. Birth father has, which is where the sister comes in. Julie's counter statement was submitted yesterday and is a lengthy and detailed report, which would be completely expected of Julie, given the level of detail she always puts into her work.

Please do try not to worry. The LA have completed all that is needed at this point in time, the next key step is the response of the court and if they are going to ask for an assessment of the aunt. Something we cannot rule out, although in my opinion unlikely.

Court is not too long away now, but it is a wait you could do without, I understand that.

Sorry I cannot offer anything more definite.

Pupil Education Plan.

In other news, the PEP also happened today with school. I am so proud of him and so is Alex. Jacob loves school. He is very engaged and his desire to learn has been commended by his teachers. When they speak about him, they are so complimentary and they always smile when chatting about him. He has an effect on all adults that way. He is a joy to be fair.

The session looked at his progressions at school and when the teacher showed the previous plan and his new, there was notably less 'emerging' section there than last time. There were only a couple of small points that he needed to work on, but nothing that is a concern. Even if Jacob was struggling, I would have been so supportive of him and very proud of him. To even be where he is after all of the changes and struggles, he has been superb.

Proud dad alert.

1st July - 1st School Report

I need to pick up where I left off being the proud dad. Jacob had his first report from school today and I am so happy for him. The content and achievements are very important, but I was more proud of him that it read *'Jacob is the happiest and most polite little boy'*. That is nearly the job done. Reading it in front of Alex, I wanted to let out a little happy tear but I kept it in. I don't consider myself to be an emotional person, but since Jacob came home, I just can't help myself. I used to take the mickey out of those dads on the TV who cried over their sons or daughters getting through to the next round of the X Factor. I would be joining them now. I completely get it.

He doesn't stop amazing me and I love him more and more each day.

7th July - Court Update

I was absolutely shattered this afternoon and went to have a lie down at about 2pm. I was classing it as my 'lunch hour'. Just as I started to read my book, I got an unexpected call from Julie. She usually calls Alex first (maybe I ask too many questions) but she couldn't get through as he was out food shopping. I dialled in Alex so we had a 3 way conversation and Julie talked us through the update. She came across a lot more positive than in previous calls the confidence level had clearly risen in regard to the anticipated outcome. Of course it came with a prerequisite of caution and to not get ahead of myself.

Let's just wait and see. That's all we can do.

9th July - Court Date

The birth father can just piss off. He is being selfish based on the needs of Jacob. Nearly 5 years of not caring, giving a shit and zero information supplied and all of a sudden the court seems to be favouring and giving his side of the family a chance to be considered to care for Jacob. I'm absolutely fuming and devastated that they continually keep considering the birth family's needs over Jacobs; that's certainly how it seems. I am fully aware that they are ticking all the legal boxes and all, but this is just a farce. It feels as though the process favours the birth family and we get zero input into the outcome. It would be devastating and cause irreversible damage and pain to this little boy should he have to move.

I need to take 10 minutes to myself. I am upset and emotionally charged. I'm a rational person usually, but right now I just can't be.

Now I've calmed down… Julie called us whilst we were playing in the garden with Jacob. Once we finally managed to get him to stay there and play football, we got started. There was no small talk which frankly I was happy with. Julie had the sense not to make us wait for the information she was offering.

'It's not bad news' was the opening line. My first thought however was that it also didn't seem to be good news either. The other line that jumped out was *'In my time of twenty-odd to thirty years experience, neither myself, the local authority I work with and legal council have come across this before…'*

The long and short of it is that although the birth mother didn't put in her statement of intent to contest, the judge has allowed her more time. Why? How many more chances and how much more time does she need. She clearly can't be bothered. The next part is that the birth father has ruled himself out, but there has been a significant push for the aunt to continue the process to be considered. After some legal terminology and jargon, the judge has said that she has to be considered and so has been offered time over the next few weeks to write her statement of intent detailing the reason why she WANTS to adopt Jacob. Again the frustrating part - I'm using the word frustrated a lot regarding the process - is that she has shown desire only because she has had pressure from the birth family. The social workers and the independent guardian have both said that in their court report, so why do they need to give her some more consideration time. It's madness.

Playing with him this evening has been so emotional as I can't get it out of my head that these times could be the last few times we get. I know that's the irrational and 'worst case scenario' playing out in my head, but I can't get rid of it.

I don't know what to do and think right now. I despise those people. How dare they think this is remotely a good thing for Jacob. I hope they find sense, but I don't hold out hope.

10th July - Daddy's Day Out

We are going to York races today. I didn't sleep very well last night and had a weird dream about Jacob not being with us and the worst-case scenario was clearly my thought pattern when I was asleep. Just as I woke up, Jacob came through - he usually wakes me up scurrying to the bathroom - and I can't describe how much my heart melted. It was an amazing feeling and one of pure love for this little boy. Thankfully, he is oblivious to this whole situation, so he was his complete and playful self. He hopped into bed as he always does, and we had a massive cuddle and kiss to the point where he told me *'too much Daddy Joe'*. Knowing Jacob and his love of both kisses and cuddles is saying something.

I rolled over and stared at the ceiling. It just put me into thought mode again and I had some more tears. I blamed it on the pollen count.

29th July - Madness from the Aunt

Julie called through this afternoon whilst I was at work. At the 11th hour before the court case tomorrow, the aunt has written an email to the social workers to say she is no longer wanting to be considered to adopt Jacob. Come on now... The only thing that we have assumed from the start of her rearing her head is that she has been put under family pressure to try and bring Jacob back to the birth family. We believe she has done that with the hope that the courts will reject her for whatever reason and the decision will be made for her. With that in mind, she would still be able to appease her family by showing willingness.

It's madness.

30th July - Birth Dad is a Joke

We had another hearing today and the adoption order was still not granted.

From Jacob's birth mother's side, she didn't attend the hearing because she said her back was sore. She was offered a virtual meeting but she then said her mouth is sore. I mean, come on... The judge has said that the local authority must employ a legal representative to take her place in proceedings as she is unreliable and doesn't have the mental capacity to understand what is fully happening and the implication of her actions. Why this wasn't done in the 1st place is beyond us?

The birth father's sister, Jacob's aunt, had emailed court yesterday saying she was pulling out as she believed the whole situation is not fair to Jacob and us. Julie has advised that she thought this would be the best scenario for us now there has to be another hearing.

Jacob's birth father attended court and has accused local authority and social workers of putting too much pressure on his sister (aunt) not to pursue her application to adopt Jacob. The judge has to take this as a serious allegation. Alex summed it up for me by calling this birth father an *'unbelievable man'*. How the hell can he come in at the 11th hour and try this is beyond me. He has had absolutely zero interest in Jacob since birth and now…

Overall the judge has now recognised this is putting a tremendous amount of stress and time for us as the adopters (finally) and so has set a new date for next Friday. The whole process completely favours everyone but the adopters and that is a tough pill to swallow. The court has said evidence must be provided to show pressure has been put on her to pull out and must attend if she wants to be considered. The judge is basically trying to ensure everything is covered so if anyone requests an appeal to the human court of justice it will not be looked at.

Alex messaged me *'You can't make it up. Julie is absolutely raging! I'm not surprised because the whole thing is a joke'* and I can completely resonate with both him and Julie. Julie has been so supportive throughout the whole process and has been the biggest cheerleader for Jacob to be adopted and become one of our family, legally.

6th August - Birth Mum has Withdrawn

Jacob's birth mother has withdrawn from the process. It was said that she has done this citing the best interest for Jacob's future and with the knowledge that both Alex and I love him so very much. She also expressed her love for him too, and I am really glad that she did to be honest. I want him to know how much he is loved by his birth mother as I am sure it will help him as he grows older. It could also make things harder, but only time will tell.

The judge had also denied both applications from the birth father and his sister (aunt) and that means there needs to be another date set for what we hope will be the final hearing and where a decision is made. The birth father has not accepted it so he legally has 21 days to appeal the decision

Additionally, the judge had stated he has to prove a significant change in circumstance and it's in Jacob's best interest and welfare that he should be removed from us. The judge has said to him that he will have an incredibly difficult and uphill battle to prove this. We have also been told by Julie that it is very common for birth parents to appeal and it's their human right to be allowed 21 days to do so, which we understand but are still frustrated with. I still think the whole process favours the birth parents' side.

The Judge did not have a diary in front of him so Julie will be speaking to court on Monday to get the court date agreed. Earliest could be Friday 27th.

8th September - Monthly Call

It was another call with Patrick. The usual monthly one. We are in such a routine and consider ourselves to be a 'normal family' and we just want to be left to get on with our lives.
That's a poor term to use and that we are not 'normal' for obvious reasons, however having the social workers still involved must surely be confusing for Jacob. Not only that, but there also isn't really much value being added from Patrick; probably through no fault of his own, it's just that we are getting on with things and not needing his specific support.

The only real take away we got from the 45 minute call was that he believes that the court case due on the 14th will be '100% the last and final one' and that he has no doubt that it will go in our favour.

14th September - Court Case Day

I woke up early today, it's about 6.00am and I am on my phone scrolling mindlessly. I wasn't particularly aware that I was thinking about the court case, but I know it is on my mind now. I really hope nothing goes wrong today and sincerely hope that the judge has enough supporting evidence to make a final and overall decision (in our favour). I am also feeling some empathy towards the birth parents as they have tried to the best of their abilities, recently, to fight the overall case. Albeit too little, too late in my opinion, but I am glad there was some energy consumed by them to at least show interest. I am sure it will benefit Jacob in future knowing this was the case. We certainly know that his birth mother loves him; we aren't sure regarding his birth father's motivations frankly. The case goes in at 11.00am, so going on previous sessions, we will likely get a call at 4-5.00pm. They seem to go on forever. Anyway, I had best get out of bed and try to switch on for work; it's business review day and I am leading them so I need to.

11.48am and 2 minutes before my third review of the day, I got three calls and rejected them as they were from a number I hadn't recognised. I was expecting Julie to call through and give us some (hopefully good) news, so assumed this one was PPI or something to that effect. As I hung up the Microsoft Teams call I was on, I received another attempt from the same number, so this time I answered it. It was Julie's manager and she told me she had some great news but had to apologise that Julie wasn't able to be the person to deliver the news. Officially the judge had ruled that the adoption order was to be granted; meaning Jacob was now officially and legally one of our forever family. I found I had two emotions at that point. The first emotion was the feeling of being overwhelmed and relieved. I certainly had small welling up of the eyes that I couldn't control. These did however quickly move to the second emotion. This was to be actually quite underwhelmed too. When I reflected on it, I believe it was down to the fact that we have never seen Jacob as anything other than one of us and part of our forever family anyway.

I called Alex and he felt pretty much the same. He actually asked me if he should feel bad about not being massively overwhelmed with the outcome, but I explained my thoughts too. Nothing has changed for us really; although so much has changed. It all feels very bizarre.

On my way home from work I called my mother and explained what had happened and the outcome we had received. I think she swore (that's not like her) and she was so happy for us as a family.

18th September - Congratulations

Patrick messaged us both today to congratulate us again and significantly book a time and method for his 'goodbye visit'. He asked if we would prefer a home visit or online and we were pretty quick to reply that we'd want a phone call only. We really don't want to confuse Jacob with more visits and potentially associate them with moving. With respect to them, we are desperate to get on with our lives, so the faster the call, the better.

FOREVER FAMILY

29th September - Patrick's 'goodbye visit'

At 5.30pm we had a call from Patrick. It was the final call and the 'goodbye visit'. It's hard to articulate this part, but frankly it was nice to get it over and done with. Albeit he's a nice guy and has been instrumental to us getting approved and finding Jacob, we are all glad to finally end the scheduled calls and visits. We've nothing against him, but we just don't see the value of them any longer. It's a box ticking exercise.

Anyway, the call was about thirty minutes of awkward small talk and Patrick explaining to Jacob that this will be the last time we would speak with him and that his 'job is now done, so you can get on with being a forever family'.

We do honestly have to say that we will be forever grateful for Patrick's efforts to help us get through the adoption process, gain sign off, and then to find Jacob. Overall he did his part and then tried to back off so we could be a family.

1st October - Chasing for Paperwork

We chased the social worker up today via email regarding the paperwork. It seems Julie is still off. We hope she is OK and on the mend.

4th October - Contact from Julie

Alex got a message back today from Julie. She is still off but wanted to update us to advise that she is over the moon for us and Jacob. She has been such a strong guiding force for us and we are going to be forever grateful to her for helping make Jacob's journey as smooth as possible. Of course, the information and guidance she has offered us has also been invaluable. She has been so invested in Jacob and his future that we couldn't have asked for a better social worker for him.

Additionally and I think finally - which is a mega shame - she has advised that there is no need for a 'final meeting or call' from her side and the local authority, but she would love to have some progress pictures and updates in due course. The 'later in life book' will be completed after Christmas as there is no rush for that as it is given to him when he is 18.

Although we want to move on and away from social workers as a family, I am a little gutted to lose the connection with someone who cared so much about our little boy. She will certainly be spoken about in his future as a very influential figure in us all finding our forever family.

She will be missed, a lot.

5th October - School Name Change

Another superb landmark happened today. Jacob's school have messaged back as they are now able to change Jacob's surname at school away from 'known as' to his new and real name, ours. It's quite a small thing in the grand scheme of things, but it's nice that we can change it. Next stop, passport.

6th October - Out of Character

Jacob has been a pain in the arse over the last few days with him crying at small things, not listening and being out of character. It's been a funny few days to the point that now he has been into his cupboard where his teddies are and pulled out one that we think came from his birth mother. I could be wrong, but I am sure there is some attachment to it and it's been done purposely for him. I am jealous about the teddy, no doubt... still. Pushing my emotions aside for him, I do feel like that if it makes him comfortable then it's fine. I just wish he would just be able to articulate how he feels. Of course, being 5, that's pretty tough for him. Not only that I do also think he still wants to please us so we don't reject him. We certainly won't do that.

We love him with all of our hearts.

It's really tough thinking he may be feeling some emotions that are ones that we can't help him with. We will just continue to show and tell him how much we love him.

7th October - No 'Daddy'

Jacob woke up in a funny mood today and even called me 'Joe' without the 'Daddy' part. That's quite tough to mentally process and take and even hurts my feelings. Something is going on in his mind, but I've no idea what. I'm glad I have a busy day at work today so I don't have to think about it.

I've just got home and I came straight into Jacob wanting to show me a love heart picture he made at school accompanied by a nice cuddle. It says next to it 'I love my Daddy's'. I can't explain how much my heart melted. I wonder if he did it knowing what was said hurt my feelings and he is trying to redeem himself?

Regardless, he's a beauty and he is in a tough situation.

8th October - Triggers

This morning I had the time to do breakfast with Jacob before work. I loved it. We wrote a letter to Grandmums, put £10 in for a McDonalds tea and had a dance to our favourite song from Nothing But Thieves (Impossible).

Not only that, I had a brain wave as to why he may have been a little off and why had got an old teddy from his birth mother out while I was in the shower. I would guess that because of the subject at school being history and the children looking at toys they used to play with, I think it brought up some memories. As he is so young, they could likely be subconscious memories, but nonetheless, he had a trigger of some sorts.

It's crazy how there are so many triggers and things that are minefields for memories. Some of which have knock on effects that he probably doesn't even know what happened.

I must keep reminding myself we are always learning and will continue each day.

20th October - Email Address

Our friends have suggested creating an email address for Jacob so we can send messages, pictures, notes and anything else we want. I think it's an amazing idea and we are going to do it.

22nd October - Wedding

We went to a wedding of some of our lovely friends yesterday. I am so hungover that I'm worried about parenting. Not for safety reasons, of course, but the fact my head may fall off. I can't do hangovers anymore, I am too old for them. When I was 18, I would get in at 5am and be shooting rifles (in the Navy) at 8am and be absolutely fine. Not anymore!

Last night was amazing. It was the first time we had seen a lot of our friends for some time due to the pandemic, yet all of them showed a fascination and interest in Jacob asking a variety of questions about him, how he is getting on and how he has settled in. They all have their own stories too, yet they wanted to know ours. It's great having great friends.

Back to the hangover. Jacob had a little bit of a lie in today as Grandad (who looked after him last night) let him stay up a little later. What are grandads for, right? The lie-in was only until 08.30am and I was not happy getting up; but needs must in this case. I somehow survived.

After that, Jacob had to go to swimming lessons. I drew the short straw of having to take him, but I think it did me some good too. Whilst he's in the lesson I also get into the other half of the swimming pool and just relax. It's a warm pool so it's actually quite good for me. When he finishes his session, we now seem to have fallen into a routine of our own 30 minutes in the pool together. Today I was so pleased with him; he managed to go under the water and pick up things from the bottom. Remembering the level of interaction he came from, it's a miracle he's doing so well. I am super proud of him.

24th October - Meeting an Uncle

I got a text from my brother at pretty short notice for us to meet up this afternoon for dinner at a local restaurant with our mother. He lives on the South coast and he's not often up North and close enough for us to see one another. The last time I saw him was when I had my surgery and he travelled up to see me. I love my brother so much and miss him more than he knows. We used to call each other pretty much daily, but recently he's not been so receptive to answering.

I am so very pleased that Jacob and my brother got to meet each other today. They interacted beautifully and Jacob enjoyed the time with him. I even managed to get a rare photo of my brother, and in this instance with Jacob too. It is a photo I will treasure forever.
I feel as though I think about family more so now I have a child too.

There is now only one uncle for Jacob to meet.

25th October - Pumpkin Picking

We went pumpkin picking and for a long walk today. As we got home and started carving the pumpkin, Jacob leaned over and told me out loud and in front of Alex that *'You are my favourite Daddy'*. My heart nearly fell out as I really don't want this to be the case of him favouring either one of us and the other Daddy feeling a bit crap over the comments. We discussed it with Jacob that he should love us both the same as we are a forever family. I guess this is what kids do as they don't understand the implications of some of their words. Personally and honestly, I felt great that he has a lot of love for me to be able to verbalise it, but I really don't want Alex feeling second best, because he is not. It is likely because I am the one who has the luxury of having lots of fun with him, whereas Alex has the boring stuff to do like the school run and getting ready for it.

Alex doesn't show that it hurt his feelings, but I am sure it does. I would find it tough if Jacob said that the other way around.

26th October - Adoption Order Letter

I was just getting into my work this morning when the *Ring Doorbell* chimed and the postman dropped off a letter. Alex collected it and I thought nothing of it. I finished the online call that I was on and made my way downstairs to collect my thoughts and get a drink. Jacob was playing and ready to head off to grandads. Alex whispered into my ear that he left the paperwork upstairs for me to read. When I got to it, it was the paperwork advising that the adoption order has formally been issued. I had a quick flutter in my heart, but once again it was quick-lived. Jacob has always been one of us and it's hard to get excited over what we already believe is the 'norm'. The contrast however, is that I am overjoyed that it's now formal, of course.

We still have to wait up to 4 weeks for the birth certificate to be issued and we can then do what we have always wanted more than anything, the passport. This seems to be our milestone and final waypoint for Jacob to become formally one of our family.

30th October - Birth Certificate

Although the adoption order has already been granted, I am desperate for that birth certificate to now arrive. It will complete the process for us. I am not counting on the local authority and people who issue birth certificates to be quick though. We will have to just sit tight and wait and with a couple of years of the adoption process behind us, we are used to that already.

5th November - Hospital Visit

Jacob was wheezing and coughing all night and we thought it was just the cough that he has had for the last few days, but it got to a point that at hourly intervals he was waking up and having really bad coughing fits and struggling to breathe; and when I say struggling, I mean he really had to try hard to get the oxygen in and fighting for breaths. I am usually calm and not quite the hypochondriac however I know - as did Alex - that this wasn't good. We were both panicking. Internally I felt sick at the thought that he was hurting and struggling; of course the 'worst case' thoughts that went through my head. We had no experience with anything similar so it was hard to judge what the hell to do. It was 2.00am and so we called 111 who advised us they were to get an ambulance to come out as a precaution; they were very reassuring to us that we had done the right thing. I know that is all part of their job and all, but it was certainly well received from us both. We made the call whilst close to Jacob and he heard the call. The operator asked us who we were calling about and we advised Jacob, to which point they asked his surname. That was a tough scenario to navigate through as we didn't want a big set back regarding his identity and him questioning his surname.

Approximately 45 long and worrying minutes later, and when the ambulance crew arrived, a lovely Irish woman and a local guy came in to check on Jacob. I had to whisper to them about his surname as they came through the door to ensure it wasn't spoken out loud and they acknowledged very respectfully. They sat down and checked Jacob's vitals, but it was clear that he was going in from the start, so I ran around and collected a load of stuff in readiness for an overnight stay (I have done enough of them). The paramedic advised us both to come along, but with a caveat that the hospital may not let us both stay due to COVID pandemic restrictions; even though it's (hopefully) nearly over. I sure as hell wasn't not going and the same for Alex. Jacob took all of this in his stride and just got on with it. His resilience was amazing. I was - and still am - so proud of him.

When we arrived, I parked my car in my usual spot (I've been here enough myself to know where to park without needing to pay) and rushed to meet them at the entrance of A&E. This was also where the ambulances came into the hospital. The paramedics were all very relaxed, as was Jacob. They had clearly done a good job whilst onboard the ambulance making him feel comfortable. I wish the same could be said for Alex and I as we were worried sick. Once they had checked us in they took us all to the children's ward, where we were told only one of us to stay. Alex and I had a quick conflab and decided Alex should stay. I am a little better at managing my emotions and anxieties, so it made sense for him to be there, although I can't deny that I was gutted to have to leave Jacob in hospital at 3am in a poor and exhausted state. We told Jacob and he cried that I was having to leave and wait at home.

I walked back to the car pretty beat up and full of differing emotions.

It's just past 10.00am and I just did a FaceTime with the boys who are still in hospital. The content was based around the treatments and of course the food they got for breakfast and lunch. Whilst on the video, I am so glad Alex was on the bed cuddling up to Jacob. I know this will be a superb additional bonding thing for them both; in the face of adversity often comes positivity… and all that stuff. On the face of it, Alex seemed to be handling this pretty well too, but I would place a small bet that he is doing that for the benefit of Jacob to try and reassure him that it is all OK and that he will be fine. He, similarly to Jacob, must be shattered too. I know I am tired and yet I managed a couple of hours of sleep after being sent home.

Finally I got to pick them both up from the hospital at about 4.00pm. As they walked to the car, they both looked lethargic and tired, bless them. Jacob just wanted to get home and feel comfortable and safe. We believe there is a little bit of a negative connection to the hospitals from previous, but we can't be sure.

Jacob also asked for a McDonalds and we couldn't say no really. He had been so brave and frankly we couldn't be bothered to cook either. It certainly cheered him up.

Regarding the medication, we have to give him 6 puffs of the inhaler at 4 hour intervals and do this for the next 4 days as a minimum. I can't wait to get up throughout the night, honest.

6th November - Hell

Last night was hell. I was so worried all night, that I hardly slept and each time Jacob went quiet I had to go in to check he was still breathing. The anxiety was strong. I administered the medicine as advised, yet he still coughed most of the night with some small intervals in between. He must have been shattered.

We will be missing swimming today, of course.

7th November - Emotions

Another day of worry, anxiety and sheer exhaustion. Alex and I are bloody knackered. I used to poo-poo parents when they moaned about being tired because of their kids. I get it and I apologise to all parents I ever mocked and told them that it was 'your choice to have kids.'

Jacob struggled through the day and the night again. I am worried as it doesn't seem to be getting much better.

8th November - More of the Same

Much more of the same. I need sleep, please God I will believe in you if you sort out this asthma and cough. I am struggling.

10th November - Fatigue

I am so tired. I need sleep. I need our child to feel better. I am worried for him and really want him to feel better. I feel helpless as a father and protector as I can't do anything for him.

11th November - 111 Non-Emergency Line

We have called 111, again. We tried the doctors first, but Sod's law is that the local NHS is having a Doctors conference today; it's already hard enough to get an appointment. Last night we must have had only a couple of hours sleep between us all with Jacob coughing and struggling and we are very worried about him. It has been close to a week since this started and I am exhausted. We had called 111 as Jacob had a very bad night coughing and wheezing. It just doesn't seem to ease up for him, especially when he is led down.

I spent 15 minutes on the line and again the person on the other end was super helpful, respectful and polite. This time we knew to be out of earshot of Jacob when they asked about surnames etc. The outcome being that we need to wait for a call later on from someone who has more experience with this medical concern. I hope they have a fix and something that will help Jacob. We all need it.

Finally, it is tough navigating this around 'real life' and work. Things can't just stop and stand still.

12th November - Waiting

We are still waiting for the birth certificate for Jacob to arrive. This is the final stage for us to be fully and mentally a Young. It is actually hard to explain. The adoption order has been granted, he has been here for what seems like forever, but that one final mental hurdle will be completed when we get that certificate.

15th November - Laughing

Finally, the cough seems to have gone. Last night Jacob woke me up at about 2.00am, yet this time as opposed to a cough, he woke me up because he was laughing. I thought he was awake, but upon checking him, he was asleep and dreaming. I asked him in the morning what he was dreaming about and he told me *'I was dreaming about monkeys waking up all of the babies'*. Where the hell does their imagination take them? I don't remember me doing this as a kid. He makes me laugh so much.

Anyway, finally I got some good sleep. Woop.

This parenting lark is so much harder than I expected, but it is also so rewarding too. I can't believe how relieved I am with Jacob feeling better and with him being able to express it. I don't know how parents with young children cope, especially as their children can verbalise how they are feeling.

16th November - Unexpected ISA

We got a message off Julie today advising us that Jacob had an ISA set up, yet nobody actually knows the details of it and who set it up. She will investigate and come back to us, but suspects it is from the local authority. We wonder if it could have been set up from birth parents? Often the unknown is a theme within the adoption journey. We are used to it now.

On a lighter and a bit of a ruder note, Jacob ran into the bedroom this morning, farted and then said *'this is a Christmas present for you'* whilst laughing. I found it hilarious, but where the hell has he got that from? It must have been someone from school, which makes me laugh as they surely have got it from parents playing the fool. I'm not the only one then.

17th November - Names

Alex had just been to pick up some medicine from the pharmacy and when he came back the packaging still had Jacob's previous name on it. Alex made a valid point too regarding the name after he made a throw-away comment of *'I just wish they would use his proper name'*. His birth name is part of Jacob's identity and will always be and we don't want to change that, of course, but we don't want to muddy the water and his brain about who he is now.

There is a constant battle of wanting him to be ours and forget about the crappy past, but also we acknowledge the importance of it being a part of his identity. I am sure that will always be an ongoing mental battle and rightly so, frankly.

We are nearly at the end of this journey now and we just want to get on with the rest of our lives as a relatively normal family.

19th November - Health Visitor

Jacob's previously assigned health visitor called this morning and it was quite out of the blue and unexpected. She called just to get an update and most importantly finalise the health related files that they hold on Jacob, which by definition added in another layer of confirmation that the process is complete, bar the birth certificate in our hands, which will be the complete and utter end of the process for us. It shouldn't be long now either.

20th November - It's Arrived

We are all done and I am over the moon. That sounds so exhilarating and emotional to say. Jacob's birth certificates have come through and show his final and formal adoption as completed; that is it, he is a Young forever.

I was in the kitchen when the envelope arrived and as soon as we collected it from the doormat we could tell it was from the birth certificate place. I was overcome with anticipation and emotion at this point and couldn't wait for Alex to open it and confirm it was what we thought it was. I went a little weak at the knees when we read it out loud. *'Jacob Young'*. It is official. Alex and I embraced and just held each other for a few minutes taking in the implication of that one piece of paper. Emotions were high.

The certificate has always been the marker for us to psychologically be 100% a fully completed forever family; it is all done.

As daddies we are struggling to process it all. We have gone through nearly 3 years of all kinds of emotions to fulfil our dream of completing our forever family and now it is done. Jesus, that's weird to say. We are a complete family and with that knowledge I have had some happy tears today.

The mentality shift having that birth certificate in our hands is just pure amazing and joyous. It is so hard to describe how we are feeling, but if you think about the exhilaration and adrenaline of winning the lottery and then double it, then that is how we are feeling right now. Jacob has brought us so much love and happiness and completed our forever family. It's amazing when you think about what challenges he has overcome in his life and has come through it the person he has. I am in complete awe of the resilience and strength of character of Jacob. Each and every day he amazes me and we are so proud of him.

This process has been the most challenging thing I have done in my life, yet I am sure the coming years will offer many more as Jacob grows up. What it has also been is the most rewarding, challenging, immersive, emotional (I feel emotional writing about it now as a wave just came over me of adrenaline and/or relief) and fulfilling life event I have ever had to date.

I think we just need to sit down and process it all.

I can't wait for the rest of our lives.

Jacob Young. Joseph Young. Alex Young.

Forever Family.

Final Thoughts.

Some final thoughts from myself as I thought it is important that I should offer a summary of advice based on the experience that we have had over the past few years. But first I want to reiterate that all journeys are going to be different; some in process but all in personal circumstances and emotions.

For those that are thinking of adopting a child or children, I would encourage you to explore it. The process is not easy and the emotional rollercoaster you will go on will be like nothing you have ever experienced before. It will challenge you to the edge of your capabilities and you will learn so much about yourself in this huge self discovery process.

At present it has been forecast that there are likely to be 100,000 children in the care system in the next 3 years and it's likely to continue to grow if adopters don't come forward. If you are one of those people or families that come forward, I would always recommend

- Be honest throughout the whole process
- Be yourself
- Be in the knowledge that it changes your whole life
- Challenge your social workers
- Have an outlet - we had our adoption support group - as it's such a valuable resource
- Document your journey as it is amazing to look back on it
- Enjoy it

And to close my diary…

'I would lay down my life for any of my children. When you are a father, I know you will understand what I mean.'

Well, mother, you are correct as always. I wouldn't have a second thought or have any hesitation to give Jacob my heart if he needed it. He is our world, and we are humbled that through shocking adversity our gorgeous little boy has graced our lives with love, joy and so many cuddles and kisses. Here's to our forever family...

Thank you for reading. I sincerely hope this has helped you with your journey.

Please, please, please....

May I kindly ask that if this diary offered you guidance and helped you understand the adoption journey, then please **_LEAVE A REVIEW_** and share with your network.

Thank you for reading our story.

The Youngs

Printed in Great Britain
by Amazon

78972027R00163